The RENAISSANCE

AN ENCYCLOPEDIA FOR STUDENTS

The RENAISSANCE

AN ENCYCLOPEDIA FOR STUDENTS

Paul F. Grendler, Editor in Chief

PUBLISHED IN ASSOCIATION WITH THE RENAISSANCE SOCIETY OF AMERICA

Volume 4

PRINTING AND PUBLISHING—WRITING

CHARLES SCRIBNER'S SONS®

THOMSON

GALE

New York • Detroit • San Diego • San Francisco • Cleveland • New Haven, Conn. • Waterville, Maine • London • Munich

THOMSON

GALE

The Renaissance An Encyclopedia for Students

Paul F. Grendler, Editor in Chief

Copyright © 2004 Charles Scribner's Sons.
Developed for Charles Scribner's Sons by
Visual Education Corporation, Princeton, N.J.

For Scribners

PUBLISHER:
Frank Menchaca

EDITORS:
John Fitzpatrick, Sharon Malinowski

COVER AND INTERIOR DESIGN:
Jennifer Wahi

IMAGING AND MULTIMEDIA:
Lezlie Light, Robyn Young, Mary Grimes, Dave
Oblender, Leitha Etheridge-Sims, Dan Newell,
Christine O'Bryan

COMPOSITION:
Evi Seoud

MANUFACTURING:
Rhonda Williams

For Visual Education Corporation

PROJECT DIRECTORS:
Darryl Kestler, Amy Livingston

WRITERS:
John Haley, Mark Mussari, Charles Roebuck,
Rebecca Stefoff

EDITORS:
Tobey Cloyd, Cindy George, John Kennedy

ASSOCIATE EDITOR:
Sarah Miller

COPYEDITING SUPERVISOR:
Helen Castro

ELECTRONIC PREPARATION:
Fiona Shapiro

For more information, contact
Charles Scribner's Sons
300 Park Avenue South
New York, NY 10010
Or visit our Internet site at
http://www.gale.com/scribners

Since this page cannot legibly accommodate
all copyright notices, the acknowledgments
constitute an extension of the copyright
notice.

For permission to use material from this
product, submit your request via Web at
http://www.gale-edit.com/permissions, or you
may download our Permissions Request form
and submit your request by fax or mail to:

Permissions Department
The Gale Group, Inc.
27500 Drake Rd.
Farmington Hills, MI 48331-3535
Permissions Hotline:
248-699-8006 or 800-762-4058

LIBRARY OF CONGRESS CATALOG-IN-PUBLICATION DATA

The Renaissance : an encyclopedia for students / Paul F. Grendler.
    p. cm
        Summary: An encyclopedia of the Renaissance with articles on various
        aspects of social, cultural, and political history such as literature, gov-
        ernment, warfare, and technology, plus maps, charts, definitions, and
        chronology.
        Includes bibliographical references and index.
        ISBN 0-684-31281-6 (set hardcover : alk. paper) — ISBN 0-684-31282-4
        (v. 1) — ISBN 0-684-31283-2 (v. 2) — ISBN 0-684-31285-9 (v. 3) — ISBN
        0-684-31284-0 (v. 4) — ISBN 0-684-31424-X (e-book)
        1. Renaissance—Encyclopedias, Juvenile. [1. Renaissance—
        Encyclopedias.] I. Grendler, Paul F. II. Encyclopedia of the Renaissance.
        III. Title.

CB361.R25 2003
940.2'1'03—dc22

This title is also available as an e-book
ISBN 0-684-31424-X (set)

Contact your Gale sale representative for ordering information

Printed in the United States of America
10 9 8 7 6 5 4 3 2 1

Table of Contents

VOLUME 1
Academies—Cromwell

VOLUME 2
Daily Life—Julius II

VOLUME 3
Kepler—Princes and Princedoms

VOLUME 4
Printing and Publishing—Writing

Maps

DEC - - 2004

Genealogical Charts

Color Plates

Printing and Publishing

The development of printing was one of the most important events of the Renaissance, with a major impact on many aspects of society. Printing promoted literacy by making the written word available to a larger public. It was also a key element in the spread of religious, social, and artistic ideas throughout northern Europe.

ORIGINS OF PRINTING

Before the invention of printing, books were produced and copied by hand, which made them both rare and expensive. In addition, the earliest books in Europe had pages of parchment—an expensive material made from animal skins. As a result, book ownership was largely limited to very wealthy individuals and institutions such as monasteries.

In the early 1100s, the Islamic world introduced paper to Europe. Although paper was less durable than parchment, it was much cheaper. Paper quickly became popular because it helped meet a large demand for books in universities. By the late 1300s, a growing interest in books among powerful secular* individuals created a demand for books outside universities.

* **secular** nonreligious; connected with everyday life

Early Printing. Three different individuals claimed credit for the invention of printing around the same time. A 1499 text names Laurens Coster, from the Dutch city of Harlem, as the inventor of printing. Another document states that Procopius Waldvogel of Prague owned molds for printing in 1444. However, no printed books have ever been traced to either of these figures. Most historians give the credit to Johann GUTENBERG, who formed a printing company in Strasbourg in the late 1430s. He moved to Mainz and formed another company with Johann Fust in 1450, and by 1454 the printing technique he used was well developed.

The printing press combined several existing technologies. A steel punch, like that used to make coins, impressed the image of a letter into a soft metal. A metalworker then turned this imprint into a mold to create forms, or units of type, for this letter. A compositor arranged the type inside two frames to create the text. The letters in these frames made up the text for two sides of the same page. An inker set the frames in the press, one above the other. He smeared ink on the letters and placed a sheet of paper between the frames. The press operator then swung a lever that brought the frames together to make the print. This type of mechanism, known as a screw press, had long been used for making wine, linen, and paper.

A good press team could print 1,000 sheets a day, but training a good team and purchasing equipment could be very expensive. In addition, it took time for a publisher to make money from his books. Many early printers went bankrupt; even Gutenberg had to sell his business. In its first years, the printing industry was restricted to a small region along the Rhine River in Germany. Printers closely guarded the secrets of their trade, limiting the spread of the business. In 1462, however, attackers

Each member of a Renaissance printing shop was responsible for a specific task. One person set the letters in two frames, another covered them with ink, and the third swung a lever that brought the frames together to make a print, as shown in this 1520 engraving.

* **sack**   to loot a captured city

sacked* the Rhine city of Mainz, and some of the city's printers fled to Italy and France, bringing their knowledge with them.

Spread of Printing. In 1465 two printers established a press near Rome. Over the next three years the price of books in that city dropped 80 percent. By 1480 printers had established themselves in 50 Italian cities, outstripping the 30 printing centers in Germany. Paris had a press by 1470, but only eight other French towns followed its lead in the next 10 years. Spain and England also set up their first presses in the 1470s. Book prices continued to drop steadily over the next two decades. In Venice, the price of a basic reading textbook fell by 75 percent between 1484 and 1488, making it affordable to most people. Wealthy collectors and average citizens joined schools and monasteries as large consumers of books.

Despite the number of presses, a small number of cities dominated publishing in each country. The leading publishing centers of the late

1400s and early 1500s were Venice in Italy, Paris and Lyon in France, Basel in Switzerland, and Cologne, Augsburg, and Nürnberg in Germany. Within those cities, two or three publishers usually controlled 40 to 60 percent of the business with several smaller ones competing for the rest.

GROWTH OF RENAISSANCE PRINTING

By the late 1400s, merchants and investors had financial interests in the publishing industry. However, the second generation of printers faced new challenges and problems. One major concern for publishers was protecting their financial interest in a book. Printers often made illegal copies of other printers' works, and these pirated copies took money out of the pocket of the original publisher. In Germany, cheap imported copies drove locally produced books out of profitable academic markets.

Words and Images. Most early printed works used the Latin alphabet, but printers soon began publishing in other languages. By 1475 there was a small but steady market for Hebrew language works. In the early 1500s, the Aldine Press in Venice concentrated heavily on Greek texts. It built a reputation as a leading publisher of works in Greek, including grammars and texts for the study of the New Testament in its original language. Other publishers printed works in Slavonic, Cyrillic, and Arabic.

* **woodcut**   print made from a block of wood with an image carved into it

As printing became more sophisticated, publishers expanded the number and type of illustrations in their works. Books often included woodcut* illustrations and decorative capital letters. A publisher also might leave space in the text to be filled in by an artist hired by the customer. Combining an image with text on the same page helped to explain a passage or to make a work accessible to those who could not read. However, illustrated books were difficult and expensive to produce. From 1490 to 1499 only 26 illustrated books went to press in Strasbourg, but from 1500 to 1509 the total was 91.

The printing of music posed other technical challenges for printers. Combining notes, staffs, and text on the same page was very complex. In many cases one of these elements had to be added by hand. It was not until the 1490s that printers designed moveable type that fit accurately enough to set all elements of music with the press.

* **humanist**   referring to a Renaissance cultural movement promoting the study of the humanities (the languages, literature, and history of ancient Greece and Rome) as a guide to living

Renaissance Publishers. Various publishers of the Renaissance specialized in certain types of books. Humanist* publishers joined forces with intellectuals in the effort to revive the culture of ancient Greece and Rome. Other presses focused on religious works, a more reliable source of income. Two of the most important publishers of the Renaissance were the Froben and Aldine presses.

For almost a century—from 1491 to 1587—the Froben press in Basel, Switzerland, was among the leading printing and publishing establishments of Europe. It produced over 900 titles. Its founder, Johannes Froben, began his career publishing religious works. Although Froben

* **Protestant Reformation** religious movement that began in the 1500s as a protest against certain practices of the Roman Catholic Church and eventually led to the establishment of a variety of Protestant churches

was not a scholar, he knew enough to look for quality manuscripts. He also took great care with the appearance of his books. Known for its variety of elegant type, the Froben press set the technical standards for other printers.

During the 1510s and 1520s, Froben's workshop became a meeting place for young humanist scholars. They brought the printer manuscripts, gave editorial advice, provided translations, and acted as proofreaders. Froben printed a great deal of humanist literature, including most of the writings of the Dutch scholar Desiderius ERASMUS, who became his close friend. Erasmus wrote of Froben's press, "No workshop can serve the interests of the great authors better than his."

The Aldine Press was an Italian publishing company, active in Venice and Rome from 1495 to 1597. Aldo Manuzio, a scholar and printer, established the press in Venice with the help of other investors. The press was the first to print the bulk of the classics of ancient Greece. During the early years of the 1500s, when Greek studies were spreading throughout Europe, it was the only press that produced Greek texts.

Like Froben, Aldo was concerned with the appearance of his books. He set his Greek books in type that resembled script. This type helped to blur the lines between print, a new form of communication, and manuscripts, a more highly regarded form. In 1501 Aldo introduced two important new ideas in printing books—he made books more convenient by reducing their height to about seven inches, and he pioneered a cursive, or "italic," type for the Latin alphabet. He also experimented with his use of illustrations and page designs.

PRINTING AND SOCIETY

Printing had a profound effect on cultural and religious movements in the Renaissance. It played a particularly important role in the success of the Protestant Reformation*.

Religion and Publishing. Printing helped spread the ideas of Protestant reformer Martin LUTHER throughout Europe. In a single month—August 1520—one publisher in the city of Wittenberg distributed 4,000 copies of Luther's *Address to the Christian Nobility of the German Nation.* Two years later the first printing of his German New Testament sold out in three months. In 1523, 418 of 498 texts printed in German were either Luther's works or works about his ideas. Modern scholars claim that the use of woodcut illustrations in these books greatly increased the impact of Luther's words. Many works in support of Protestant ideas included woodcuts borrowed from other works. Originally designed as monsters, these images appeared in Protestant works as demonic monks or cardinals.

Protestant reformers in France and Switzerland also had a close relationship with the press. Some French reformers were scholars who had worked with humanist publishers in Paris since about 1500. In 1534 the publication of an anti-Catholic pamphlet turned the king against the Protestants and the printers who aided them. Several publishers fled

France and settled in Geneva, Switzerland, eventually turning it into a major center of Protestant publishing. Religious reformer John CALVIN aided in this effort. Between 1525 and 1550 six presses operated in the city and published 42 titles. Between 1550 and 1564, the number of presses grew to 40. Over the course of this period Geneva's presses produced 527 books, 160 of which were works by Calvin.

* **hierarchy**   organization of a group into higher and lower levels

The Catholic Church hierarchy* seems to have treated printing with suspicion from almost the beginning. When Pope Paul III established the Roman INQUISITION in 1542, one of its main duties was to draw up lists of forbidden books. These lists had a dramatic effect on Italian publishing. For example, before 1560 over half of the books published by the Giolito press in Venice were secular works. However, during the 1570s more than 70 percent of its titles were religious.

* **papacy**   office and authority of the pope

Catholic and Protestant leaders competed with one another for the services of leading publishers. Catholic officials entertained French printer Henri Estienne II when he visited Italy in the 1550s. In 1560 Pope Pius IV asked Paolo Manuzio, the son of Aldo, to become the official printer to the papacy*. Manuzio used an earlier offer from a Protestant leader to improve his bargaining position with the pope. Printer Christophe Plantin worked for Philip II, the Catholic king of Spain, from 1568 to 1576—but nine years later he took a job as printer to the Protestant University of Leiden in the Netherlands.

Effects on Society. With the growth of printing, book production became concentrated in a few cities and in the hands of a few publishers. This small group of people had considerable power over what the public read. Their influence created new cultural divisions in Europe. During the Middle Ages, all types of people had had access to the main sources of culture—markets, festivals, and wandering entertainers. Printing changed this, widening the gap between city and country as well as between literary and popular culture. As printing spread, professionals and intellectuals turned to solitary reading instead of public lectures or presentations. Over time they shared less and less with the majority of illiterate or semi-literate people. (*See also* **Bible; Books and Manuscripts; Catholic Reformation and Counter-Reformation; Censorship; Humanism; Ideas, Spread of; Index of Prohibited Books; Literacy; Protestant Reformation.**)

Professions

In Renaissance Europe, the word "profession" referred not to a career in general, but to a career in one of several high-prestige fields, such as law, medicine, the church, civil service, or teaching. Those who entered the professions earned more than most nonprofessionals, aside from nobles and wealthy merchants. Most professionals also held high social positions.

All professionals needed to be able to read, write, and speak Latin. Boys preparing for the professions began studying the language around age six or seven. Future lawyers and some physicians continued their education at universities. In southern Europe, boys entered universities

* **theology** study of the nature of God and of religion

* **guild** association of craft and trade owners and workers that set standards for and represented the interests of its members

at age 17 or 18 and received a doctorate in law or medicine after five to seven years of study. In northern Europe, boys of 13 or 14 received instruction from masters and older students. After four years they received a bachelor's degree and could continue on to earn a doctorate in law, medicine, or theology*.

After completing this formal training, a person had to be accepted into a professional organization, such as a guild* or college, in order to practice. Guilds were more likely to accept locals—especially those with male relatives in the guild—than strangers. Most professionals came from families in which several generations of men had entered the same profession.

Levels of training varied within each profession. For example, only some medical professionals held university degrees. Others took up practice as surgeons and empirics (practical doctors who treated wounds or fractures). These doctors could enter a medical guild after passing an examination, but they did not enjoy the status or income of university-trained physicians. Similarly, teachers needed a degree to instruct students in a university or even a secondary school. However, teaching elementary school did not require a degree. This position offered little in the way of pay or prestige. It was also the only profession open to women.

* **hierarchy** organization of a group into higher and lower levels

The church gave boys from poor or nonprofessional families more opportunities than other professions. For example, Pope Pius V (reigned 1566–1572) was the son of a peasant. The church offered a variety of positions for priests, secretaries (who served popes and bishops), and lawyers for religious courts. These different positions called for varying levels of training. Parish priests needed little formal schooling. However, those who wished to rise in the church hierarchy* needed a university degree—usually in the field of law. Most of the Italian popes, cardinals, and bishops during the Renaissance had degrees either in church law or in both church and civil law.

* **apprenticeship** system under which a person is bound by legal agreement to work for another for a specified period of time in return for instruction in a trade or craft

The professions of law and civil service expanded throughout the Renaissance. As Renaissance states grew, so did the demand for civil servants such as judges and secretaries. Some states established special schools to train boys for government careers. Professionals who recorded legal agreements, known as notaries, were also essential. Most notaries learned their profession through apprenticeship*. (*See also* **Clergy; Education; Guilds; Law; Medicine; Notaries; Universities.**)

Protestant Reformation

The Protestant Reformation was a religious movement that began in Germany in the 1500s and eventually spread throughout western and central Europe. Before the Reformation, the Roman Catholic Church was the center of Christianity in Europe. By the end of the 1500s, however, various rival churches had formed to challenge its dominance. These changes in religion had profound effects on political, social, economic, and intellectual life. They also contributed to the outbreak of civil wars in Germany, France, the Netherlands, and Scotland.

Roots of the Movement. The Protestant Reformation grew out of the religious conditions of the late Middle Ages. Historians disagree about the state of the Catholic Church during this period. Some believe that the church was in a period of spiritual decline, while others claim that most Christians were satisfied with it. In any case, it is clear that there were problems in the Catholic Church at this time. For example, the popes of the period often focused on politics and neglected important religious matters.

Many Catholics sought reforms within the church. Some of the most powerful voices for reform belonged to the humanists* of the early Renaissance. In the early 1500s, Christian humanists such as Desiderius ERASMUS of the Netherlands and Jacques Lefèvre d'Etaples of France hoped to renew religion by returning to the original sources of Christianity. Their interest in classical* thought led many humanists to produce new translations of ancient texts, including the Scriptures.

Lutheran Reforms. Martin LUTHER (1483–1546), a German monk, brought these tensions to a head in the early 1500s. A biblical scholar, Luther developed a new theology* that challenged many Catholic beliefs. In 1517 he issued a series of statements, known as the Ninety-five Theses, which questioned certain practices of the Roman Catholic Church. Humanist scholars soon adopted Luther's ideas and helped spread them. Publishers distributed his works throughout Germany, bringing him wide fame. The Catholic Church, however, accused Luther of heresy*. In 1521 the pope excommunicated* him and Holy Roman Emperor* Charles V declared him an outlaw. To avoid arrest, Luther went into hiding.

Meanwhile, Luther's followers were debating ways to put his ideas into practice. Eventually, they proposed a series of moderate changes in religious ritual and belief. Many German states and independent cities accepted these reforms. Close cultural and economic ties between Germany and the Scandinavian countries helped spread Lutheran ideas in northern Europe. At first, students and preachers played an influential role in the reform movement there. Later, the kings of Denmark and Sweden adopted the new faith as a way to weaken the power of Catholic bishops and to create state churches under their own control.

The Lutheran reforms caused a significant amount of social upheaval in Germany. Tension developed between supporters and opponents of the new movement. In 1524 the PEASANTS' WAR broke out, with farmers and townspeople protesting the policies of local lords and church leaders and demanding various rights. Troubled by these events and by the possibility of a permanent split in the church, a number of writers who had once supported Luther drew back. In 1524 Erasmus published an attack on one of Luther's major religious ideas. Many other humanists also turned against the Reformation, although some became preachers of the new faith.

Movements in Switzerland. Former humanists also took up the cause of reform in Switzerland. Between 1520 and 1525, Swiss preacher

* **humanist** Renaissance expert in the humanities (the languages, literature, history, and speech and writing techniques of ancient Greece and Rome)

* **classical** in the tradition of ancient Greece and Rome

* **theology** study of the nature of God and of religion

* **heresy** belief that is contrary to the doctrine of an established church

* **excommunicate** to exclude from the church and its rituals

* **Holy Roman Emperor** ruler of the Holy Roman Empire, a political body in central Europe composed of several states that existed until 1806

See color plate 12, vol. 4

German monk Martin Luther, shown here in a 1533 portrait by Lucas Cranach the Elder, led the Protestant Reformation that began in 1517. His ideas challenged the traditional beliefs and practices of the Roman Catholic Church.

* **authoritarian** referring to strong leadership with unrestricted powers

See color plate 11, vol. 4

Huldrych Zwingli persuaded the city of Zurich to adopt drastic religious reforms. Other Swiss cities followed a few years later. However, Zwingli disagreed with Luther on certain central religious ideas, causing a split between the groups led by the two reformers. Protestantism remained divided from this point forward.

The pace of change in Zurich was not rapid enough to satisfy some of Zwingli's followers. One group, known as the Anabaptists, organized its own rival churches. In 1534, Anabaptist extremists seized control of the German city of Münster. They established an authoritarian* government, banned all books except the Bible, and expelled or massacred all people whom they considered "godless." Eventually, Catholics and Lutherans who had been exiled by the Anabaptists stormed the city and regained control. Thereafter, the Anabaptist movement all but disappeared.

Calvinism. Beginning in the 1520s, humanists known as evangelicals helped bring about a reformation movement in France. They drew their beliefs from the writings of French reformer John CALVIN. In 1536 Calvin published *Institutes of the Christian Religion,* a powerful statement of religious ideas drawn from Luther, Zwingli, and other writers.

Calvin settled in the Swiss city of Geneva, where he developed a church organization that became a model for Protestants throughout Europe. His plan depended on cooperation between church and state. Calvin also emphasized the importance of education in reformed Christianity. At his urging, Geneva founded an academy that provided a humanist education and training in theology to future ministers. Many individuals who studied there went on to play leading roles in the Reformation.

As Calvinism spread into Catholic societies, it became a source of both political and religious conflict. In France, the Netherlands, and Scotland, independent Calvinist churches were linked together in a tightly woven structure. As a group, they tended to oppose royal policy and often found themselves in conflict with Catholic monarchs. In 1562, the first of a series of WARS OF RELIGION between Catholics and Protestants broke out in France. The wars continued until 1598, when the Edict of Nantes legalized the French Reformed Church.

Meanwhile, the Netherlands was under Spanish rule. In 1572, the Dutch rebelled and began to fight for their independence. Although the war began as a political struggle, it soon became a religious one as well. The Calvinist northern provinces won their independence, but the southern provinces remained under the control of the Catholic king of Spain.

In Scotland, Protestants led by preacher John KNOX opposed the Catholic queen, MARY STUART. In the 1560s, they forced the queen into exile, rejected the authority of the pope and bishops, and established the Calvinist church as a major force in Scottish life. Calvinism also gained a following in eastern Europe, especially in Poland, Bohemia, and Hungary.

* **succession**   determination of person who will inherit the throne

* **annulment**   formal declaration that a marriage is legally invalid

The Reformation in England. The Protestant movement triumphed in England partly as a result of problems with the royal succession*. In the late 1520s, HENRY VIII sought an annulment* from his first wife, CATHERINE OF ARAGON, who had failed to produce a male heir. When the pope denied his request, England dissolved its ties with the Catholic Church. The doctrine of the new English church remained officially Catholic for the rest of Henry's life. However, two of Henry's close advisers, Thomas CRANMER (the archbishop of Canterbury) and Thomas CROMWELL (the chief minister), were influenced by Lutheran ideas.

Under EDWARD VI (ruled 1547–1553), England made further progress toward becoming a Protestant nation. Archbishop Cranmer oversaw the publication of an English-language prayer book that kept the outer forms of Catholic worship but was based on Protestant theology. When MARY I took the throne in 1553, she attempted to restore Catholicism. However, because she reigned only briefly and failed to produce an heir, the change did not last.

In 1558 ELIZABETH I came to power and took a moderate position favoring Protestants. The following year, she approved the Act of Supremacy, which denied the authority of the pope and recognized the queen as head of the English church. Most people accepted Elizabeth's policies and began to use the new English prayer book. However, some Protestants, known as Puritans, objected to Elizabeth's control of the church. They formed an active minority and continued to seek additional reforms into the 1600s. (*See also* **Bible; Catholic Reformation and Counter-Reformation; Christianity; Humanism; Preaching and Sermons; Puritanism; Religious Thought.**)

Ptolemy

ca. 100–170
Egyptian scientific scholar

* **astrology**   study of the supposed influences of the stars and planets on earthly events

The ancient Egyptian scientist Claudius Ptolemy wrote works on a wide range of topics, including ASTRONOMY, geography, mathematics, and music. Although Ptolemy's writings were over a thousand years old by the time the Renaissance began, they had a great influence on the scientific thought of the time.

Modern scholars know little about Ptolemy's life. He appears to have spent his whole life in Alexandria, a city in Egypt, which was then part of Roman territory. His first name is Roman in form and his last name Egyptian, suggesting that he came from a mixed family.

Ptolemy believed that the study of the skies was more than a science. In his major work on astronomy, *The Almagest,* he argued that studying astronomy led people to think about God, whom he considered to be the cause of all heavenly motions. This view of astronomy was very influential during the Renaissance. In another work, the *Quadripartitum* (Four Parts), Ptolemy expressed his belief in astrology*. He claimed that the heavenly bodies had a physical influence on all earthly matters, including geography, climate, and even human lives.

The Almagest covered all aspects of mathematical astronomy known to ancient scholars. It also explains Ptolemy's vision of the universe—a sphere with a tiny, unmoving Earth at its center. Other ancient astronomers believed in this geocentric, or earth-centered, view of the universe, but they had trouble making it fit with their observations of the movements of heavenly bodies. The irregular motions of the planets, for example, did not match perfectly circular orbits around Earth. Various astronomers came up with theories to fix this problem. Some suggested that the orbits of the planets were not quite centered on Earth, while others proposed more complicated adjustments. Ptolemy cleverly combined these different schemes in a new mathematical theory that fit very well with observations of the heavens.

Ptolemy's system defined the common view of the Earth and the heavens for much of the Renaissance. A few Renaissance astronomers argued with some of the points of the system, but their work was inferior to Ptolemy's. By the early 1500s, however, the Polish astronomer Nicolaus COPERNICUS had begun to formulate a heliocentric, or Sun-centered, model of the solar system. His work sowed the seeds of a new system that would in time destroy the Ptolemaic vision of the universe. (*See also* **Science.**)

Puritanism

Puritanism was a Protestant reform movement that developed within the Church of England in the 1500s. It had a major influence on English social, political, and religious thought. Followers of the movement, known as Puritans, sought purity of heart, mind, and worship. They viewed the Bible as the foundation of their faith and rejected any practices that lacked scriptural authority.

Roots of the Movement. Puritanism emerged during the reign of the Protestant king EDWARD VI (from 1547 to 1553). It began with opposition to the use of certain vestments (garments) by church officials. The Anglican* church required members of the clergy to wear the vestments. However, reformers objected because the use of these garments was not based on the Bible. When MARY I, a Catholic, took the throne in 1553, many Puritans fled to Germany, where they continued the debate over vestments and proposed reforms to the Anglican prayer book.

ELIZABETH I became queen in 1558 and restored Protestant religious practices in England. However, her policies did not satisfy the Puritans. Reformers renewed their attacks on the use of traditional vestments, and Elizabeth settled the issue by ordering all members of the clergy to wear them. In 1566 the Puritans tried to obtain religious reforms through Parliament, but their efforts failed.

Demands for Reform. The Puritan movement took on a new issue in 1570, when the reformer Thomas Cartwright called for a more democratic church organization. His proposal would have eliminated the offices of deacons, bishops, and archbishops. The following year Walter Strickland, a Puritan member of Parliament, introduced a bill to strike from the Anglican prayer book certain ceremonies of which Puritans did not approve. The failure of his bill deepened the tensions within the church. So did the decision of a church court, made around the same

* **Anglican** referring to the Church of England

* **theology**   study of the nature of God and of religion

time, ordering some prominent Puritans to support various beliefs and practices of the Anglican Church.

As tensions mounted, a new debate arose over "prophesyings"—a practice in which ministers and students of theology* met for Bible study, followed by a sermon. In 1574 Queen Elizabeth banned prophesyings, apparently viewing them as a way for Puritans to spread their demands for reform. Puritans responded by holding "exercises" or "classes," in which a minister preached a sermon, followed by a group discussion. The archbishop of Canterbury, head of the Church of England, put an end to the meetings by forcing clergy members to accept the Anglican prayer book and by using the church courts to punish outspoken Puritans.

Despite these setbacks, the Puritans remained a powerful force. In the early 1600s, they outlined a series of new demands to the new king, JAMES I. James agreed to moderate religious reforms, including better training and higher salaries for the clergy and a new translation of the Bible. However, the only reform actually carried out was the publication of the Bible.

* **dissent**   to oppose or disagree with established belief

The struggle within the Church of England reached a crisis in the 1630s. William Laud, the bishop of London and, later, archbishop of Canterbury, reinforced many traditional church practices and stifled dissenting* voices in the church. The Puritans resented Laud's policies, and their hostility contributed to the outbreak of a civil war in 1642. (*See also* **Christianity; England; Preaching and Sermons; Protestant Reformation; Religious Thought.**)

Queens and Queenship

The Renaissance produced an unusually large number of royal women who exercised cultural and political influence. Queenship is a broader and more flexible term than kingship. While kings are always rulers, queens can serve in a variety of roles. A queen regnant, for instance, is a woman who has inherited the throne and rules the state in her own right. Other queens may be the wives or mothers of kings, with varying degrees of power. A non-ruling queen sometimes serves as a regent, usually acting on behalf of a son who is too young or unable to take power.

Ruling Queens. Few women became queens regnant in Renaissance Europe, partly because the laws or customs of some countries prevented women from inheriting the throne. Those queens who did rule had the problem of marriage. Although they were expected to wed and to produce royal heirs, making an appropriate match was not easy. Renaissance society generally expected women to obey their husbands, but at the same time people feared that a queen's husband would dominate or influence her. If she chose one of her subjects as a spouse, the marriage might lead to conflict within the country. However, a foreign husband might meddle in the nation's affairs.

Two of the most important ruling queens of the Renaissance solved the marriage problem in different ways. In Spain, ISABELLA OF CASTILE

One of the most important ruling queens of the Renaissance, Isabella of Castile strengthened her kingdom through her marriage to Ferdinand of Aragon. Their union brought the two realms together to form the kingdom of Spain.

* **diplomatic**   having to do with formal relations between nations

* **Holy Roman Empire**   political body in central Europe composed of several states; existed until 1806

* **patron**   supporter or financial sponsor of an artist or writer

(ruled 1474–1504) married a neighboring monarch, FERDINAND OF ARAGON. The marriage won acceptance because it united their two realms into the kingdom of Spain. Moreover, Isabella's status as a married woman and mother of sons helped strengthen her authority. By contrast, ELIZABETH I of England (ruled 1558–1603) never married, largely because of political divisions among her advisers over the selection of a husband. Although Elizabeth failed to provide an heir to the throne, her single status became a diplomatic* tool. Until late in life, she used the possibility of her marriage to a foreign ruler as a lever in international relations.

Queens Consort. A king's wife, known as a queen consort, had one primary duty: to provide a son who could inherit the throne. If the queen failed in this duty, her husband might divorce her or even call for her execution.

Although a queen consort had no ruling authority of her own, she did have symbolic power, especially if she had been formally recognized in a coronation ceremony. Along with the king, the queen represented the majesty of the monarchy. Her influence depended on the survival of her sons, the strength of her personality, and the status of her family.

Women who served as regents held limited authority to govern. During the mid-1500s, Mary of Hungary controlled the Netherlands for her brother, CHARLES V of the Holy Roman Empire*. Although women could not occupy the throne of France, CATHERINE DE MÉDICIS (1519–1589) governed the country as regent for her sons. Occasionally queens consort acted as regents for short periods when their husbands were absent, but they usually exercised little power. Katherine Parr, the last wife of Henry VIII, ruled briefly on her husband's behalf in 1544.

Regardless of the queen's status, her position at court allowed her to be a patron* to artists, musicians, poets, and scholars. One of the greatest female patrons was MARGARET OF AUSTRIA, who served as regent of the Netherlands in the early 1500s for her nephew, Charles V. In addition, many women who married rulers of foreign realms brought cultural ideas from their homelands to their new countries and encouraged political and economic bonds between the two states. (*See also* **Court; Monarchy; Patronage; Princes and Princedoms; Women.**)

Querelle des Femmes

* **oppress**   to exercise power over others in an unjust or cruel way

The French phrase *querelle des femmes,* meaning "the woman question," refers to a literary debate about the nature and status of women. This debate began around 1500 and continued beyond the end of the Renaissance.

The first Renaissance figure to raise the issue of women's status was the philosopher Heinrich AGRIPPA OF NETTESHEIM. In 1509 Agrippa gave a lecture on the virtues of the female sex. Agrippa re-interpreted biblical, Greek, and Roman texts to support his theory that women were superior to men. He argued that men had oppressed* women not because of natural differences but for social reasons. This claim separated sex, the biological distinctions between men and women, from gender, a social construct.

Italian writer Baldassare Castiglione summarized some of Agrippa's ideas for a wider audience in *The Book of the Courtier* (1528). However, Castiglione took a far less extreme view than Agrippa. While he acknowledged that men's dominant role in society placed limits on women's freedom, but he did not question the right of men to rule. Italian poet Ludovico ARIOSTO took a much stronger position in support of women. In 1532 he made several additions to his poem *Orlando Furioso* that argued that women could be chaste* and that they were morally equal, or even superior, to men. He also encouraged women to write their own history instead of depending on men to do it for them.

In England, the *querelle des femmes* focused on the issue of women as rulers. CATHERINE OF ARAGON, the first wife of HENRY VIII, had Spanish humanist* Juan Luis Vives's *Instruction of a Christian Woman* (1523) translated for her daughter, the future MARY I. The book concluded that Mary should not govern because women are weak. Scholar Thomas Elyot countered Vives's claims in *The Defence of Good Women* (1540), arguing that women can rule as well as men, but they should do so only under special circumstances.

Protestant preacher John KNOX renewed the attack on female rule in *First Blast of the Trumpet Against the Monstrous Regiment of Women.* Written while Catholic women ruled France, Scotland, and England, the book did not appear in print until 1558, after the Protestant queen ELIZABETH I had assumed the throne of England. Elizabeth's supporters were quick to respond to Knox, arguing that God had made Elizabeth queen because she was unlike other women. Elizabeth's rule also raised another issue for women of her day: the status of women in marriage. During the Renaissance, a woman's husband was her undisputed master. This fact provided a major reason for Elizabeth to stay single.

By the end of the 1500s, most scholars agreed that virtue was the same for both men and women, and they focused on education as a way to bring equality to the sexes. The Dutch scholar Anna Maria van Schurman—one of the most educated women of her time—argued for the education of women in *Whether a Christian Woman Should Be Educated* (1638). In *The Equality of Men and Women* (1622), the French feminist Marie de Gournay declared that men and women could excel equally if they had the same education. She also mocked men for failing to take women seriously and to accept them as equals in a conversation. After 1650 social conversation between men and women began to be accepted in society. (*See also* **Feminism.**)

* **chaste**   sexually pure

* **humanist**   Renaissance expert in the humanities (the languages, literature, history, and speech and writing techniques of ancient Greece and Rome)

Rabelais, François

ca. 1494–1553
French humanist and writer

Although he is best known as a writer of satire*, French author François Rabelais pursued many careers in his lifetime. At various times, he was a monk, a doctor, a teacher, a clergyman, and an expert in languages. He gained fame for his satire *Gargantua and Pantagruel,* which promoted humanism* and religious reform. However, his comic and

* **satire** literary or artistic work ridiculing human wickedness and foolishness

* **humanist** referring to a Renaissance cultural movement promoting the study of the humanities (the languages, literature, and history of ancient Greece and Rome) as a guide to living

* **theologian** person who studies religion and the nature of God

* **patron** supporter or financial sponsor of an artist or writer

inventive writing frequently brought him into conflict with church and state authorities.

Rabelais's Life. Scholars know very little about several periods of Rabelais's life. Even his date of birth remains uncertain. Some evidence suggests that he was born as early as 1483, but most scholars consider 1494 the correct date. The son of a successful lawyer in the French town of Chinon, Rabelais may have studied to become a monk at a nearby monastery. If so, he could have begun his studies as early as 1510 or 1511, receiving a traditional education in church Latin and religious philosophy. At some point he also learned to read Greek.

By 1521 Rabelais had joined another monastery, where he fell in with a group of humanist scholars. In 1523, he experienced the first of a series of conflicts he would have throughout his life with conservative theologians* in Paris. The Faculty of Theology at the University of Paris seized the Greek and Latin books of Rabelais and his circle of friends. Although the faculty eventually returned the texts, Rabelais soon left to join another, less restrictive order of monks. Four years later he left that order and went out into the world.

Rabelais then went on to study medicine, receiving a Bachelor of Medicine degree in 1530. He practiced medicine on and off throughout his life, and his advanced language skills helped him to make a name for himself in the field. Medical schools of the time relied heavily on the works of ancient Greek medical writers such as HIPPOCRATES and GALEN. Rabelais produced new, accurate editions of these ancient texts. He also lectured on Hippocrates.

In 1531 Rabelais published his satire *Pantagruel,* which became immediately popular. However, the work offended the Faculty of Theology in Paris, who condemned it as indecent. Within a few years, Rabelais attached himself to an important patron*—Cardinal Jean du Bellay, the bishop of Paris. However, du Bellay's support was not enough to protect Rabelais from the Paris theologians, who continued to attack his work throughout his life.

In 1534 Rabelais published another satire, *Gargantua.* Like *Pantagruel,* this work poked fun at the Roman Catholic Church. Unluckily for Rabelais, a group of Protestant reformers chose the same year to post placards throughout Paris protesting Catholic practices. The Catholic Church immediately began to exercise greater control over booksellers and printers. Those who had criticized the church, like Rabelais, found themselves in a risky situation.

Rabelais received an advanced degree in medicine in 1537. For the rest of his life, he supported himself with money from his medical practice, support from his patrons, and the modest income he received for his popular writings. He also earned a small salary as a clergyman. In 1543 the Faculty of Theology condemned *Gargantua and Pantagruel,* but the king gave Rabelais permission to continue writing about the characters. Rabelais published two more volumes in the series before his death in 1553. The circumstances and exact date of his death are unknown.

Gargantua and Pantagruel. Rabelais' most famous work, *Gargantua and Pantagruel,* is a collection of five books. Rabelais published the first four books over a period of 20 years, and the fifth appeared after his death. The books' main characters—Pantagruel and his father, Gargantua—are giants that Rabelais modeled after figures in popular tales.

The first two books are similar in form to romances*, with plots that include a jumble of comic events. Throughout these adventures, Rabelais slips in satiric comments about the intellectual, religious, and professional people of his day. He also asserts the values of Christian humanism and the reform movement within the church. For example, one of his characters—Friar Jean—represents a new type of monk who is worldly and active. In later books, Pantagruel and his sidekick Panurge seek the advice of various counselors on whether Panurge should marry, eventually embarking on a mock epic* voyage to consult with an oracle. The plot of these books reflects the theme of a search for answers in an uncertain world.

Gargantua and Pantagruel celebrates the breaking of boundaries and rejects rigid points of view. As the narrator, Rabelais hides behind a number of masks—at one point he is a wise philosopher, at another a hustler. Rabelais also breaks with tradition by mixing words from both the highest and lowest realms of society. Finally, the work constantly switches its perspective, sometimes beginning with a serious commentary only to follow it with mockery. For example, when two characters encounter a riddle in a religious building, one of them reads it as a divine Christian truth, but the other sees only the rules for a game of tennis. These constant shifts deny the reader any clear statement of the author's beliefs. (*See also* **French Language and Literature; Satire.**)

* **romance** adventure story of the Middle Ages, the forerunner of the modern novel

* **epic** long poem about the adventures of a hero

Ramus, Petrus

1515–1572
French philosopher
and educator

Petrus Ramus was a controversial figure in France in the 1500s. A scholar, teacher, and speechmaker, he sought far-reaching changes in the educational system of his day. In particular, he challenged the authority of ancient writers whose works were central to Renaissance scholarship, such as the Greek philosopher ARISTOTLE and the Roman orator CICERO. Ramus drew on the work of scholars such as Rudolf AGRICOLA to create a new method of inquiry that vastly simplified the techniques of Aristotle. He claimed that his new method was useful in all fields of knowledge.

Life and Works. Pierre de La Ramée was born into a poor farming family in the French province of Picardy. He later adopted the Latin form of his name, Petrus Ramus. Ramus went to Paris in 1523 and worked his way through school as a servant for richer students. In 1537 he began his teaching career in Paris. He soon became notorious for his attacks on Aristotle, whose system of logic had dominated the curriculum for centuries.

In 1543 Ramus published his two chief works, *Training in Dialectic* and *Remarks on Aristotle*. In these works, he harshly criticized the followers of Aristotle, both ancient and modern. He also proposed a plan to change the entire curriculum of the Renaissance university. Ramus's ideas infuriated many of his colleagues. The following year his critics persuaded the French king, FRANCIS I, to ban Ramus from teaching either logic or philosophy. However, the next king, Henry II, lifted the ban in 1547.

In 1551 Ramus became royal lecturer at the Collège de France. He used this position to continue his attacks on Aristotle. In 1563 Ramus announced a plan for reforming the University of Paris, including firing professors, doing away with student fees, teaching physics in the arts curriculum, and adding professorships in astronomy, botany, and pharmacy. His plan, however, was short-lived. Within a year, the WARS OF RELIGION had broken out between Catholics and Protestants in France. Ramus, who had converted to Protestantism in 1562, had to flee Paris.

For several years Ramus moved between France, Germany, and Switzerland. While he was living in France in 1572, a wave of religious violence, known as the St. Bartholomew's Day massacre, occurred. During the course of the massacre, Ramus was murdered in his room. Some scholars believe his killers were assassins hired by a long-time academic enemy.

Ramus' Method. In the early Renaissance, university students learned logic and rhetoric* largely from the writings of Aristotle. His system of rhetoric involved five basic parts: invention, arrangement, style, memory, and delivery. Invention, according to Aristotle, was the art of selecting the best arguments to prove a point. This process, he claimed, belonged to the field of dialectic (logic) as well as to rhetoric.

* **rhetoric**   art of speaking or writing effectively

Several scholars of this time, including Agricola, Lorenzo VALLA, and Juan Luis VIVES, attempted to simplify Aristotle's system of logic. They came up with a new system based on invention and judgment—the art of laying out arguments in the most useful way. Ramus took up their ideas and carried them further. He sought to create a single method, with easily memorized rules, by which anyone could learn any subject.

In Ramus' method, students used the process of invention to find the relationship between a subject and the facts that could be stated about the subject. To take a simple example, in the sentence "Hot is the opposite of cold," the word "opposite" lays out the relationship between hot and cold. Ramus developed a list of 14 different arguments that could represent a relationship between subjects. To solve a problem, a student had to run through this list of arguments and select the best one for the topic. After choosing arguments, the student would then use the process of judgment, or arrangement, to assemble them in a useful order.

* **artisan**   skilled worker or craftsperson

Ramus believed that students could use this approach to solve any kind of problem. After observing artisans* at work in Paris and in Germany, he began to see connections between mechanical and philosophical theories and practical problem solving. As a teacher, Ramus promoted his classes not to philosophers but to young men seeking success in the world of commerce, government, and the professions. Ramus's ideas spread quickly. By the year 1650 there were more than

1100 printings of his works in Europe. His method found favor among practicing lawyers, orators, and teachers, especially in northern Europe and Protestant countries. (*See also* **Logic; Philosophy.**)

Raphael

1483–1520
Italian artist

* **composition**   arrangement of objects in a work of art

* **altarpiece**   work of art that decorates the altar of a church

* **patron**   supporter or financial sponsor of an artist or writer

Raphael Sanzio has been hailed as one of Europe's greatest painters. Critics of his own day and later have called him—along with MICHELANGELO and LEONARDO DA VINCI—one of the most important artists of the Renaissance. They have praised Raphael's versatility, coloring, and composition*, as well as the sweetness of his style. Although Raphael lived only to age 37, he had a substantial influence on many artists who came after him.

Early Career. Raphael was born in Urbino in central Italy and learned to paint from his father, an artist named Giovanni Santi. After Santi's death in 1494, the boy became an assistant in the workshop of PERUGINO, the most famous painter of the region at that time. Raphael quickly mastered Perugino's style, and the two artists' paintings from these years are hard to tell apart.

Raphael's first commission was for an altarpiece*, *St. Nicholas of Tolentino* (1500). Then he received several assignments from the duke of Urbino, including a painting of *St. George Fighting the Dragon*. In 1504 Raphael went to Florence, where he studied the works of Michelangelo and Leonardo. From Leonardo, Raphael learned sfumato, a technique that uses gentle shading rather than sharp outlines to define forms. From Michelangelo, Raphael learned to broaden his figures and to focus more on anatomy.

Raphael spent four years in Florence, applying what he was learning from other artists and experimenting with composition. He also worked for prominent patrons*. He produced numerous religious paintings, some featuring Mary and the infant Jesus, and others showing larger groups of individuals. The most complex of these works, the *Canigiani Holy Family,* includes five figures. He painted many portraits as well, and some of these show the influence of Leonardo's *Mona Lisa*. By the end of Raphael's time in Florence, the influence of Perugino had nearly disappeared from his work. Instead, his paintings reflected what he had learned from Michelangelo, Leonardo, and other artists working in the city.

A New Market for Art

Raphael was one of the first artists to sell prints of his work. In the early 1500s, there was a growing demand for affordable, mass-produced works of art. Raphael took advantage of this emerging market to test a new way of producing and selling pictures. He formed a partnership with an engraver who produced prints of his drawings and a businessman who sold them. Raphael controlled the process closely, providing the printer with detailed instructions about reproducing the images. He also received most of the profits from the prints, which helped spread his style across Europe.

Later Career. Some of the information about Raphael's career comes from Giorgio Vasari (1511–1574), a Renaissance painter and biographer. According to Vasari, in about 1508 the young artist heard from the architect Donato BRAMANTE (a distant relative) that Pope JULIUS II had work for him. As a result, Raphael left Florence and went to Rome.

The pope asked Raphael to decorate a room called the Stanza della Segnatura in the Vatican Palace. Pleased with the result, Pope Julius assigned the artist to paint the neighboring audience chamber, the Stanza d'Eliodoro. Julius died before the work was finished, but the new pope, LEO X, ordered Raphael to continue. Then Leo commissioned

RAPHAEL

Raphael's serene portraits of the Madonna, the mother of Christ, became models for other artists. His *Madonna of the Fish,* shown here, dates from around 1513.

* **humanist** Renaissance expert in the humanities (the languages, literature, history, and speech and writing techniques of ancient Greece and Rome)

* **papal** referring to the office and authority of the pope

* **fresco** mural painted on a plaster wall

* **classical** in the tradition of ancient Greece and Rome

See color plate 2, vol. 1

Raphael to paint two more rooms, including the meeting chamber of the supreme church court.

Popes Julius II and Leo X surrounded themselves with humanists*. Raphael had not received a classical education, but these scholars supplied him with subject matter for his art drawn from the works of ancient Greek and Roman writers. Under their influence, Raphael developed a style inspired by ancient culture that perfectly suited the papal* court. Raphael became so popular with Rome's patrons that he had more work than he could do. He painted altarpieces and portraits, including one of Pope Julius, as well as frescoes* of biblical and classical* subjects.

The years that Raphael spent in Rome, from 1508 to 1520, were the most productive ones of his life—and also one of the most creative periods of the Renaissance. While Raphael was decorating the Vatican rooms, Michelangelo was painting the ceiling of the Vatican's Sistine Chapel, and Bramante was building the new church of St. Peter. Around 1515 Pope Leo placed Raphael in charge of all classical structures in Rome and asked him to create a map of the city as it had looked in ancient times. For the next five years, Raphael also served as architect of St. Peter's and several other churches and palaces, and he produced drawings for a set of tapestries to be hung in the Sistine Chapel. In 1518 Raphael completed two paintings commissioned as gifts for King FRANCIS I of France: *St. Michael* and *Holy Family of Francis I.* Raphael's last work, completed just a few days before his death, was *Transfiguration,* which illustrates passages from the New Testament.

Artistic Methods and Influence. Raphael helped change the way artists' workshops functioned in the 1500s. Other masters, such as Perugino, had operated large workshops where they supervised assistants who helped them produce pieces. Raphael gave the artists in his workshop considerable responsibility. As his fame grew, so did the

* **apprentice** person bound by legal agreement to work for another for a specified period of time in return for instruction in a trade or craft

* **perspective** artistic technique for creating the illusion of three-dimensional space on a flat surface

* **relief** type of sculpture in which figures are raised slightly from a flat surface

See color plate 14, vol. 4

demands on his time, and he gathered more artists around him. By 1515 Raphael had what was probably the largest painting workshop that had ever been assembled. Vasari reported that 50 artists accompanied the painter to the Vatican each day. Some were assistants and apprentices*, but others were mature artists who functioned as partners.

Raphael was involved in every stage of a project in his workshop without taking complete responsibility for any step after the initial idea. The other artists not only copied and enlarged designs on sketches, but also drew new studies of live models. Raphael seems to have treated the workshop as a cooperative venture, rather than a strict master-apprentice relationship, and other artists of his time considered him a generous teacher.

Raphael invented new types of composition and new ways of using color, often adapting the methods of others to create his own distinctive techniques. In composing his paintings, he experimented with several different types of perspective*. He also tried to imitate ancient relief*. In *Battle at the Milvian Bridge* (on the wall of one of the Vatican rooms), he combined traditional perspective with relief. Designed by Raphael and painted by his workshop after his death, the scene shows the emperor Constantine and his army, moving like a procession from left to right.

Raphael was the first artist to adapt his colors to each individual commission. Before Raphael, artists usually used only one style of coloring, which they taught to their apprentices. Raphael combined Leonardo's subtle, smoky sfumato tones with the Florentine taste for beautiful color effects. The result was a style called *unione,* which Raphael used when he wanted to express harmony. For more dramatic scenes he turned to chiaroscuro, a style marked by deep shadows and high contrast between dark and light colors. In his final masterpiece, *Transfiguration,* Raphael used *unione* in the upper part of the painting, which is dominated by an image of Christ. In the lower part, a scene of earthly struggle, he employed chiaroscuro. Raphael's experimentation with color styles encouraged the next generation of artists to make their paintings more expressive by combining colors in a creative way. (*See also* **Art, Education and Training; Art in Italy; Rome.**)

| **Reformation** | **See** *Catholic Reformation and Counter-Reformation; Protestant Reformation.* |

| **Religion** | **See** *Bible; Christianity; Clergy; Islam; Jews; Missions, Christian; Popes and Papacy; Preaching and Sermons; Religious Literature; Religious Orders; Religious Thought.* |

Religious Literature

Because Christianity played such a major role in the social and intellectual life of the Renaissance, almost all the literature produced in Europe at that time had some religious content. However, many types of works were specifically Christian in nature. Religious writers produced poetry, stories, essays, and dialogues, written both in Latin and in

* **vernacular**   native language or dialect of a region or country

* **laypeople**   those who are not members of the clergy

* **humanism**   Renaissance cultural movement promoting the study of the humanities (the languages, literature, and history of ancient Greece and Rome) as a guide to living

* **epic**   long poem about the adventures of a hero

* **medieval**   referring to the Middle Ages, a period that began around A.D. 400 and ended around 1400 in Italy and 1500 in the rest of Europe

vernacular* languages. All these works fell under the broad heading of devotional literature, which aimed to help the reader lead a more holy life.

Devotional writing changed in several ways during the late Middle Ages and the Renaissance. For example, by the middle of the 1300s, the growing use of the vernacular in writing had helped to create new forms of religious literature. At the same time, a large new audience for books emerged among laypeople*. During the Renaissance, other factors such as the development of printing and the intellectual movement known as humanism* produced further changes in religious literature. However, people continued to read older religious texts, including works written by church fathers (individuals who shaped Christianity in its early centuries). Also, new religious works continued to focus on themes that had been traditional throughout the Middle Ages.

Major Themes. The most popular devotional texts of this period advised readers about following the example of Jesus Christ. This theme appeared in such works as *Life of Christ* by Ludolph of Saxony and *Imitation of Christ* by Thomas à Kempis. These works taught that believers could recreate Christ's sufferings in their own minds and bodies, an idea that became a focus of spiritual exercises for Catholics and some Protestants in the late Renaissance. For Catholics, literature of this type focused largely on the physical details of Christ's suffering.

Another major figure in devotional literature was the Virgin Mary. Catholic authors of this period wrote about the Virgin in epics*, lyric poetry, sermons, and meditations. These works discussed Mary's various roles as a wife and mother, a worker of miracles, and a person who pleads on behalf of sinners. Devotion to other members of Christ's Holy Family, such as his cousin John the Baptist, became popular at this time as well. A cult also developed around Joseph, Mary's husband, which presented Christ's earthly father as a model for Christian fathers.

Some devotional literature focused on the ideal of isolation, which provided a contrast to a Renaissance culture centered on the life of the city and the court. Many texts described the experiences of the Desert Fathers, who fled Roman persecution in the 200s and 300s. These holy men settled in Egypt, where they lived as hermits. The image of a person alone in the desert provided a popular model for many Christians. During the 1500s, however, this ideal faded as both Catholics and Protestants stressed the importance of public as well as private devotion.

Another form of religious literature, the confessional, evolved out of the handbooks used by medieval* priests to guide them in the care of souls. With the development of printing, these works became available to laypeople as well. Confessionals might take such forms as biographies, catalogues of virtues, or dialogues. For example, a text might be presented as a conversation between the body and the soul, Jesus and a sinner, or man and the devil.

A final theme that played a large role in religious literature was affectivity. This term, based on the word *affectus* meaning love or emotion, referred to a spirituality based on experience and emotion rather than

on reason. Literature of this type became very popular during the Catholic Reformation* of the mid-1500s. Authors attempted to appeal directly to the reader's senses, to inspire sighs, groans, and tears. Many authors of affective works were women, such as the Spanish nun TERESA OF ÁVILA.

Literature of Prayer. For those who could read, literature played a central role in the Renaissance practice of prayer. During the Renaissance, Christians read religious works both publicly and privately. Some Renaissance religious scholars viewed the act of reading alone as the first step on a path leading to a greater spiritual awareness. From reading, they claimed, the soul moved to meditation, prayer, and finally contemplation, a state of mystical* awareness of God. Public reading, by contrast, was done out loud, in a group, often as part of a church service or other ritual.

Prayer, like reading, might be either spoken or silent. Although vocal prayer played an important role in certain religious rituals, devotional literature more often focused on mental prayer. The Spanish mystic St. John of the Cross described praying in silence as a conversation between the soul and God. Various texts of the late Renaissance urged readers to pray passively before the mystery of God's presence. During the Renaissance, various disagreements about the nature of prayer arose between Protestants and Catholics, as well as within each group. However, both Protestant and Catholic literature about prayer—like devotional literature in general—took up the most basic theme of modern literature: the self. (*See also* **Catholic Reformation and Counter-Reformation; Latin Language and Literature; Religious Thought.**)

Religious Orders

During the Middle Ages and Renaissance, there were two types of clergy members. One group, known as the secular* clergy, lived in the world and tended to the spiritual needs of laypeople*. The other type of clergy belonged to religious orders—groups of men or women who lived according to a religious "rule," usually involving vows of poverty, chastity*, and obedience. Many new religious orders appeared during the Renaissance, and many existing orders underwent reforms.

REFORMS OF EXISTING ORDERS

By the 1400s, most religious orders had strayed far from the ideals of their founders. Traditional monasteries, which followed the Benedictine Rule (a series of rules laid down in the 500s by St. Benedict), had fallen into decline in the 1200s and 1300s. They faced competition from the rise of mendicant orders, whose members lived by begging and were forbidden to own property. At the same time, a new system known as the *commenda* was placing many monasteries in the hands of people who often ran the houses purely for their own gain. During the 1300s, even the mendicant orders fell away from their basic ideal of poverty.

In 1534 Ignatius Loyola founded the Society of Jesus, the largest new religious order of the Renaissance. He appears at the center of this picture holding a copy of the order's constitution. Other noted Jesuits of the 1500s and 1600s stand nearby.

* **papacy** office and authority of the pope

All these problems helped contribute to the growing sense of need for reform within religious orders. Many orders began to return to their founding rules. For example, the Franciscans—an order founded by St. Francis of Assisi in the 1100s—had begun as a mendicant order of hermits. Over time, however, the papacy* had eased many of the strict rules under which the Franciscans lived. In the late 1300s a group of monks who followed a reform movement called the Observance sought to restore the order's original ideals. Observant houses appeared throughout Europe during the 1400s. However, other Franciscans, known as Conventuals, opposed their reforms. After years of controversy, Pope Leo X divided the Franciscan order into two parts, the Conventuals and the more rigid Friars Minor. Two even stricter groups of Franciscans, the Minims and the Capuchins, appeared in the late 1400s and early 1500s.

Reform of the Dominicans, another mendicant order, also began in the late 1300s. Dominican religious houses joined together to form larger groups called congregations that were independent of Dominican control but still linked to the order. By the late 1400s nearly all Dominican congregations, except in England, were reformed.

The old-fashioned order of the Benedictines also underwent reforms beginning in 1424. The reform movement tightened the union between abbeys and required monks to take vows to their congregation, not to a specific abbey. These reforms began in Padua, Italy, and spread throughout Europe. One congregation in Austria contained over 100 abbeys.

NEW RELIGIOUS ORDERS

Beginning in the 1500s, several new religious orders arose throughout Europe, especially in Italy. Many of these were a different kind of order known as clerics regular, or priests living under a religious rule. Although they took the traditional vows of monks, they also devoted

themselves to active ministries, mostly in schools and parishes. The largest group of this type was the Jesuits. However, a variety of smaller orders for both men and women appeared at this time.

The Jesuits. The Society of Jesus, or Jesuits, first appeared in 1534 when IGNATIUS LOYOLA and six other students at the University of Paris made a pact to travel to the Holy Land to convert the Muslims. They took vows of poverty and chastity and eventually became priests. However, war prevented them from continuing to Jerusalem. In 1539 they formed a new plan to spread the faith through preaching, hearing confessions, and performing works of mercy. They took a special vow to make themselves available for missionary work anywhere in the world. By the end of the 1500s, Jesuits had missions in India, Japan, China, Brazil, Mexico, and other parts of Spanish America.

In 1548 the Jesuits opened their first school in Messina, Sicily. Until then they had avoided permanent assignments, but the school was so successful that soon the order considered teaching its primary mission. The Jesuits thus became the first teaching order in the Catholic Church. They came to exercise a great deal of influence on education.

Like the Dominicans and Franciscans, the Jesuits remained independent from the control of local bishops. However, the group differed from other orders in several ways. They did not gather together during the day to sing hymns or pray, and they did not wear a distinctive habit. More importantly, the Jesuits used a book written by Ignatius, the *Spiritual Exercises,* as their guide to spiritual life. This practice unified and motivated the order. Ignatius also insisted on frequent correspondence between Jesuit leaders and the members of the order. This helped to promote a common outlook among Jesuits. Their letters have since provided a highly valuable resource for historians of the Renaissance. Humanism* had a profound impact on the Jesuits. Because of their emphasis on teaching, many Jesuits became expert in subjects such as science, philosophy, and theology. The Jesuits played a leading role in the spread of humanist ideas.

Other Male Orders. Most of the new Italian orders dedicated themselves to charitable acts such as helping the poor, tending the sick, or educating children. One major teaching order was the Piarists, founded by St. José Calasanz. In 1597 he opened a free school in Rome, paid for by donations from wealthy clergy members. The school educated poor boys in the catechism* and in other subjects that helped them to earn a living. Pope Clement VIII approved the order in 1604. The order grew rapidly, but this caused several problems. Standards fell as the Piarists rushed poorly trained teachers into classrooms. Also, the Jesuits grew to resent the Piarists as a rival teaching order. In 1642 the Roman Inquisition* briefly arrested Calasanz and forbade the order to take in new members. However, the Piarists thrived after the pope restored them as a full order in 1669.

One of the more controversial Italian orders was the Barnabites, founded by St. Antonio Maria Zaccaria. In 1533 he and two friends set up a community of priests living the simple life of monks. A friend of

* **humanism**   Renaissance cultural movement promoting the study of the humanities (the languages, literature, and history of ancient Greece and Rome) as a guide to living

* **catechism**   handbook of religious teachings

* **Roman Inquisition**   religious court started in Rome in 1542 to deal with those accused of straying from the official doctrine of the Roman Catholic Church

* **confraternity**   religious and social organization of Roman Catholics who were not members of the clergy

* **penance**   act performed to show sorrow or repentance for sin

Woman's Work in a Man's World

During the Renaissance, the Roman Catholic Church made it difficult for women to perform missionary work. After the Council of Trent (1545–1563), the papacy would approve only cloistered orders of women. As a result, those who wished to work in the world often did so without papal approval. For example, Mary Ward of England founded the Institute of the Blessed Virgin Mary in the early 1600s. The institute opened several colleges and taught girls in many countries. However, the papacy refused to recognize it as a religious order because its members were not cloistered and because they performed tasks considered unfit for women. Pope Clement XI finally approved the order in 1703.

his, the countess Ludovica Torelli, founded a similar order for women, known as the Angelics. Several of Zaccaria's married friends then set up a confraternity* called the Devoted Married Laity of St. Paul. Many church leaders saw these three organizations as being too closely linked. The order further damaged its image by its public acts of penance*, in which mixed groups of priests and nuns painted their faces and whipped themselves. The Barnabites fell under suspicion from the Inquisition but eventually received approval from Pope Clement VII in 1533.

New religious orders arose in France partly in response to problems within the Catholic Church, which had been heavily drained by the extended WARS OF RELIGION that ended in 1598. The most influential new congregation was the Oratory of Mary and Jesus, founded by Pierre de Bérulle in 1611. Bérulle saw the priesthood, not the vows of religious orders, as the source of all holiness in the Church. Thus, he established an order of priests who lived together without taking vows and devoted themselves to training new clergy members. Several other orders arose either directly or indirectly from the Oratory, including the Congregation of St. Nicholas-du-Chardonnet and the Congregation of Jesus and Mary.

In 1625 Vincent de Paul established the Congregation of the Mission, another order of priests. Its members, known as the Lazarists, preached, taught catechism, heard confessions, and tended the sick. One of Vincent's followers, Jean-Jacques Olier, founded St. Sulpice seminary, which became a leading center for the training of priests in France.

Orders of Women. The role of women in the Roman Catholic Church underwent a profound change during the Renaissance. Developments within society and the church encouraged women to take a more active role in religious life and to engage in charitable work aimed at helping the poor, the sick, and orphans.

In the late 1300s the Dutch priest Geert Grote founded an order called the Sisters and Brethren of the Common Life. His goal was to promote a religious life devoted to prayer and meditation. Unlike nuns, members of the Sisters came mostly from noble or middle-class backgrounds, did not take vows, and maintained the right to own property. These secular features made the order more acceptable to the public, which feared the growth of religious groups that did not pay taxes. Over time, however, religious and secular authorities began pressing the Sisters to adopt a religious rule. Many of them formed convents and placed themselves under the authority of the church.

In 1535 Angela Merici, a young Italian woman, established a confraternity called the Company of St. Ursula for women who wished to devote themselves to God but could not afford the entrance fee required by most convents to help support the new nun. The order sought to protect the virginity of its members, but did not require them to take vows. The Ursulines taught catechism to young girls and promoted female education. In France, the Ursulines eventually formed traditional convents, and French Ursuline nuns established the first female mission in Canada in the early 1600s.

The Angelics of St. Paul, the female counterpart to the Barnabites, also led a religious life that included performing acts of charity. Their main work involved reforming convents and helping the sick, orphans, and former prostitutes. In time, the independence of the Angelic Sisters aroused opposition from church leaders, and in 1552 the order adopted a cloistered life, shut away from the public. (*See also* **Clergy; Confraternities; Devotio Moderna; Education; Inquisition; Missions, Christian; Women.**)

Religious Thought

* **theology** study of the nature of God and of religion

* **classical** in the tradition of ancient Greece and Rome

* **mystical** based on a belief in the idea of a direct, personal union with the divine

The Renaissance brought many new ideas and trends to the study of theology*. Religious scholars began to reexamine sacred texts in the light of classical* knowledge. They studied the Bible in its original languages (Greek and Hebrew) and applied the doctrines of ancient philosophers to religious ideas. The Kabbalah, a mystical* Jewish system of interpreting the Scriptures, also played a major role in the ideas of both Christian and Jewish thinkers during this period.

CHRISTIAN THOUGHT

During the Middle Ages, most Europeans were members of the Roman Catholic Church. However, a number of different schools of religious thought existed within this single church. Catholics differed over such issues as whether the pope should be subject to the authority of church councils. These theological divisions became more pronounced during the Renaissance. Scholars began to question many traditional doctrines of the Catholic Church and to adopt new views based on their reexamination of ancient religious texts.

Attacks on Scholasticism. Religious scholars of the Middle Ages had favored a philosophy known as Scholasticism, which combined Christian faith with the ideas of the Greek thinker ARISTOTLE. The most important explanation of this belief system appeared in *Summa Theologica,* by St. Thomas Aquinas (1225–1274). During the Renaissance, however, many scholars attacked Aquinas' work because it relied heavily on abstract ideas and formulas. Humanists* such as Desiderius ERASMUS (ca. 1466–1536), as well as some Protestant reformers, favored another approach. They urged Christians to follow the example and teachings of Jesus. The Roman Catholic Church responded to attacks on its doctrines at the Council of Trent, which took place between 1545 and 1563. The church reaffirmed the views of Scholastic thinkers that it had supported throughout the Middle Ages.

* **humanist** Renaissance expert in the humanities (the languages, literature, history, and speech and writing techniques of ancient Greece and Rome)

Christians and the Bible. Biblical studies blossomed during the Renaissance as humanist scholars began reviving the original Greek and Hebrew versions of the text. For most of Christian history, theologians had relied on a Latin version of the Bible known as the Vulgate. Renaissance scholars such as Lorenzo VALLA compared the Vulgate with the original texts and found many flaws in the translation. Their work helped translators such as Erasmus prepare new versions of the Bible that followed the original sources more closely. Erasmus also wrote a set of "paraphrases" of the New Testament. The paraphrases aimed to make biblical passages easier to understand by rewriting them in simpler terms.

The Protestant Reformation* of the early 1500s spurred efforts to interpret and analyze the Bible. Martin LUTHER, the central figure of the Reformation, viewed the Bible as the sole source of religious knowledge and placed a great deal of importance on understanding it. In his commentaries on the Bible, he focused on the relationship between the Old and New Testaments. He noted that while the Old Testament had value for Christians on its own terms, its chief value lay in its hidden links to characters and events in the New Testament. Other Protestant leaders, such as Philipp MELANCHTHON, Huldrych Zwingli, and John CALVIN, also prepared commentaries on the Bible designed to help spread Protestant doctrines and train clergy members.

Patristics. Another major development in Christian thought at this time was the recovery of patristic works. The term *patristics* refers to the writings and doctrines of the church fathers, the theologians of the early Christian era. Throughout the Middle Ages, the writings of the church fathers often had been available only in translations or in incomplete versions. During the Renaissance, however, renewed contact between the Roman Catholic Church and the Orthodox Church, centered in the city of Constantinople, helped restore the original texts to western Europe.

Renaissance humanists, aiming to recover the wisdom of the ancient world, made the revival of patristics an important part of their studies. Humanists such as Erasmus discovered, edited, and translated the writings of the major Greek and Latin church fathers or the 300s and early 400s, including AUGUSTINE OF HIPPO, St. Jerome, and John Chrysostom. Unlike scholars of the Middle Ages, humanists viewed the church fathers less as authorities on doctrine than as sources of Christian teaching. They believed the church fathers had special understanding of Christianity because they had lived so close to the time of Jesus. Many humanists also praised the church fathers for their knowledge of languages and literature.

New Directions in Christian Thought. During the Renaissance, many humanists sought to revive the ideas of the ancient Greek philosopher PLATO. These scholars, known as Neoplatonists, had a major impact on religious thought. Various factors shaped the growth of Neoplatonism, including the expanding knowledge of Greek, the increased contact between eastern and western churches, and the renewed study of the church fathers. Scholars such as Marsilio FICINO (1433–1499) sought to replace the ideas of Aristotle, which had held a central place in Scholastic thought, with those of Plato. They saw Plato's works as being closer to the philosophy of the Greek church fathers, especially St. Augustine.

---

* **Protestant Reformation** religious movement that began in the 1500s as a protest against certain practices of the Roman Catholic Church and eventually led to the establishment of a variety of Protestant churches

---

Renaissance and Reformation

In some ways, the humanist ideas of the Renaissance played a crucial role in the spread of the Protestant Reformation in the 1500s. Protestant reformers relied on the text of the Bible as the chief source of religious authority. Thus, their ideas rested on the work of humanists who had helped to recover biblical texts in their original Greek and Hebrew versions. However, the reformers disagreed with humanist thinkers on many points of theology. For instance, the reformers placed a great deal of emphasis on the idea of original sin. They saw humans as sinful, fallen beings whose only hope lay in the grace of God.

Several religious thinkers of the Renaissance urged Christians to model their lives on the example of Jesus. German theologian Thomas à Kempis, shown here, advanced this idea in his famous work of the early 1400s, *On the Imitation of Christ.*

The Neoplatonists played a key role in one of the biggest debates in Renaissance theology, the question of whether the human soul was immortal. The roots of the conflict lay in the writings of Averroes, an Arab philosopher who had commented on Aristotle in the 1100s. According to Averroes, Aristotle's works denied the immortality of the soul. For centuries, followers of Averroes—known as Averroists—continued to claim that only faith, and not reason, could prove that the soul was immortal. Throughout the Renaissance, various Italian scholars attacked the views of the Averroists. Ficino took a strong stand against them, making the immortality of the soul a key part of his belief system. However, another noted thinker, Pietro POMPONAZZI, claimed that according to reason, the soul must be mortal.

Many Neoplatonic thinkers also took an interest in mysticism. Several of them became students of the Kabbalah, a Jewish system of seeking hidden symbolic meanings within the Scriptures. Armed with a new-found knowledge of Hebrew, philosophers such as Giovanni PICO DELLA MIRANDOLA (1463–1494) and Giordano BRUNO (1548–1600) explored the Kabbalah to seek a deeper understanding of Christian beliefs.

JEWISH THOUGHT

Many of the same ideas that affected Christian scholarship during the Renaissance also played a role in Jewish thought. Like Christians, Jews explored the links between their faith and the ideas of ancient philosophers such as Aristotle. They also studied and wrote commentaries on the Bible and other sacred works.

Religion in Jewish Philosophy. Throughout the Middle Ages, Jewish philosophy and theology were closely connected. One of the most influential Jewish philosophers was Moses Maimonides of Spain (1135–1204). His work sought to link the divine wisdom of the Torah (the most sacred Jewish religious text) with human wisdom, as revealed in the works of Aristotle. Followers of Maimonides believed that Greek philosophy and the Torah taught the same truths in different ways.

During the 1400s Jewish thinkers in Spain became more familiar with the works of Thomas Aquinas and other Christian Scholastics. Drawing on these texts, they developed the notion that the truths of theology complete and perfect those of philosophy. Some Jewish thinkers sought to prove that the Jewish faith was in harmony with reason, while Christian doctrines were not. Other Jewish philosophers explored a variety of religious issues, such as the nature of God, the origin of the universe, prophecy, miracles, and human perfection. Some scholars also blended the ideas of the Kabbalah into their worldview. They linked the hidden meaning of the Torah to the ideal order of the universe, as contained within the mind of God.

Jewish philosophy in Renaissance Italy relied heavily on the ideas of Aristotle and Maimonides. In addition, Italian Jews explored the works of Averroes and Plato. Some Jewish philosophers played a major role in the growth of Neoplatonic thought. For example, Yohann Alemanno

(ca. 1435– ca. 1504) became the teacher of the philosopher Giovanni Pico della Mirandola and introduced him to both the Kabbalah and Jewish texts on Plato.

In 1492 Spain forced all its Jews to leave the country. Many Jewish exiles fled to the Ottoman Empire* and spread their philosophy there. Scholars in eastern cities began to focus their attention on the Bible and other sacred texts. A leading philosopher of the 1500s was Moses Almosnino, who developed a moral philosophy based on Scholastic sources, Jewish and Muslim thought, and the Kabbalah. His belief system declared that humans could achieve union with God through moral action.

Jews and the Bible. The Bible played a key role in Jewish scholarship during the Middle Ages. Jews studied the Old Testament in terms of both its language and its role in Jewish law and custom. The understanding of the Bible also informed the study of secular* philosophy and mysticism. Most scholars drew on all these areas of knowledge—language, tradition, philosophy, and mysticism—in their teaching.

During the Renaissance, Jewish exiles from Spain brought their studies to other regions, especially in eastern Europe. Most of these biblical scholars saw the Torah as the ultimate source of human knowledge. However, they also believed that the Scripture was vastly complex, filled with symbols and allegories* that required explanation. To unearth the layers of meaning within the Bible, they used a method borrowed from Christian Scholasticism. This technique involved laying out a series of questions and objections and then resolving them in a long discussion. Jewish scholars tended to focus on complex issues rather than straightforward ones, and they enjoyed discovering hidden connections between distinct fields of knowledge.

Jewish Messianism. Several Jewish thinkers in the 1400s and 1500s argued that the end of the world, or apocalypse, was near. They believed that this coming crisis would bring forth a Messiah—a hero who would save the Jews both as individuals and as a people. The Messiah, some claimed, would bring God's revenge upon the enemies of the Jews and establish a miraculous kingdom on earth. Many also believed that the coming of the Messiah would put an end to death and restore the dead to life.

Several writers of the late 1400s and 1500s predicted the arrival of the Messiah. A few even claimed to be the Messiah or someone else who would play a major role in the apocalypse. One of the most important messianic writers was Isaac Luria (1534–1572), a student of the Kabbalah. He claimed that the Messiah would be a spiritual leader, rather than a political or military one. This figure, he argued, would restore the power of God on earth and would fight the forces of evil.

ISLAMIC THOUGHT

In most parts of the Islamic world, philosophy fell into decline in the 1100s. Theologians in the east opposed the study of metaphysics*,

* **Ottoman Empire**   Islamic empire founded by Ottoman Turks in the 1300s that reached the height of its power in the 1500s; it eventually included large areas of eastern Europe, the Middle East, and northern Africa

* **secular**   nonreligious; connected with everyday life

* **allegory**   literary or artistic device in which characters, events, and settings represent abstract qualities and in which the author intends a different meaning to be read beneath the surface

* **metaphysics**   branch of philosophy concerned with the nature of reality and existence

which they saw as being in conflict with the revealed word of God in the Qu'ran, the sacred text of Islam. As metaphysics sank in importance, religious scholars turned to mysticism. The most noted mystical thinker of this period was Muhyi al-Din ibn al 'Arabi of Spain. His works and those of his students focused on such themes as the divine unity of all creation and the powers of rare individuals who are "friends of God."

In the late 1200s and early 1300s, many Muslim thinkers rejected mysticism, which they feared would dissolve the legal and ethical system of Islam. Scholars such as Ibn Taymiya of Damascus, Syria (1263–1328), insisted that the goal of Islam was not to understand or love God but to obey him. According to Ibn Taymiya, the only way to do this was to return to the teachings of the Qur'an and the practices of the Prophet Muhammad, the founder of Islam. Similar ideas arose in the Muslim empire of India in the 1600s, where scholars called for a purification of religion through a return to the Qur'an and Islamic law. (*See also* **Christianity; Classical Scholarship; Ideas, Spread of; Jewish Languages and Literature; Jews; Philosophy; Religious Literature.**)

Renaissance: Influence and Interpretations

Writing in the 1430s, Matteo Palmieri of FLORENCE celebrated "this new age, so full of hope and promise" with a greater collection of "nobly-gifted souls" than the world had seen in a thousand years. Like others of his day, Palmieri believed he was living in a special time, a period of tremendous intellectual and artistic creativity inspired by the ancient world. That era came to be known as the Renaissance, and ever since Palmieri's day historians have discussed its causes, characteristics, and importance.

IDENTIFYING THE RENAISSANCE

For centuries, scholars have seen the Renaissance as a distinct period of history. However, most have used more than just dates to identify the time. They have also examined intellectual movements, political changes, technological advances, and other factors in an attempt to understand Renaissance society.

Defining the Era. The cultural changes that launched the Renaissance began to take shape around 1350. At about that time, new developments in learning, the arts, politics, and society emerged in Italy. Many Italian intellectuals became interested in humanism* with its focus on ancient Greek and Roman culture. By the late 1400s these developments had spread to the rest of Europe, aided by the invention of printing. In northern Europe, other factors, such as new religious ideas, influenced Renaissance thought.

No single date marks the end of the Renaissance. Nevertheless, historians generally agree that, by the mid-1600s, the artistic and intellectual trends of the period had run their course and new ideas were emerging. Events such as the THIRTY YEARS' WAR (1618–1648) had

* **humanism** Renaissance cultural movement promoting the study of the humanities (the languages, literature, and history of ancient Greece and Rome) as a guide to living

changed the political map of Europe. By then, humanists had revived the learning of ancient Greece and Rome and made it part of the curriculum at European schools and universities. A few developments after the mid-1600s, such as the later works of the English poet John MILTON (who died in 1674) are also often included in the Renaissance.

The Renaissance View of the Era. The notion of an age focused on reviving the best features of ancient culture began with the Italian poet PETRARCH in the mid-1300s. Scholars of the 1400s and 1500s, especially Italians, further developed Petrarch's ideas about the Renaissance and his belief that it was a unique period of history.

Petrarch changed the European view of history. Earlier, scholars had considered the birth of Christ to be a major turning point, marking the end of the dark pagan* times and the beginning of the Christian age. But Petrarch viewed the writing and scholarship of the MIDDLE AGES as inferior to the learning and languages of the classical* world. He divided history in a new way, with its turning point in the A.D. 300s, when the Roman Empire adopted Christianity. For Petrarch, this marked the end of the classical era and the beginning of a less civilized time. He began calling the two eras "ancient" and "modern," and he clearly valued the ancient more highly.

By the time of his death in 1374, Petrarch had acquired followers who shared his vision. They contributed to the burst of CLASSICAL SCHOLARSHIP—especially the recovery and publication of many texts from ancient Greece and Rome—that fueled the humanist movement.

The humanist historian Flavio Biondo (1392–1463) promoted the idea of dividing history into three distinct periods: antiquity*, marked by great learning; a middle period of about one thousand years; and an era of cultural rebirth beginning about 1400. Other humanists developed the view that the Middle Ages had been a time of darkness and ignorance. "It is but in our own day," wrote Palmieri, "that men dare to boast that they see the dawn of better things." Writers like Palmieri and Giorgio Vasari (1511–1574) claimed that the rebirth of culture began in literature with Petrarch, in art with the painter GIOTTO, and in Latin with Leonardo BRUNI, a humanist scholar who worked to restore what he considered the classical purity of the language. This view of the origins of the Renaissance became widespread in Italy during the 1400s and 1500s.

Other Europeans agreed that a new age had dawned after the long medieval* period. French humanists acknowledged that the Renaissance had begun in Italy, but also credited French figures, such as king FRANCIS I (ruled 1515–1547), for their efforts in encouraging a cultural rebirth. Some northern European thinkers, including the philosopher Desiderius ERASMUS (ca. 1466–1536), saw the Renaissance in religious terms, as a return to the pure and authentic beliefs of early Christianity as well as to classical culture.

Beginning in the 1500s, the Protestant Reformation* influenced the way some people thought about the Renaissance. Protestant historians of the time accepted the concept of ancient and medieval periods giv-

* **pagan**   referring to ancient religions that worshiped many gods, or, more generally, to any non-Christian religion

* **classical**   in the tradition of ancient Greece and Rome

* **antiquity**   era of the ancient Mediterranean cultures of Greece and Rome, ending around A.D. 400

* **medieval**   referring to the Middle Ages, a period that began around A.D. 400 and ended around 1400 in Italy and 1500 in the rest of Europe

* **Protestant Reformation**   religious movement that began in the 1500s as a protest against certain practices of the Roman Catholic Church and eventually led to the establishment of a variety of Protestant churches

Giorgio Vasari, shown in this self-portrait from the 1560s, was one of several Renaissance writers who described their own time as a glorious age of cultural rebirth. His influential work *The Lives of the Most Excellent Architects, Painters, and Sculptors* claimed that the great art of the ancient world had fallen into decline during the Middle Ages. He saw the work of artist Giotto de Bondone in the early 1300s as the beginning of a major revival in art.

* **papacy**   office and authority of the pope

ing way to a rebirth. However, they emphasized some of the problems of the Middle Ages, blaming the papacy* for its cultural backwardness and its religious errors and abuses. They also saw their own age as the time in which true religion was restored. Although Italian writers paid little attention to religious matters when describing the Renaissance, Protestant historians often viewed the period in terms of both a revival of scholarship and religious reform.

INTERPRETING THE RENAISSANCE

Scholars have been studying the Renaissance since it ended. They have compared the Renaissance with the periods before and after it; noted the

forms it took in various parts of Europe; examined the relationship between the Renaissance and the Protestant Reformation; and traced the influence of the Renaissance on later culture. For centuries, most historians shared the view of the period as a rebirth after the darkness of the Middle Ages. More recently, scholars have expanded and sometimes challenged that interpretation.

The 1700s and 1800s. Intellectuals of the 1700s inherited from the humanists the division of history into three eras. They tended to emphasize the contrast between the Middle Ages and the modern era. In *Essay on the Manners and Spirit of Nations* (1756), the French writer Voltaire argued that during the Middle Ages the church had joined forces with certain governments to suppress individual freedom and reason. During the 1300s, 1400s, and 1500s, Italians and then the French had begun to shake off the chains of religion and take rational steps forward. Following Voltaire's lead, French art historian Jean-Baptiste Seroux d'Agincourt (1730–1814) identified the Renaissance with the art of the period between the Middle Ages and the 1700s.

Three scholars shaped the view of the Renaissance as a unique period of history. French historian Jules Michelet, in *The Renaissance* (1855), was the first to conceive of the Renaissance as a distinct period in European civilization, with a unique spirit that expressed itself in every aspect of life. That spirit, he wrote, was "the discovery of the world and the discovery of man." Michelet focused on the revival of classical antiquity, scientific discoveries, and geographic exploration.

Four years later, German historian Georg Voigt published a detailed study of Italian humanism. He saw a sharp break between medieval culture and the Renaissance, which he considered the beginning of modern culture. Voigt credited Petrarch with launching the Italian Renaissance and discovering "the new world of humanism." In Voigt's view, one of the key features of the Renaissance was individualism—an awareness of and emphasis on the individual. He identified Petrarch as displaying this characteristic because the poet expressed his personal interests rather than following an established philosophical system.

Swiss historian Jakob Burckhardt was the most influential Renaissance scholar of the 1800s. In *The Civilization of the Renaissance in Italy* (1860), Burckhardt summed up the views of the historians of his day and influenced other scholars for a century. His book covers six aspects of Italian Renaissance civilization: politics, individualism, the revival of antiquity, science, society, and religion.

In the section on politics, Burckhardt describes the origins of the Italian city-states. In discussing individualism, he argues that medieval people were aware of themselves only as members of families and other groups, but Renaissance people saw themselves as independent individuals. The third section of his book covers the revival of antiquity, which guided Renaissance humanists as they developed their interests and talents. The fourth section deals with Renaissance advances in scientific and geographic discovery. Next, in a discussion of society, Burckhardt claims that Renaissance cities developed a social structure in which status depended on culture and wealth, not birth. In the last section, on religion, the author suggests that excessive individualism led to a break-down in morals and a loss of respect for religion in Italy. Individualism also contributed to the country's decline in the 1500s. However, by that time the Italian Renaissance had succeeded in bringing Europe into the modern world.

Burckhardt's views on the Italian Renaissance were widely accepted, but scholars differed in their interpretations of the Renaissance in northern Europe. Most agreed that it was a break from the Middle Ages and that humanism was a key element. They disagreed, however, on the role of the Protestant Reformation. As a result, the northern Renaissance was never as clearly defined as the Italian Renaissance. In addition, some historians tended to think that the modern world originated in northern Europe in the 1500s, not in Italy in the 1400s.

From the 1900s Onward. From Petrarch through the 1800s, the Renaissance was seen as a revolt against the Middle Ages. The 1900s brought a reaction from scholars who specialized in medieval studies. Some accepted the existence of the Renaissance but placed its beginning back in earlier times. Others claimed that the Renaissance brought nothing new, that it was just a continuation—or even a decline—of medieval culture. The most influential attack on the Renaissance by a medievalist came from Charles Homer Haskins. In *The Renaissance of the Twelfth Century* (1927) he argued that the modern world had really begun in the 1100s and that the Italian Renaissance was a minor historical episode.

Renaissance scholarship increased dramatically after the end of World War II in 1945. Most scholars accepted the idea of the Renaissance but did not attempt sweeping studies of it. Instead, they focused on distinct aspects or phases of the Renaissance.

The major contribution of historians after the 1940s was identifying humanism as the unifying force of the Renaissance. In *The Crisis of the Early Italian Renaissance* (1955), Hans Baron distinguished between the early humanism of Petrarch and his followers, who advised withdrawal from active life in favor of study, and the later humanism of Leonardo Bruni and other Florentines, who believed that scholars should be involved in public affairs. Paul Oskar Kristeller (1905–1999), perhaps the most important Renaissance scholar of the 1900s, concentrated on humanism. He defined humanistic studies as the study of grammar, rhetoric*, poetry, history, and moral philosophy based on the standard ancient authors in Latin and sometimes Greek. Many other scholars accept this definition.

* **rhetoric** art of speaking or writing effectively

Another strand of Renaissance study has consisted of art criticism and art history. During the 1800s, John Ruskin and Walter Pater and other critics wrote extensively about the works of artists such as MICHELANGELO, GIORGIONE, and LEONARDO DA VINCI. The leading authority on Italian Renaissance painting for much of the 1900s, Bernard Berenson, viewed the Renaissance as a golden age. His influential studies focused on the qualities of works of art, rather than on the social and intellectual climates that produced them.

Since the mid-1900s scholars have examined the Renaissance from multiple angles, such as its religious expressions and political organiza-

tion. Specialists called social historians have increasingly turned away from politics and famous individuals to study the entire range of human activities and social groups. Sifting through mountains of historical data, social historians have provided detailed information about such aspects of life as courtship, marriage, poverty, crime, and the roles and rights of women.

Most scholars today still regard the Renaissance as different from the Middle Ages and as the beginning of the modern era. Some, however, deny that the Renaissance was a unique period, or they dismiss it as concerned only with the culture and experiences of elites*. Further research and interpretation will no doubt continue to influence thinking about the Renaissance.

* **elite** privileged group; upper class

INFLUENCE OF THE RENAISSANCE

In the traditional view, the Renaissance affected every area of human activity and knowledge, from art to zoology. It transformed Europe and, eventually, the rest of the world. In addition, it left a legacy that still shapes many aspects of modern life.

Education and History. Renaissance humanists created a school curriculum based on classical languages and literature. This system dominated European education for centuries. Students seeking to enter universities had to know Greek and Latin, and the classics were a key part of their studies. The English and French carried this humanist curriculum to North America, where, until the early 1900s, certain universities required students to know classical Latin.

Before the Renaissance, some people had thought of history as shaped by divine forces. By contrast, the humanists viewed history as a fully human activity. They also began to distinguish different ways of writing about history: as an art, like literature; as a way of teaching a moral or political lesson; or as a scientific quest for truth. The notion of history writing as a technical discipline based on facts began with the Renaissance historians.

Art and Science. The art and architecture of the Renaissance had a lasting influence on later centuries. Masterpieces by Michelangelo, Leonardo, RAPHAEL, and other Renaissance masters became standards of greatness. In addition, later artists continued trends begun during the Renaissance. For example, the method Filippo BRUNELLESCHI invented for showing perspective* is still taught and used today. The Renaissance also revived the classical idea of portraits as realistic images of individuals, a move toward modern portraiture.

* **perspective** artistic technique for creating the illusion of three-dimensional space on a flat surface

Renaissance architects drew on classical models and, in turn, were imitated by later designers. Andrea PALLADIO's writings and villas* have influenced many structures built over the years. Examples in the United States include the White House and Monticello, the home of Thomas Jefferson.

* **villa** luxurious country home and the land surrounding it

Science advanced when Renaissance humanists discovered and spread ancient works on mathematics, medicine, and other topics.

Renaissance Tales Retold

Renaissance playwright William Shakespeare borrowed plots from a variety of sources for his plays. In turn, many modern moviemakers have borrowed *his* plots. The science-fiction classic *Forbidden Planet* (1956) follows the story of Shakespeare's play, *The Tempest.* Japanese filmmaker Akira Kurosawa based *Throne of Blood* (1957) and *Ran* (1985) on *King Lear* and *Macbeth.* Shakespeare's comedy *The Taming of the Shrew* inspired the musical *Kiss Me Kate,* filmed in 1953. Eight years later, the movie version of the musical *West Side Story* recreated Shakespeare's *Romeo and Juliet* in New York City of the 1950s.

* **guild**   association of craft and trade owners and workers that set standards for and represented the interests of its members

Certain important scientific ideas took root during the Renaissance, including the value of precise measurement, the notion that the universe is mathematically harmonious, and the belief that technological progress is possible. These ideas laid the foundation for modern science. In addition, medicine was revolutionized in the Renaissance by two new practices: an emphasis on the study of anatomy and teaching medical students through direct observation of patients. Both of these elements remain important to medical training today.

Popular Imagination and Culture.   The general public draws ideas and images of the Renaissance from school, museums, books, television, and movies. Major Renaissance figures, such as Michelangelo and William SHAKESPEARE, are familiar to people all over the world, and the term "Renaissance" has entered the common vocabulary.

Because the Renaissance produced individuals with a wide range interests who excelled in a number of different areas, someone who is accomplished and successful in several fields is often called a "Renaissance man" or "Renaissance woman." Writers have referred to the outpouring of literary and artistic activity among African Americans of the 1920s as the Harlem Renaissance. In the 1970s, the city of Detroit, Michigan, rebuilt a downtown area to bring new life to a declining urban core. The area was named the Renaissance Center to convey images of rebirth and cultural achievement.

Shakespeare has had more influence in the popular imagination than any other Renaissance figure. Schools and universities teach his plays, which are performed more often than any other English plays. Phrases from his works, such as "To be or not to be," have become part of everyday language. Many of Shakespeare's plays have been filmed and or made into operas.

Other operas have drawn on Renaissance figures and settings. Gaetano Donizetti's *Lucrezia Borgia* (1833) offers a sensational and dramatic treatment of the life of a member of the powerful BORGIA clan. Giuseppe Verdi's *Don Carlos* (1867) alters the facts of history to create an exciting story set in Spain during the reign of PHILIP II. *Benvenuto Cellini* (1838), by Hector Berlioz, dramatizes the life of the great sculptor, while Richard Wagner's opera *Die Meistersinger* (*The Mastersinger of Nuremberg,* 1868) is based on the story of a German singers' guild* of the 1500s.

Historical fiction and films have also contributed to the popular image of the Renaissance. In novels such as *The Life of Cesare Borgia* (1912) and *Columbus* (1942), Rafael Sabatini depicts various larger-than-life characters who peopled the 1400s and 1500s. *The Agony and the Ecstasy* (1961), a novel by Irving Stone about Michelangelo, portrays the artist as a heroic genius struggling against society to create great works. It was later filmed. These and other works have shaped a dramatic and colorful vision of the Renaissance that is popular, although not entirely accurate. This view is summed up in the 1949 film *The Third Man,* when a character played by Orson Welles says, "In Italy for thirty years, under the Borgias, they had warfare, terror, murder, and bloodshed, but they produced Michelangelo, Leonardo da Vinci, and the Renaissance." (*See*

also **Art; Classical Antiquity; Europe, Idea of; History, Writing of; Humanism; Ideas, Spread of; Individualism; Literature; Science.**)

Representative Institutions

Representative institutions emerged in Europe during the late Middle Ages. Before that time kings ruled with the advice and support of the clergy, known as the first estate, and the nobility, known as the second estate. As towns became more important economically, they gained a voice in government as the third estate. Representatives of the estates met in an assembly, variously called the Parliament, Estates General, Cortes, Diet, or Landtag in different places. In Italy important towns became autonomous* and set up representative institutions to govern themselves.

ITALY

Governments with representative institutions were generally called republics. Renaissance writers used the term *republican* to describe a form of government dominated by leading merchants with little participation by others. Some scholars explain the enthusiasm for republican government as a result of the numerous independent city-states in Italy and the great interest in classical* culture. Republican governments with representative institutions took different forms.

Communes. Between the 1000s and 1200s, a number of northern and central Italian towns shook off the rule of local princes* and bishops. Each of these cities set up a commune—an association of citizens that took over many of the functions of government. These citizens usually came from the wealthy and merchant classes. Most communes had an elected executive committee of consuls and a larger assembly with which the consuls were supposed to consult. The assemblies acquired the power to approve laws that were binding on all citizens.

In the 1200s growing interest in the classical world led scholars to study the government of the ancient Roman republic. They admired the Roman principles of justice, peace, equality, and the common good, and adopted these ideals in forming communes. Brunetto Latini, chancellor of Florence in the 1250s, wrote that the commune was the best form of government because its members are elected and advised by the citizens and must follow the communal laws.

Guild Republics. Early communes represented mainly the interests of the wealthy classes. However, as urban economies developed and became more specialized, the associations of artisans* and tradespeople known as guilds grew dramatically. In many urban areas, they formed alliances and demanded representation. In Bologna, Padua, and Florence, groups of guilds even took over city government on several occasions.

Like the communes, these guild-based republics followed the example of ancient Rome, quoting the Roman principle "that which touches all

* **autonomous** self-governing; independent

* **classical** in the tradition of ancient Greece and Rome

* **prince** Renaissance term for the ruler of an independent state

* **artisan** skilled worker or craftsperson

* **humanist**   Renaissance expert in the humanities (the languages, literature, history, and speech and writing techniques of ancient Greece and Rome)

* **patronage**   support or financial sponsorship

* **aristocracy**   privileged upper classes of society; nobles or the nobility

* **elite**   privileged group; upper class

* **autonomy**   independent self-government

must be approved by all." However, they applied this principle in a limited way, extending rights only to those who lived in the city. People in the surrounding area controlled by the town had no say in government.

Influential humanists*, such as the poet PETRARCH and the Florentine chancellor Coluccio SALUTATI, supported the concept of republican government. Nevertheless, by the end of the 1300s republicanism based on the people and the guilds had begun to decline. In northern Italy, nobles reacted against the demands of the lower classes for greater representation and turned to despots—individual rulers with sweeping powers. In places where republicanism remained, the nature of government changed. The upper classes shared power but made it difficult for other groups to join the administration. In Florence members of the middle class came to depend upon the patronage* of the city's aristocracy*, which helped stifle political opposition. Those in control promoted the image of the city as a family, with the rulers as parents looking after the needs of their children.

Florence and Venice. Florence and Venice were the two Italian cities most closely associated with republican government. Florence had become a commune by 1138, and republican government survived in the city until the 1500s. By the 1430s the powerful MEDICI family controlled political life in Florence, but they ruled through existing republican institutions. When France invaded Italy in 1494, the Medici were banished from Florence and the monk Girolamo SAVONAROLA restored the republic. However, the Medici returned in 1512, and in the 1530s they abolished republican institutions and established themselves as dukes.

Although Venice was praised by many Renaissance observers as a model republic, its government was actually less representative than that of Florence. A Great Council made up of members of the elite* classes elected an executive officer, called the doge, and other officials to administer city business. Although the Great Council contained over 2,000 members, it had been closed to newcomers since 1297. Thus, an upper class of wealthy traders and investors held power in the city. Venice remained a republic until the French conquered it in 1797.

OTHER EUROPEAN STATES

Most towns in northern and eastern Europe did not attain the degree of independence reached by Florence and Venice. However, representative institutions existed in many provinces and at a national level, and, in some places, towns had a substantial amount of autonomy*.

The Netherlands. Towns in the Netherlands set up independent governments similar to those in Italian city-states. The upper classes dominated the towns until the 1300s, when challenged by urban wool workers. Eventually merchants and artisans gained the right to have representatives. In the southern provinces, guilds drew up lists of candidates for the town council, with the first burgomaster (similar to a

* **Flanders** region along the coasts of present-day Belgium, France, and the Netherlands

mayor) chosen from the aristocracy. In the north, the council and burgomaster all came from among the wealthiest citizens.

In Flanders* the towns of Ghent, Bruges, and Ypres ran the whole province, instead of the three estates that governed elsewhere. When Flanders became part of the duke of Burgundy's lands in the late 1300s, assemblies representing the first and second estates (the clergy and the nobility) were added. However, throughout the Netherlands, the town leaders (the third estate) still dominated political life because of their economic power. Although the duke could summon the assemblies to raise revenues, the councils of every province had to approve any new taxes. A veto by one of the estates or even by a single member of one commune could prevent the government from raising taxes.

In the 1500s the Netherlands came under the control of the HABSBURG king of Spain. Opposition to Spanish domination led to a revolt in the 1570s, and for a time the estates controlled the entire country. The southern provinces eventually accepted the return of Spanish rule, but the northern provinces remained independent until the late 1700s.

The Iberian Peninsula. The Spanish kingdoms of Castile and Aragon each had an assembly called the Cortes, with representatives from the clergy, the nobility, and the towns. In Castile, the clergy and the nobility paid no taxes, so they saw little reason to attend meetings of the Cortes. This left the towns to face the power of the monarch alone. Originally, a general assembly of the heads of families elected the representatives from the towns. However, by the 1300s representatives chosen by the monarchy held most of the power in the Cortes.

Aragon had a separate Cortes in each of its three provinces (Aragon, Valencia, and Catalonia). These assemblies possessed more independent power than the Castilian Cortes. In response to a political crisis of 1626, for example, the Cortes of Aragon and Valencia agreed to raise taxes for the crown but refused to send troops.

France. French kings began to summon representatives of the three estates to a national assembly, known as the Estates General, in the early 1300s. Deputies to the Estates General could not raise taxes but could recommend such an action to the assemblies of their provinces. The Estates General did not meet between 1484 and 1560. As a result, no taxes were authorized and the monarchy faced financial difficulties. The king often had to approach the estates of the provinces to raise money or approve treaties.

In France, the nobility and the clergy generally outvoted the representatives of the towns. Moreover, people in the countryside did not have their own representatives, but relied on local nobles to speak on their behalf. During the 1600s and 1700s, the crown worked to undermine the power of the estates. No Estates General met between 1615 and the beginning of the French Revolution in 1789.

England. By the time of the Renaissance, Parliament had been established as the representative institution in England. Parliament consisted of two bodies: the House of Lords (made up of members of the nobility)

Parliament, the representative assembly of England, met whenever the monarch called it into session. Here Elizabeth I presides over a meeting of Parliament.

Milites Provinciarum & Burgenses (quos vocant) utrinq. qui Cameram Parlamenti inferiorem constituunt Prolocutorem conducentes.

* **burgher** well-to-do middle class inhabitant of a town or city

and the House of Commons. In the early Renaissance, the House of Commons included two burghers* from each town and two knights from each rural county. Later, the towns began electing knights as well. As a result, most members of Parliament belonged to the aristocracy.

A New Estate

Scandinavia was the only region of Europe in which peasants gained representation in the national assembly. In Denmark, the nobility and clergy became so powerful that, in 1468, the king replaced the old assembly with a new body that included members from the nobility, clergy, burghers, and free peasants. Peasants also won representation in Sweden's national assembly in return for their support for a rebellion against the Scandinavian Union. In the 1400s Swedish opponents of the union—made up of Denmark, Norway, and Sweden—invited representatives of the burghers, miners, and peasants to a parliamentary meeting. Sweden succeeded in breaking free of the union, and later Swedish rulers frequently summoned the national assembly.

Some English monarchs summoned Parliament rarely, while others called members together for lengthy sessions. In the 1530s, HENRY VIII consulted Parliament as he broke away from the Roman Catholic Church and introduced religious changes in England. Later, Parliament oversaw the efforts of ELIZABETH I to lay the permanent foundations for the Church of England. In the 1600s, conflicts between Parliament and the king led to civil war. Between 1629 and 1640, CHARLES I refused to summon the members of Parliament and tried to govern without consulting them. In 1649 they had him executed.

Germany. Representative institutions in Germany took many forms. The clergy usually formed the first estate, but in many places they did not attend the local assembly, called the Diet or Landtag. In other areas, the nobility refused to participate in the Landtag to assert their independence from the local prince. They would only attend the Reichstag, the imperial assembly summoned by the emperor. Peasants generally had no representatives in the Landtag.

Many German towns achieved a good deal of autonomy, with guilds dominating town councils. Most towns were subject to the authority of a territorial prince. However, some became powerful enough to gain status as "imperial cities" under the emperor.

German princes often had their own sources of revenue. As a result, they did not need to rely on the Landtag to pass taxes. During the 1500s, many Protestant princes took over monasteries and other church properties with the approval of the local diet. For this reason, assemblies in Protestant regions gained new privileges and influence. In Catholic Bavaria, the princes remained strong and the power of the estates gradually declined. (*See also* **City-States; Government, Forms of; Guilds; Monarchy; Political Thought; Princes and Princedoms; Social Status; Taxation and Public Finance.**)

Revolts

During the Renaissance, social, economic, and political tensions often led to popular revolts. Although commonly referred to as peasant revolts, these uprisings usually involved townspeople as well as peasants. Moreover, most revolts were carefully planned and led by individuals from the upper levels of urban and rural society. The primary goal of rebellion was to achieve justice, and most rebels respected life and property. While some committed bloody acts, they targeted only individuals viewed as enemies of the community.

* **prince** Renaissance term for the ruler of an independent state

Causes of Revolt. Protest was a normal part of relations between lords and tenants or princes* and subjects. Most protests arose because of changes in political and economic organization or in social relationships. However, protest turned into revolt when the people believed that such changes threatened the survival of the community. For example, a combination of high taxes and unequal distribution of food might trigger an uprising. In most cases, the rebels sought to restore the previous state of affairs, not to overthrow the system.

Bad harvests, excessive taxation, and abuse from soldiers were the most common causes of rebellion. People tended to accept these hardships when they affected everyone equally. However, if some people profited while others suffered, revolt was likely. In 1585, for example, an uprising in Naples specifically targeted individuals who had been hoarding food.

Theories of Resistance and Revolt. Those who led rebellions turned to religion, history, and myth to justify their actions. Many cited biblical examples of protest and just wars against tyrants*. Both ancient Roman and Germanic law provided support for the right of the people to resist bad leaders and to take back power from them. Medieval churchmen also promoted the idea of justified resistance. In 1405, Jean de Gerson of France declared that, "No sacrifice is more pleasing to God than the death of a tyrant." Within the Roman Catholic Church, councils could challenge even the authority of the pope.

The Protestant Reformation* ushered in the great age of resistance in Europe. The original Protestants were German princes who opposed the decision of CHARLES V, the Holy Roman Emperor*, to outlaw the teachings of religious reformer Martin LUTHER (1483–1546). The princes based their right to revolt partly on Luther's claims that people should be free to follow their consciences. Luther accepted that kings ruled by God's will. However, he argued that "if one may resist the pope, one may also resist all the emperors and dukes who … defend the pope." Protestant Reformer John CALVIN (1509–1564) also accepted the divine rights of kings. Calvin recommended passive resistance instead of uprisings. However, he left the door open for revolt by adding that obedience to secular* authority should never come before obedience to God.

Calvinist leaders in France took a stronger position, especially after the French king authorized a massacre on St. Bartholomew's Day, August 24, 1572, that left thousands of Protestants dead. In writings that followed this event, resistors stated that the king drew his power from the people and that it was the duty of the people to reject tyranny. French writer Philippe Duplessis-Mornay proclaimed that subjects were justified in taking up arms against an unjust ruler.

Calvinists in the Netherlands and Catholics in England and France also used some of these arguments for revolt when they found themselves in opposition to their rulers. The argument turned on the question of who ultimately held power—the monarch or the people. In either case, there was always the danger of abuse of power.

Records of Revolt. Documents from the 1430s and 1440s indicate numerous revolts in Denmark and Sweden, and in the late 1400s several uprisings occurred in Germany. Reports of revolts become much more common during the 1500s. The first recorded major peasant uprisings in central and eastern Europe took place in Hungary (1514) and Slovenia (1515).

The revolt of Spain's Castilian cities (*comuneros*) shows how revolts affected the way rulers governed. Spanish nobles were alarmed when Charles I, their king, left Spain for Germany in 1519 to be crowned Holy Roman Emperor. They feared that his absence would further weaken the

* **tyrant** absolute ruler who uses power unjustly or cruelly

* **Protestant Reformation** religious movement that began in the 1500s as a protest against certain practices of the Roman Catholic Church and eventually led to the establishment of a variety of Protestant churches

* **Holy Roman Emperor** ruler of the Holy Roman Empire, a political body in central Europe composed of several states that existed until 1806

* **secular** nonreligious; connected with everyday life

This illustration shows German peasants taking up arms in a 1525 revolt against their lords. Known as the Peasants' War, the uprising actually included a wide range of common people, such as artisans, preachers, middle-class townspeople, and even minor nobles.

---

* **artisan**   skilled worker or craftsperson

kingdom, which was already being harassed by its neighbors. They also had complaints about Charles's rule—about the many foreigners who held government positions and about a new tax.

The Spanish rebellion began in urban areas as cities rose up against the crown. Rural villages quickly took advantage of the confusion to revolt against their lords. In response, many of the lords looked for royal protection. They gave the king their full support and strengthened the royal army. Many of the rebellion's urban leaders found it too difficult to maintain one revolt while fighting off another. They soon ended their uprising. Charles generously pardoned the rebels. Although he maintained control, the Comunero Revolt made it clear that Charles could govern successfully only by seeking the support of those he ruled.

The German peasant's revolt of 1525 stands out as the classic example of a popular uprising of the time. It began with opposition to German nobles expanding their economic and political control over their subjects. The main leaders were not peasants but artisans*, preachers, minor nobles, and middle-class townspeople. They organized resistance, and violence broke out in 1524. Over the next year uprisings swept through areas of southern Germany, Switzerland, Austria, and what is now eastern France.

Much of western Europe followed Germany's lead. In 1529 in France and in the 1540s in Belgium, people revolted to defend their traditional privileges. Several major uprisings occurred in the French territory of Aquitaine beginning in 1548 protesting a new salt tax. Bad harvests and political crises in the mid-1580s led to revolts in France and Italy. Religious politics set off a revolt in Paris in 1588, when the king ordered the execution of a duke and a cardinal.

Conditions worsened in the 1590s as a result of bad harvests and rising prices. Widespread famine and increasing prices led to a peasant uprising in Finland that lasted two years and a short-lived revolt in England. Between 1594 and 1597, Austrian peasants revolted on a large scale. From 1593 to 1595, French peasants and laborers rose up to resist new taxes in the revolt of the Croquants. (*See also* **Peasants' War; Violence; Warfare.**)

Rhetoric

Rhetoric, the art of speaking or writing persuasively, was a matter of great importance to educated people during the Renaissance. In schools, students used it to express their own ideas and to analyze the works of others. The basic principles of rhetoric were so familiar to educated people that they could use them almost without thinking. Eloquent speech became the key to success in professions and at court. Renaissance scholars based their study of rhetoric mainly on the works of CICERO, an ancient Roman orator and philosopher who claimed that when rhetoric combined wisdom and persuasive speaking, it produced civil government and justice.

Roots of Rhetoric.   Scholars of the Middle Ages and Renaissance learned about rhetoric largely from two ancient sources: Cicero's *On Invention* and an anonymous text called *The Art of Rhetoric for Herennius*. These sources identified three major types of rhetoric. Judicial rhetoric was used to present a case in court, while political rhetoric aimed to persuade an audience about political issues. The third type, epideictic rhetoric, served to praise or blame a particular person or thing. Speakers might use this form of rhetoric at ceremonies such as funerals and birthday celebrations.

On Invention and *Rhetoric for Herennius* divided rhetoric into five basic parts, known as canons. The first canon, invention, referred to the way speakers selected arguments to support their positions. Scholars drew on certain basic categories of thought, which they called topics, to find their arguments. For example, in describing a person, a speaker might use such topics as appearance, education, and character. The Greek philosopher ARISTOTLE (384–322 B.C.) discussed the techniques of invention in two of his works, *Rhetoric* and *Topics*. Cicero also wrote a work called *Topics*, which attempted to explain Aristotle's ideas further.

The second canon, arrangement, dealt with the structure of a formal speech. In ancient practice, a speaker would begin by introducing his topic and laying out the facts related to it. He would then announce his thesis (the point he wished to argue) and gave a brief overview of his argument. He offered arguments to support his thesis and to counter opposing viewpoints and ended with a formal conclusion. Renaissance humanists* used this structure in formal letters and essays as well as in orations.

The third canon, style, focused on word choice and figures of speech. The *Rhetoric for Herennius* was the major Renaissance reference for style. It identified three broad levels of style—plain, middle, and grand. It also described 64 different figures of speech for writers to use and imitate. Renaissance writers, who considered style very important for expressing emotion, came up with even longer lists of such figures.

The *Rhetoric for Herennius* also devoted chapters to the two final canons, memory and delivery. Renaissance authors were not much concerned with memory, which had to do with the use of mnemonics (memory aids) to learn a speech. However, they paid some attention to delivery, the art of using voice and gestures effectively during a speech.

Rhetoric in the Renaissance. These ancient methods of rhetoric fell out of favor during the Middle Ages, as educators focused more on logic. Scholars involved in the sciences tended to rely on dialectics, a branch of logic, rather than on rhetoric, to discuss their findings. Dialectics was a method of discussion between experts, while rhetoric aimed to address the general public. Unlike rhetoric, which aimed to persuade an audience, dialectics focused on discovering the truth.

During the Renaissance, however, some of the distinctions between these two fields began to blur. As more people became interested in scholarly questions, scholars began to find rhetoric a useful tool for bringing their studies to a wider audience. As a result, rhetoric gradually regained its importance in the academic realm. It also became important in three other fields: preaching, letter writing, and poetry. Renaissance preachers favored a grand style that played on their listeners' emotions. Humanist authors paid close attention to their use of rhetoric in private letters because they often hoped to publish them for a wider audience.

* **humanist** Renaissance expert in the humanities (the languages, literature, history, and speech and writing techniques of ancient Greece and Rome)

Renaissance writers continued to rely on the *Rhetoric for Herennius* and Cicero's *On Invention* as their main sources for the study of rhetoric. However, humanist scholars also recovered other ancient Roman manuscripts on the subject. In the mid-1300s, the Italian scholar PETRARCH found works by Cicero that dealt with the art of rhetoric and the value of poetry and literature. In 1416 Italian humanist Poggio Bracciolini found the first complete manuscript of *On the Education of the Orator,* by the ancient Roman teacher Quintilian. This work described the training that a person would need to become an ideal orator, or "the good man speaking well." The book had a great influence on humanist methods of teaching rhetoric.

Greek studies also had a major impact on Renaissance rhetoric. Italian scholars began to study the Greek language in the late 1300s, and those who did not read Greek could refer to new Latin translations of Greek works. Renaissance scholars prepared new, more accurate translations of Aristotle's *Rhetoric,* which clarified many of the author's points. For example, they showed that Aristotle defined rhetoric not as the art of speaking persuasively but as the art of seeing all possible means of persuasion. They also identified three kinds of appeals that speakers could use to sway their audience. The first, *ethos,* rested on the moral character of the speaker. The second, *logos,* depended on reason, and *pathos,* the third, played on the emotions of the audience. These new translations of Aristotle's works reawakened interest in the ancient thinker's teachings on the subject of rhetoric.

Rhetoric and Education. During the first half of the 1400s, rhetoric formed the core of the humanist program of study. Teachers produced a variety of new Latin textbooks on this subject. One of the most influential manuals was *On a Course of Studies* (1512) by the Dutch scholar Desiderius ERASMUS. It laid out a curriculum that would help students master Latin, imitate ancient writers, and create original works. Vernacular* rhetoric manuals began to appear during the 1500s. They became very important in England, where the Renaissance arrived later than in the rest of Europe. In England, texts in Latin were the first rhetorical manuals. Some English rhetorics focused on a single canon, such as invention or style. Others, like Thomas Wilson's *The Arte of Rhetorique* (1553), included all five canons. Wilson took a fresh approach to rhetoric, using examples from the Bible, classical works, and his own time to show how to apply the principles of rhetoric.

Scholarly writers also produced various treatises* on the meaning and value of rhetoric. Several of them sought to clarify the differences between rhetoric and dialectic. The northern European author Rudolf AGRICOLA first took up this topic in 1479 in his *Three Books On Dialectical Invention.* Petrus RAMUS, a French educator, expanded on Agricola's ideas in his *Training in Dialectic* (1543). Ramus claimed that invention and arrangement belonged to the field of dialectic rather than rhetoric. In northern Europe, the scholar Gerhard Johann Vossius took issue with Ramus' new approach. His *Commentary on Rhetoric* (1605) dealt with the full art of rhetoric as Cicero had described it. Another critic of Ramus was the English philosopher Francis BACON. His *Advancement of Learning*

* **vernacular** native language or dialect of a region or country

* **treatise** long, detailed essay

* **civic** related to a city, a community, or citizens

(1605) echoed Cicero's idea that the complete art of rhetoric played an important role in civic* life. (*See also* **Classical Scholarship; Education; Humanism; Logic.**)

Ricci, Matteo

**1552–1610
Italian missionary to China**

* **Jesuit** refers to a Roman Catholic religious order founded by St. Ignatius Loyola and approved in 1540

* **classical** in the tradition of ancient Greece and Rome

Matteo Ricci was the first Jesuit* missionary to promote the Roman Catholic faith in China. During his 28 years there, Ricci introduced Chinese scholars to European technology and learning. At the same time, he launched the European study of Chinese culture.

Born in Macerata, Italy, Ricci began his Jesuit training in 1571. He studied law, philosophy, mathematics, and astronomy before volunteering to serve as a missionary in Asia. Ricci became a priest in India in 1580, and a few years later Chinese officials invited him to settle in a province of southern China. He eventually settled in the capital city of Peking (now known as Beijing), where his residence became the center of the growing Christian community. He also became acquainted with many Chinese scholars and government officials.

Ricci learned to speak Chinese and had a deep appreciation for Chinese culture. He became the bridge connecting China to the Europe of the late Renaissance. Ricci introduced the culture of China to the West by translating the major works of Chinese philosophy into Latin. He also developed a system for spelling Chinese names and words in the European alphabet. In addition, he carried Western ideas into China by writing Chinese books based on classical* sources. Ricci also translated a world map into Chinese, which he presented as a gift to the emperor of China.

Ricci argued that Christianity and Confucianism, one of China's traditional belief systems, could exist side by side. China's prime minister shared this view and became a Christian. Together the two men translated European books on mathematics, astronomy, and geography into Chinese. Upon Ricci's death, the emperor of China granted him a burial place near Beijing. Known today as the Matteo Ricci cemetery, it holds the tombstones of more than 60 Jesuits and other missionaries. (*See also* **Missions, Christian.**)

Rome

* **classical** in the tradition of ancient Greece and Rome

* **papacy** office and authority of the pope

* **humanist** Renaissance expert in the humanities (the languages, literature, history, and speech and writing techniques of ancient Greece and Rome)

* **patron** supporter or financial sponsor of an artist or writer

Renaissance Rome had various identities related to Christianity, classical* culture, and Renaissance art. The city was considered the headquarters of the Roman Catholic Church, even though the papacy* was not based in Rome for most of the 1300s. Rome also became known as an important site of classical art and architecture. Humanists* and artists flocked to the city to study its ancient buildings and ruins. Over the course of the Renaissance, Rome gained a reputation as a center of artistic activity as popes and other patrons* commissioned works from leading painters, sculptors, and architects.

The City of Rome. In 1350 Rome was an agricultural town with a population of about 30,000 people. The withdrawal of the papacy to Avignon in southern France in 1309 had left the city without a ruling prince. However, by 1410 governmental institutions had emerged in

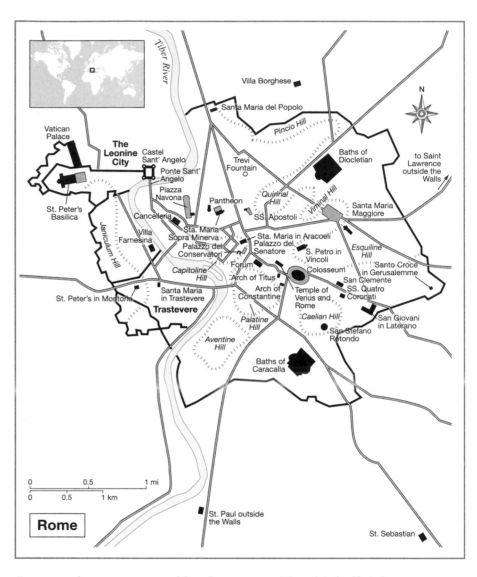

Rome

Rome and were supported by the papacy. The chief officials were a senator, appointed by the pope, and three conservators, chosen by lots from the city's urban districts. The senator, a foreigner, headed Rome's highest court; the conservators oversaw the markets, guilds*, and city councils. The officials were housed in two palaces on the Capitoline Hill. The artist MICHELANGELO redesigned them to form a unified urban ensemble around a statue of the ancient Roman emperor Marcus Aurelius.

During the 1500s, two city councils developed in Rome. The larger or public council was open to any Roman citizen (male) over 20 years old who was approved by five gentlemen from his district. This inclusive rule opened city offices and institutions to immigrants, who had acquired Roman citizenship and were not servants or artisans*. Rome welcomed and absorbed foreigners of all classes to a greater degree than most Renaissance cities.

The flow of migrants to the city helped swell Rome's population to 55,000 by 1520 and 100,000 by 1600. The population included a small community of Jews, perhaps 3,000 to 4,000 people. However, after 1555 Jews had to live in the ghetto, a gated enclosure that was locked at night. Men outnumbered women in the city's population, partly because Rome had large numbers of unmarried churchmen. Commerce and manufacturing played a much smaller role in the city's economy than agricultural produce and income from positions in the curia, the bureaucracy of the papacy.

Humanists and architects contributed to the knowledge of the ancient city beneath Renaissance Rome. The humanists revived interest in the city's antiquities*, unearthing ruins and hunting for ancient texts, objects, and statues. On the surface, the city's appearance was transformed by urban planning and buildings based on classical principles such as symmetry*, the use of classical columns, and straight streets. By 1585, however, the cityscape inspired by classical models began taking on a stronger Christian tone. Statues of saints and religious inscriptions appeared on ancient monuments, illustrating Christianity's victory over the pagan* beliefs of the classical world.

The Sack of Rome. In the 1520s Pope Clement VII joined with France and several Italian city-states in an alliance against Charles V, the Holy Roman Emperor*. Charles sent an army against Rome. On May 6, 1527, the imperial troops laid siege to the city and conquered it the following day. The pope and about 1,000 others fled to a fortress within the city and watched as the soldiers looted the city and terrorized, raped, robbed, and murdered its citizens. The army did not leave the ruined city until February 1528.

Historians disagree about Charles's responsibility for the military attack on Rome, but it seems clear that the brutality and destruction that followed horrified him. Known as the Sack of Rome, the event shook European Catholics to the core. The city, once celebrated as the head or center of the world, had been shown to be vulnerable, and the papacy's attempts to remain politically independent and powerful had suffered a severe blow. Some Protestants saw the Sack of Rome as divine punishment of a corrupt church. But both Protestant and Catholic humanists grieved for the damage done to Rome's libraries and its reputation as a center of learning. Some humanists died in the sack; many writers and artists fled the city to escape it.

Rome regained political and economic strength under Pope Paul III, who reigned from 1534 to 1549. Once again the city became a magnet for artists and writers, but the sack had dimmed hopes for Rome's future. For many people, all that remained was a lingering nostalgia for the golden age of Renaissance culture that had ended in 1527. (*See also* **Art in Italy; Cities and Urban Life; Holy Roman Empire; Popes and Papacy.**)

* **antiquity** era of the ancient Mediterranean cultures of Greece and Rome, ending around A.D. 400

* **symmetry** balance created by matching forms on opposite sides of a structure

* **pagan** referring to ancient religions that worshiped many gods, or, more generally, to any non-Christian religion

* **Holy Roman Emperor** ruler of the Holy Roman Empire, a political body in central Europe composed of several states that existed until 1806

See color plate 2, vol. 3

Ronsard, Pierre de

1524–1585
French poet

* **classical**   in the tradition of ancient Greece and Rome

* **ode**   poem with a lofty style and complex structure

* **sonnet**   poem of 14 lines with a fixed pattern of meter and rhyme

* **epic**   long poem about the adventures of a hero

Pierre de Ronsard, the leading French poet of the 1500s, is best known for his love poems. Ronsard's works inspired many French poets in the late 1500s, and his influence spread to the Netherlands, Germany, Italy, and England.

Early Work. Born to a noble family in Vendôme, in central France, Ronsard served in the households of several royal and noble French families. Ronsard began writing poetry in both Latin and French in the 1540s, and he also took up the study of Greek. In the 1550s Ronsard became part of a group of young poets who called themselves the "Brigade." (They later renamed themselves the Pléiade, a name drawn from Greek mythology.) Inspired by classical* and Italian poets, these writers wanted to create a French literature in the grand tradition of ancient Greece and Rome.

In 1550, Ronsard published his first collection of poetry, *The First Four Books of the Odes*. The ode was one of the young poet's favorite forms. In an ode published in 1552, Ronsard described both poetry and the political order that it praises as being inspired by God. This verse expresses the ideals of the poets who made up the Pléiade.

Love Poems. Within a couple of years, however, Ronsard had turned away from classical models and toward the sonnet*, a more personal verse form. In 1552 he published his most celebrated work, *Loves,* a collection of love sonnets modeled on the *Canzoniere* (Book of Songs) of the Italian poet PETRARCH. Ronsard referred to his beloved in these poems as Cassandre, the name of the daughter of a wealthy Italian merchant. In many of the verses he played on the fact that Cassandra was also the name of a prophetess in Greek mythology.

In 1555 Ronsard produced a second collection of love poems addressed to a new mistress, Marie, whose name is an anagram of the French word *aimer,* meaning "to love." When he published his collected works in 1578, Ronsard added two more sets of love poems: one dedicated to French noblewoman Françoise d'Estrées and one inspired by Hélène de Surgères, a lady at the court of CATHERINE DE MÉDICIS. In this last collection Ronsard plays on the name Hélène, linking his beloved to the mythical figure Helen of Troy.

Other Works. Though he was most famous for his love poetry, Ronsard's true ambition lay in the field of the epic*. The growth of French as a literary language brought with it a demand for a French national epic, which Ronsard attempted to address. The first four books of Ronsard's epic, *La Franciade,* appeared in 1572. This work drew on the model of the Aeneid, by the ancient Roman writer VIRGIL, which described the adventures of Aeneas, the legendary founder of Rome. Ronsard presented his hero, Francus, as a survivor of the Trojan War and the ancestor of French royalty. However, Ronsard lost his royal patron, Charles IX, in 1574, and the poet never finished his national epic.

* **pastoral** relating to the countryside; often used to draw a contrast between the innocence and serenity of rural life and the corruption and extravagance of court life

Ronsard composed a great variety of other poems during his life, including hymns in honor of nature, pastoral* poetry, and *Last Verses*, the sad sonnets he wrote on his deathbed in 1585. Ronsard also contributed to the field of poetic theory. His *Summary of French Poetics* (1565) offered practical advice on how to write in French and urged poets to take pleasure in variety. (*See also* **French Language and Literature; Poetry.**)

Rouen

* **guild** association of craft and trade owners and workers that set standards for and represented the interests of its members

L ocated in the northwestern province of Normandy, Rouen was the leading port of Renaissance France and the country's second-largest city. The city's population grew from about 40,000 in 1500 to a peak of 75,000 in 1550. During these years, Rouen served as a major commercial hub, a seat of regional government, and a center of religious reform.

Rouen's ability to handle ocean-going ships made trade a key part of the economy. Local merchants had contacts with England, Italy, the Netherlands, Portugal, Spain, Africa, and South America. Major industries included woolens and hosiery. However, restrictive guild* regulations eventually drove many wool and hosiery makers out of the urban area.

Rouen was an important administrative city as well. It had many royal courts and its archbishop oversaw more than 1300 parish churches. Yet, despite its commercial and political prominence, Rouen did not develop a large artistic or intellectual community. The city's main cultural event was an annual poetry contest in honor of the Virgin Mary.

* **Protestant Reformation** religious movement that began in the 1500s as a protest against certain practices of the Roman Catholic Church and eventually led to the establishment of a variety of Protestant churches

Normandy emerged as a center of religious reform during the Protestant Reformation*. In 1557 Protestants founded a Reformed church in Rouen. Five years later, they took over the city and held it for six months. When Catholic troops regained control, they executed several of Rouen's Protestant leaders. Although the Reformed church reestablished itself and grew steadily, relations between Catholics and Protestants remained tense. In September 1572, a large massacre of Protestants occurred in Rouen. But after this the city escaped much of the religious violence that raged across France in the 1570s and 1580s. However, in 1589 Catholic activists took over Rouen, and three years later the city endured a five-month siege* by Protestant forces. Finally, in 1594 Rouen accepted the Catholic convert Henry of Navarre as king HENRY IV, ending the civil wars in the region. (*See also* **Economy and Trade; France; Wars of Religion.**)

* **siege** prolonged effort to force a surrender by surrounding a fortress or town with armed troops, cutting the area off from aid

Rubens, Peter Paul

1577–1640
Flemish painter

P eter Paul Rubens was the most successful and influential northern European artist of the 1600s. Following the tradition of the Italian Renaissance masters, he produced glowing paintings of religious and mythological subjects as well as portraits and landscapes. His robust, larger-than-life figures represent the essence of the Baroque* style of art. Rubens also excelled in several other fields—so many that a friend said of him, "Of all his talents, painting is the least." Scholar, humanist*,

* **Baroque**   artistic style of the 1600s characterized by movement, drama, and grandness of scale

* **humanist**   Renaissance expert in the humanities (the languages, literature, history, and speech and writing techniques of ancient Greece and Rome)

* **classical**   in the tradition of ancient Greece and Rome

* **apprentice**   person bound by legal agreement to work for another for a specified period of time in return for instruction in a trade or craft

* **guild**   association of craft and trade owners and workers that set standards for and represented the interests of its members

* **villa**   luxurious country home and the land surrounding it

* **Catholic Reformation**   reform movement within the Roman Catholic Church that focused on spiritual renewal, correcting abuses, and strengthening religious orders; it began in the late Middle Ages and continued throughout the Renaissance

* **secular**   nonreligious; connected with everyday life

diplomat, and businessman, Rubens was an outstanding example of a "Renaissance man," someone of great knowledge, ability, and accomplishment in a variety of areas.

Early Career.   Rubens's parents fled the Netherlands in the late 1500s to escape religious persecution. Peter Paul was born in the small German town of Siegen, but the family later returned to ANTWERP in the Netherlands. There young Rubens received a classical* education. Then he served as an apprentice* to various local painters, including Otto van Veen, the city's leading artist. In 1597 Rubens completed *Portrait of a Young Man,* his earliest dated work, and was accepted into the painters' guild* the following year.

Many artists from the Netherlands traveled to Italy to study and work. Rubens made the journey in 1600, visiting Venice and Mantua. The following year he arrived in Rome, just as the Baroque style of painting was emerging. Rubens studied the paintings of Italian artists such as MICHELANGELO, RAPHAEL, and CARAVAGGIO. He also focused on ancient sculpture, which he sketched in such a lifelike manner that the pictures seem drawn from live models rather than marble statues.

In Rome, Rubens accepted a major commission to prepare three large murals for a chapel. He also received his first assignment as a diplomat, when the duke of Mantua asked him to carry gifts to king Philip III, ruler of Spain and the Netherlands. In 1605 Rubens went back to Rome and began an intensive study of classical art and literature. He also began collecting Roman sculpture, coins, and other ancient objects.

When Rubens returned to Antwerp in 1608, he found a peaceful political climate and promising opportunities. He received a commission for a painting called *Adoration of the Magi* to be placed in the Town Hall. In addition, the local Spanish rulers named him their court painter. Rubens married Isabella Brant and set up a studio in Antwerp. For his own home, he designed a magnificent Italian Renaissance villa* set in the heart of the city.

Rubens completed an enormous number of projects between 1610 and 1620. Among his religious commissions were two triptychs (three-panel pieces), *Raising of the Cross* and *Descent from the Cross*. Rubens's extensive output of religious pictures established him as northern Europe's leading artist of Catholic Reformation* themes. However, he also painted many secular* works, including hunting scenes, portraits, and images from history and mythology. His great productivity was partly the result of his large, well-organized studio. Often, Rubens would start a picture by drawing the basic outline in chalk, then his assistants would begin painting, and he would finish it. For one commission, a series of 39 ceiling paintings for a new church in Antwerp, Rubens painted preparatory sketches in oils, leaving other artists to complete the canvases. Although fire later destroyed the paintings, the surviving sketches reveal Rubens's creative genius and lively style.

International Activity.   In 1621 Rubens began acting as agent for Spain in peace negotiations between warring sections of the

Although famous as a painter, Peter Paul Rubens was also a distinguished scholar. In *The Four Philosophers,* painted around 1611, the artist portrayed himself, standing on the left, with three important scholars of his time.

* **allegory**   literary or artistic device in which characters, events, and settings represent abstract qualities and in which the author intends a different meaning to be read beneath the surface

* **patron**   supporter or financial sponsor of an artist or writer

Netherlands. His fame as a painter allowed him to move freely among royal courts. He met with princes and officials, who often discussed politics while posing for their portraits.

The following year Rubens went to Paris to fulfill a commission for a series of scenes celebrating the life of MARIE DE MÉDICIS, former queen of France. Drawing on his broad knowledge of classical mythology and allegory*, the artist sketched grand, dramatic images. His assistants created large paintings based on the sketches, and Rubens added the finishing touches.

When the artist returned to Antwerp, he continued to receive commissions from prominent patrons*. Important paintings of this period include another *Adoration of the Magi* (1624), surrounded by sculptures designed by Rubens; *Ludovicus Nonnius* (ca. 1627), a portrait of the painter's friend and physician; and *Landscape with Philemon and Baucis* (1625), a troubled view of nature with a hint of a rainbow suggesting the return of peace and order. Rubens also designed a series of tapestries that created the illusion of additional tapestries within the larger scene. Based on religious subjects, the series expressed Rubens's Catholic faith.

In 1626 Rubens's wife died, and he set forth on a number of diplomatic* missions. He arranged for England and Spain to exchange ambassadors as a first step toward a formal peace treaty. Eventually Rubens was knighted by these two countries—the only painter to receive this honor from both monarchies. He also received notable commissions, such as painting the ceiling of the banquet hall in England's Whitehall Palace.

Later Career. Back in Antwerp, Rubens married Helena Fourment and retired from diplomatic work to devote his time to his family and to art. He took on several significant projects, such as designing a group of nine arches for the procession of a new ruler through the streets of Antwerp. He also created a vast series of mythological paintings for the hunting lodge of King Philip IV of Spain. To complete the series, Rubens employed most of the artists in Antwerp. He painted more than 60 oil sketches for the paintings, based on tales from *Metamorphoses* by the Roman poet Ovid. The sketches are some of Rubens's liveliest and most inventive works.

Rubens was troubled with attacks of gout, a disease that causes joint pain, during his final years. Nonetheless, he managed to complete a number of works, including two masterpieces in the late 1630s: *Self-Portrait*, in which the artist presents himself as a knight, and *Het Pelsken*, a painting of his wife Helena that offers a view into his private life.

After Rubens's death, his fame spread far beyond the Netherlands. In Italy, the late Baroque painters and the sculptor Gian Lorenzo Bernini studied his style. His work also inspired the Spanish painter Diego Velázquez and various French Baroque painters. Rubens's lasting influence ranks him with earlier Renaissance masters such as Michelangelo, TITIAN, and Raphael. (*See also* **Art in the Netherlands; Baroque; Netherlands; Spain.**)

The Creative Life

Some critics and art historians have identified genius with torment, dwelling on the image of solitary artists who struggle against economic, social, and spiritual obstacles to fulfill their lonely vision. Peter Paul Rubens is proof that not all great artists fit this image. Far from being a solitary genius, he was a capable businessman who produced great works in collaboration with many other artists. Successful, happy, respected, a devout Catholic and devoted husband and father, Rubens was a thoroughly balanced man of his time as well as a creative genius.

---

* **diplomatic** having to do with formal relations between nations

---

Rudolf II

1552–1612
King of Hungary and Bohemia, Holy Roman Emperor

* **patron** supporter or financial sponsor of an artist or writer

* **Holy Roman Emperor** ruler of the Holy Roman Empire, a political body in central Europe composed of several states that existed until 1806

Although a great patron* of the arts and learning, Rudolf II was an incompetent ruler who suffered from periods of severe depression. Holy Roman Emperor* from 1576 to 1612, he focused more on artistic than on political matters and exercised little control over the religious conflicts that threatened the stability of his empire.

The son of Holy Roman Emperor MAXIMILIAN II, Rudolf spent eight years of his youth at the court of his uncle, PHILIP II of Spain. In 1572 Rudolf became king of HUNGARY. By 1576 he was also ruler of BOHEMIA, AUSTRIA, and the Holy Roman Empire.

Rudolf moved the imperial capital from Vienna to Prague, which became a center of Renaissance culture. His personal collections were the wonder of the age and included paintings, sculpture, decorative arts, musical instruments, natural objects, and scientific devices. A patron of leading philosophers, mathematicians, and astronomers, Rudolf also

See color
plate 15,
vol. 3

had a strong interest in the occult—the study of mysterious forces believed to affect the world.

Like other HABSBURG emperors, Rudolf hoped to unite Christian Europe. However, rather than give full support to the Roman Catholic Church, he backed individuals who were not tied to either Catholic or Protestant organizations. This policy led to political chaos. Rudolf's most disastrous plan, however, was his attempt to lead a crusade against the Ottoman Turks* in the 1590s. The project resulted in a war, which lasted until 1606, and the revolt of his Hungarian subjects. Increasingly alarmed by Rudolf's incompetence, other members of the Habsburg family eventually forced him to yield most of his titles to his younger brother Matthias. Rudolf died in 1612, but his misguided actions led to the THIRTY YEARS' WAR (1618–1648). (*See also* **Holy Roman Empire; Prague; Vienna.**)

* **Ottoman Turks** Turkish followers of Islam who founded the Ottoman Empire in the 1300s; the empire eventually included large areas of eastern Europe, the Middle East, and northern Africa

Russia

See color
plate 14,
vol. 3

* **humanism** Renaissance cultural movement promoting the study of the humanities (the languages, literature, and history of ancient Greece and Rome) as a guide to living

Russia missed the Renaissance, most historians agree. Religious and political barriers prevented the ideas of Italy and other parts of western Europe from taking hold in Russia during the 1400s and 1500s. However, regions around Russia did absorb some elements of Renaissance humanism*.

Religion was the major obstacle to the Renaissance in Russia. The Orthodox Church, the version of Christianity that dominated the country, rejected almost everything Western, including the realistic religious art of the Renaissance. In Europe, the invention of movable type had hastened the spread of Renaissance ideas. In Russia, however, the church's traditional suspicion of books and learning stood in the way of the print revolution.

Politics also hindered the spread of the Renaissance into Russia. In eastern Europe, Renaissance thought and art flourished in the neighboring countries of POLAND and Lithuania. They represented Roman Catholicism, the Latin language, and Western art and architecture. However, because of the rivalry between the Polish-Lithuanian state and Russia over control of various regions, the Russians rejected Polish-Lithuanian cultural influences. In addition, Russia was preoccupied with foreign wars and internal crises—conditions that Italian humanist Enea Silvio Piccolomini, later Pope PIUS II, noted were unfavorable to the growth of the culture and the arts.

The states of Kievan Rus', long under Polish-Lithuanian influence, developed separately in political and cultural realms from Moscovy, the area around Moscow. Renaissance humanism took root in Kievan Rus', although weakly. Today this region, the present-day states of Ukraine and Belarus, has closer ties to Western culture and to Greek and Roman literature than to Russian traditions.

Moscow became the center of Russian political and religious life during the 1400s. Under the influence of the monk Andrei Rublev (ca. 1370–ca. 1430), a distinctive Russian style of art began to develop. Contacts with the Western world through centers such as Kiev dwindled, and Muscovy grew more isolated from the rest of Europe. The grand dukes of Muscovy deliberately emphasized the Russian values of tradition and stability over the foreign tendency toward innovation and change.

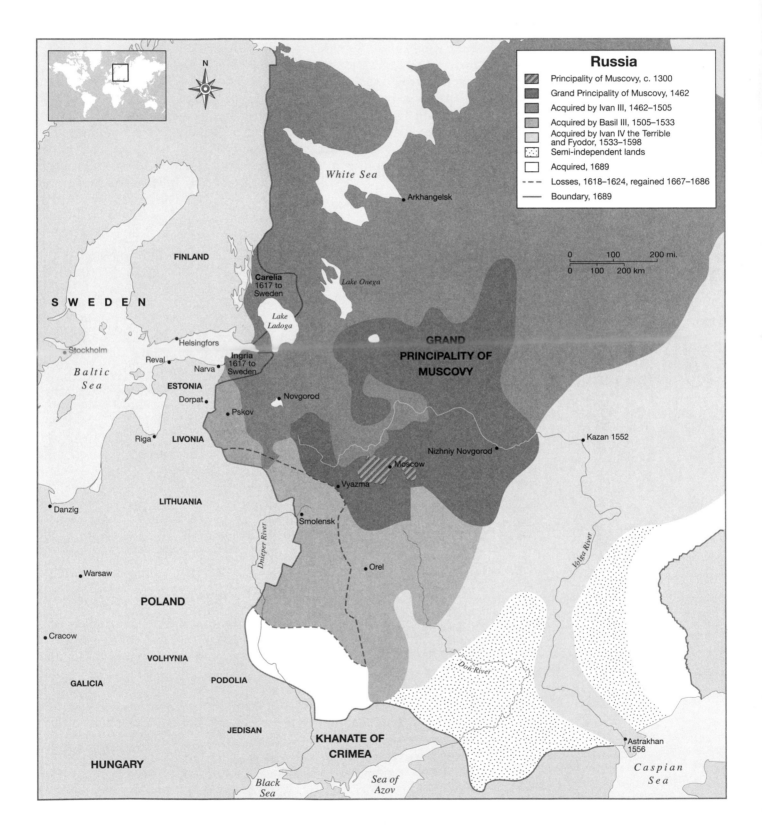

Russia

- ◨ Principality of Muscovy, c. 1300
- ◼ Grand Principality of Muscovy, 1462
- ◼ Acquired by Ivan III, 1462–1505
- ◼ Acquired by Basil III, 1505–1533
- ◻ Acquired by Ivan IV the Terrible and Fyodor, 1533–1598
- ⬚ Semi-independent lands
- ◻ Acquired, 1689
- - - - Losses, 1618–1624, regained 1667–1686
- —— Boundary, 1689

N

White Sea

Arkhangelsk

FINLAND

Carelia
1617 to
Sweden

Lake Onega

SWEDEN

Lake
Ladoga

Helsingfors

Stockholm

Reval

Ingria
1617 to
Sweden

Narva

Baltic
Sea

ESTONIA

Dorpat

Novgorod

GRAND
PRINCIPALITY OF
MUSCOVY

Pskov

Riga

LIVONIA

Nizhniy Novgorod

Kazan 1552

Moscow

Vyazma

LITHUANIA

Danzig

Smolensk

Dnieper River

Volga River

Warsaw

Orel

POLAND

Cracow

VOLHYNIA

Don River

GALICIA

PODOLIA

JEDISAN

KHANATE OF
CRIMEA

Astrakhan
1556

HUNGARY

Black
Sea

Sea of
Azov

Caspian
Sea

0   100   200 mi.
0   100   200 km

* artisans skilled worker or craftperson

Although thousands of foreign merchants, artisans*, and soldiers lived in Muscovy during the reign of Grand Duke Ivan III (1462–1505), they had little influence on the Russian people around them. Russians were suspicious of Catholics, Protestants, and Jews, and they disliked foreign ways. Few Russians traveled abroad, and as a result they had little idea of what the Renaissance had achieved elsewhere or what it could do for Russia. Diplomats from England or central Europe who visited Muscovy at the time were struck by the exotic character of the Russians, who shared so little of the culture that was the pride of educated Westerners. (*See also* **Baltic States.**)

Salons

Salons were gathering places that played a key role in European social and intellectual life in the 1600s. Like the Italian ACADEMIES of the 1400s, a salon provided a place for people to meet and discuss interesting issues. Salons, however, brought together a far greater variety of people and ideas than other social groups. In the context of the salon, women mingled with men, writers with the wealthy and powerful, oral culture with written texts, and social life with intellectual discussions.

The roots of the salon date back to the royal courts of the Middle Ages, and forerunners of the salon existed in Italy in the 1400s. However, the salon truly came into its own in France in the 1600s. Salons had a major impact on the culture of Paris, but they also appeared in other European cities, including Berlin, Vienna, and London.

The salon was one of the few settings for discussion that offered a major role to women. Each salon, in fact, had a woman who served as its hostess, inviting guests of both sexes into her home and guiding the conversation among them. Salons provided hostesses with a way to pursue their education and to gain cultural influence. Many writers, in fact, criticized the salon culture for placing too much power in female hands.

The subjects discussed in salons varied. In Paris in the 1600s, most salon gatherings focused on matters of language, such as how to express ideas clearly in writing. Other topics included the nature of love, marriage, and male authority. The salon also provided a fertile ground for literature. Many writers found patrons* among the women who ran salons or among the wealthy individuals who gathered there. A number of women in French salons published their own writings, which often drew on the ideas discussed in the salon setting.

* patron supporter or financial sponsor of an artist or writer

The salons of Paris helped promote new cultural ideas, such as the importance of talent over noble birth. They also provided a private setting for people to debate political ideas without interference. The salon culture gave birth to a new class of informed citizens, independent of the nation's political leaders. As a result, salons were often attacked by those who feared changes to the social order. (*See also* **Feminism; Women.**)

Salutati, Coluccio

1331–1406
Italian intellectual and politican

* **humanist** Renaissance expert in the humanities (the languages, literature, history, and speech and writing techniques of ancient Greece and Rome)

* **papacy** office and authority of the pope

* **medieval** referring to the Middle Ages, a period that began around A.D. 400 and ended around 1400 in Italy and 1500 in the rest of Europe

* **pagan** referring to ancient religions that worshiped many gods, or, more generally, to any non-Christian religion

* **republican** refers to a form of Renaissance government dominated by leading merchants with limited participation by others

Coluccio Salutati was the leading humanist* of his generation. An official in the city of FLORENCE for more than 30 years, he helped make the city the center of the humanist movement.

Salutati was born in Stignano, a small village under the control of Florence. After receiving an education in Bologna, he held a series of positions in government—first in the region around Stignano and later in the cities of Rome and Lucca. In 1374 he became supervisor of election procedures in Florence, and a year later he assumed the post of chancellor, or head of state. Around the same time Salutati took office, Florence went to war with the papacy*. The new chancellor gained fame throughout Europe with a series of brilliant *missive,* public letters written in defense of Florence's cause. Salutati produced thousands of *missive* during his life, including some written just days before his death.

Salutati's fame as the author of the *missive* made him a leader of the humanist movement in Italy. Although his writing style was medieval*, it reflected humanist ideas in its use of examples from Greek and Roman sources. In addition, he made a strong case for humanist education by claiming that knowledge of history was essential for a political leader. In 1397 Salutati helped bring Manuel Chrysoloras, a Greek scholar and teacher, to Florence. The scholar's arrival played an important role in reintroducing Greek learning to western Europe. Salutati also made scholarly studies of a number of ancient texts. However, he did not follow the lead of earlier humanists, such as the Italian poet PETRARCH. While Petrarch longed for the ancient world and showed no interest in history after the A.D. 100s, Salutati sought to trace historical and literary developments across the centuries between ancient times and his own.

Over the decades Salutati gathered around him a group of followers who became the leaders of the next generation of humanists in Italy. Toward the end of Salutati's life, however, these followers became critical of some of his views, which they found old-fashioned. For instance, Salutati tended to regard Christian wisdom as superior to pagan* culture and thought. He also argued that monarchy was the best form of government and rarely expressed republican* ideas in his writing. Salutati's influence declined, but his central role in developing Italian humanism and in establishing Florence as its capital has remained. (*See also* **Greek émigrés; Humanism.**)

Sannazaro, Jacopo

1458–1530
Italian poet

* **pastoral** relating to the countryside; often used to draw a contrast between the innocence and serenity of rural life and the corruption and extravagance of court life

Jacopo Sannazaro of Italy gained fame for his poetry in both Latin and Italian. He is best known for his works in the pastoral* style, especially his romance* *Arcadia,* which had a great influence on the development of the pastoral form.

Born to a noble Italian family, Sannazaro grew up in and around NAPLES in southern Italy. Early in his career, he composed verses in the style of the famous Italian poet PETRARCH (1304–1374). He also wrote farces* for the court of the Duke of Calabria. In the 1490s he began writing poetry in Latin. Sannazaro spent the years from 1501 to 1504 in exile in France with Frederick of Aragon, the former king of Naples.

* **romance**   adventure story of the Middle Ages, the forerunner of the modern novel

* **farce**   light dramatic piece that features broad comedy, improbable situations, stereotyped characters, and exaggerated physical action

* **epic**   long poem about the adventures of a hero

Sannazaro's *Arcadia* became one of the most popular books of the 1500s. It first appeared in print in an illegal copy in 1502, and two years later another version came out with two additional chapters. *Arcadia* tells the tale of Sincero, an unhappy lover from Naples who enters an ideal world of poetic shepherds (Arcadia). The text presents the life of Arcadia as an endless cycle of games, feasts, and songs. Eventually, the hero leaves the happy life of Arcadia and returns to his homeland, only to find that the woman he loved has died. This pattern of entering and then leaving a blissful rural world would influence most of the European pastorals that followed. It also reflects the period of exile Sannazaro experienced in his own life.

In his Latin epic* *On Giving Birth by the Virgin* (1526), Sannazaro applied the pastoral style to the story of Christ's birth. Influenced by the verse of the ancient Roman poet VIRGIL, this poem presents the birth of Christ from the viewpoint of the joyful shepherds. However, like *Arcadia,* this work also contains notes of sorrow and lament. One of the poem's most moving sections describes Mary at Christ's death, weeping bitterly at the foot of the cross. (*See also* **Pastoral; Sidney, Philip.**)

Satire

See *Literature.*

Savonarola, Girolamo

1452–1498
Preacher, reformer, and prophet

* **Dominican**   religious order of brothers and priests founded by St. Dominic

* **humanist**   referring to a Renaissance cultural movement promoting the study of the humanities (the languages, literature, and history of ancient Greece and Rome) as a guide to living

* **patron**   supporter or financial sponsor of an artist or writer

The Dominican* friar Girolamo Savonarola was a leading political and religious figure in FLORENCE in the 1490s. Savonarola, who claimed to possess the gift of prophecy, attacked the wealthy and powerful in his sermons. He urged the people of Florence to reform their government and to transform the city into a New Jerusalem that would become the center of a worldwide Christian empire.

Early Life and Career. Born in Ferrara, Savonarola received a humanist* education before entering the monastery of San Domenico in Bologna in 1475. During his seven years there, he became a priest. In 1482 he was transferred to the monastery of San Marco in Florence, where he began to preach. His sermons at this time focused on the ideas of sin, punishment, and the redeeming power of Christ's love. They gained little notice from the people of Florence. A few years later, however, he attracted attention as a visiting preacher in San Gimignano, where he announced that God planned to punish the sinful world, especially the church, and bring about a great reform. He preached this message in various cities over the next few years.

In 1490 Savonarola returned to San Marco at the request of Lorenzo de' MEDICI, the leader of Florence. Lorenzo felt that the friar's presence would add prestige to the monastery and its patrons*, including himself. Savonarola's new, sensational style of preaching appealed greatly to the common people. It also won the admiration of several noted artists and scholars, including Giovanni PICO DELLA MIRANDOLA, Marsilio FICINO, Sandro BOTTICELLI, and MICHELANGELO BUONAROTTI. Savonarola soon

Dominican friar Girolamo Savonarola dominated the political scene in the city of Florence in the 1490s. Claiming to have the gift of prophecy, he preached about the dawn of a glorious age in which Florence would become the center of a new Christian empire. However, he eventually fell from favor and was arrested, tortured, and hanged.

* **tyrant** absolute ruler who uses power unjustly or cruelly

* **sack** to loot a captured city

* **secular** nonreligious; connected with everyday life

* **excommunicate** to exclude from the church and its rituals

* **conspirator** one who plots with others to commit a crime

became the prior, or head, of San Marco and restored the order's original strict rules. His powerful sermons increased the monastery's fame. It attracted many new recruits, including some from prominent families.

The French Invasion. Savonarola's preaching soon became more outspoken. He attacked tyrants* and condemned the church's alliance with the wealthy and powerful at the expense of the poor. Between 1492 and 1494 he began to claim that God was sending him visions of a kingly warrior who would cross the Alps and conquer Italy. In late summer of 1494, Charles VIII of France invaded Italy, seeking to conquer the kingdom of Naples. His arrival appeared to confirm the friar's prophecies.

It also placed Florence in peril. Piero de' Medici, the city's new leader, had refused to let Charles pass through Florence's territory. The king responded by threatening to sack* the city. To preserve peace, Piero had to surrender important fortresses and towns within Florence and agree to pay Charles a large sum of money. The news of this bargain led to an uprising in Florence and forced the Medici family to flee the city. Charles entered Florence on November 17 and demanded that the Florentines restore the Medici to power. However, after an anti-French riot and a series of talks with Savonarola, Charles agreed to leave the city in exchange for a smaller payment than that promised him by Piero.

The New Jerusalem. After driving out the Medici, the people of Florence pressed for serious changes in the structure of city government. Savonarola proposed that the city model itself after Venice, which had a single council made up of some 2,000 nobles. In December, Florence set up a new assembly called the Grand Council, made up of 3,000 male citizens. Savonarola hailed the new council as a "government of the people" and claimed credit for it.

The friar now began to preach almost daily about the coming age of the Antichrist. He predicted that Florence would join forces with the king of France to lead the world into an age of universal Christianity and peace. Florence would be the center of a Christian empire, a New Jerusalem for the new age. In addition to his rousing sermons, Savonarola and his supporters staged processions and "bonfires of the vanities," in which citizens publicly burned books, paintings, clothing, playing cards, and other items the friar viewed as immoral.

Various groups challenged the policies of Savonarola and his followers, whom opponents called the Piagnoni (wailers). Conservative clergy members criticized his involvement in politics and disputed his claim to prophecy. Secular* political opponents blocked several of his measures, such as regulating women's dress. Gangs of young nobles disrupted his sermons and processions. In 1497 Pope Alexander VI excommunicated* Savonarola and threatened to take economic measures against Florence for supporting him. Later that year Savonarola learned of a plot to restore Piero de' Medici to power. He had the conspirators* executed without granting their right to appeal their sentence. This action severely weakened the friar's moral standing with the people of Florence.

Savonarola's End. In early 1498 one of Savonarola's chief followers accepted a challenge to test the truth of the friar's claims to divine favor. The test would be a trial by fire. If the flames did not kill Savonarola, it would prove that he was truly favored by God. On the day scheduled for the event, however, both sides argued so long about the details of the trial that rain eventually put out the flames. People took this as a sign of God's disapproval, and the city guard dispersed the angry crowd. The next day a mob attacked San Marco. The guard stepped in once again, arresting Savonarola and his two closest deputies. Questioned under torture, Savonarola admitted to faking his prophecies. On May 23, 1498, the three were hanged and their bodies burned.

After Savonarola's death, Florence's nobles took control of the city, and in 1512 the Medici returned to power. However, the Piagnoni remained a force in the city. In 1527 they played a role in driving out the Medici and establishing a short-lived republican* government. Within a few years, however, the Medici returned and became hereditary dukes of Florence. Nonetheless, Savonarola's ideas continued to circulate widely outside of Italy. They exerted a great influence on Catholic reformers of the 1500s, and Protestant leaders such as Martin LUTHER hailed him as their forerunner. (*See also* **Medici, House of.**)

* **republican**   refers to a form of Renaissance government dominated by leading merchants with limited participation by others

Saxony

* **Holy Roman Emperor**   ruler of the Holy Roman Empire, a political body in central Europe composed of several states that existed until 1806

* **duchy**   territory ruled by a duke or duchess

* **elector**   German prince with a vote in choosing the Holy Roman Emperor

* **humanist**   referring to a Renaissance cultural movement promoting the study of the humanities (the languages, literature, and history of ancient Greece and Rome) as a guide to living

* **Protestant Reformation**   religious movement that began in the 1500s as a protest against certain practices of the Roman Catholic Church and eventually led to the establishment of a variety of Protestant churches

Saxony emerged as a leading state in northeastern Germany during the Renaissance. In 1423 the Holy Roman Emperor* Sigismund awarded the duchy* of Saxony-Wittenberg to Frederick of Meissen and Thuringia. In 1485 the duchy was split between Frederick's grandsons into Ernestine Saxony, which carried the title of elector*, and Albertine Saxony. This lasting division created complicated boundaries that would prove troublesome in the future.

At first Ernestine Saxony, centered in Wittenberg, overshadowed Albertine Saxony, based in Dresden. Under Elector Frederick III, "the Wise", Saxony-Wittenberg prospered and gained influence in the Holy Roman Empire. In 1502 Frederick founded a new university in Wittenberg that welcomed humanist* scholars and attracted an Augustinian monk named Martin LUTHER. Although not a humanist, Luther used humanist techniques to study the Bible. His studies led him to become a strong critic of Scholasticism, a movement endorsed by the Roman Catholic Church that blended Christian teachings with ancient philosophy. In October 1517, Luther launched the Protestant Reformation* with his famous Ninety-five Theses. The Greek scholar Philipp MELANCHTHON, one of Luther's most important supporters, was an educational reformer who turned the university into a humanistic school.

Frederick and his successors protected Luther's movement from the decrees of the church and Emperor CHARLES V and made Ernestine Saxony the center of the Reformation. The Lutheran Reformation did not gain any ground in Albertine Saxony until the rule of Duke Henry V (1539–1541). Henry's son Maurice continued to promote church reform but declined to join the Protestant Schmalkaldic League. When the league went to war with Charles V, Maurice sided with the emperor. The victorious Charles rewarded Maurice by turning over to him most of Ernestine Saxony.

Maurice and Charles soon fell out over the emperor's failure to live up to his promises. Maurice then formed a secret alliance with King Henry II of France and attacked Charles, setting off a rebellion of German princes in 1552. Charles was forced to sign a treaty and give up some of his political and religious goals. By this time, Dresden had replaced Wittenberg as the seat of power in Saxony, and Albertine Saxony had emerged as the leading Protestant state in the empire.

Saxony reached its peak under Maurice's brother, Elector August I (ruled 1553–1586). Leipzig became a center of arts, and Wittenberg was recognized as the stronghold of Lutheranism. By the early 1600s, however, Saxony was losing influence. Elector John George switched sides several times in the course of the THIRTY YEAR'S WAR (1618–1648), and Saxony was devastated during the last years of fighting. After the war, Brandenburg, not Saxony, emerged as the leading state in northern Germany. (*See also* **Holy Roman Empire; Protestant Reformation.**)

Scandinavian Kingdoms

During the Renaissance, the kingdoms of Denmark and Sweden competed for power in Scandinavia. By 1448 Denmark controlled Norway and Iceland, and Sweden ruled Finland. Both kingdoms saw a surge of cultural and intellectual activity in the 1500s as new ideas reached the region from neighboring European states. Rivalry between the two countries continued into the 1650s, when Sweden became the dominant power and the influence of Denmark declined.

Renaissance Ideas. In the early 1500s, artists from Germany and Flanders* arrived in the Scandinavian courts. They produced portraits of prominent individuals, such as the Danish king Christian II (ruled 1513–1523). At the same time, humanism* inspired various scholars in the region to study the Latin of ancient Rome and to write about the history of local cultures.

The introduction of the printing press in the late 1400s helped spread Scandinavian writing. In 1514 the Danish scholar Christiern Pedersen printed an edition of *The Deeds of the Danes* (ca. 1200) by the medieval* historian Saxo. The Swedes Johannes and Olaus Magnus published *History of All the Kings of the Goths and Swedes* and *A History of the Nordic Peoples* in the 1500s.

Protestant reform movements of the 1500s had considerable success in Scandinavia. The Swedish king, Gustav Vasa, declared Sweden a Lutheran country in 1527; nine years later, Christian III did the same for Denmark. The main inspiration for the Lutheran Renaissance in Scandinavia was the German reformer Philipp MELANCHTHON, who attempted to harmonize Christian beliefs with the ideas of classical* culture. His emphasis on the study of classical languages contributed to the development of Latin literature in the region. The vernacular* was used

* **Flanders**   region along the coasts of present-day Belgium, France, and the Netherlands

* **humanism**   Renaissance cultural movement promoting the study of the humanities (the languages, literature, and history, of ancient Greece and Rome) as a guide to living

* **medieval**   referring to the Middle Ages, a period that began around A.D. 400 and ended around 1400 in Italy and 1500 in the rest of Europe

* **classical**   in the tradition of ancient Greece and Rome

* **vernacular**   native language or dialect of a region or country

mostly by women writers and for religious works. Translations of the Bible appeared in Swedish, Danish, Finish, and Icelandic.

Scandinavian Cultures. The period between 1550 and 1600 was a time of great cultural development for Denmark. Frederick II (ruled 1559–1588), an enthusiastic patron* of the arts, attracted artists, musicians, and architects to the kingdom and supported the education of promising students. Leading Danish poets included Erasmus Laetus, who composed Latin epics*, and Hans Thomessøn and Hans Christensen Sthen, who wrote hymns. Among later scholars were Anders Sørensen Vedel, who collected and edited popular folk ballads in 1591, and Arild Huitfeldt, who wrote *Chronicle of Denmark* (1604).

The Danish astronomer Tycho BRAHE established Uraniborg, one of Europe's finest research centers, in the late 1570s. An accomplished writer, Brahe also composed outstanding poetry in Latin. His sister, Sophie, gained renown as the first female scholar in Scandinavia.

The Danish king Christian IV (ruled 1588–1648) built two magnificent castles: Rosenborg and Frederiksborg. When fire destroyed the

* **patron** supporter or financial sponsor of an artist or writer

* **epic** long poem about the adventures of a hero

61

Norwegian city of Oslo in 1624, Christian rebuilt it and modernized its castle, Akershus, in the style of the Renaissance.

Humanism developed a following in Norway, especially in the cities of Bergen and Oslo. Some Norwegian writers focused on Latin texts, while others studied Norse literature and history. In Iceland the cathedral schools of Hólar and Skálholt became important centers of learning. Two prominent Icelandic authors, Oddur Einarsson and Arngrímur Jónsson, produced works defending their country against foreign prejudice.

From 1600 to 1650 Sweden experienced a period of political and cultural expansion. During the reigns of King Gustav II Adolf (ruled 1611–1632) and his daughter, Christina (ruled 1632–1654), Stockholm became a gathering place for artists, architects, and other intellectuals. Christina hired a French court painter and a German architect to help build Drottningholm Castle near Stockholm.

Rival Courts. The rivalry between Sweden and Denmark inspired various works of art and literature. For example, the Swede Johannes Bureus and the Dane Ole Worm competed in collecting inscriptions written in runes—an ancient form of writing used in Scandinavia. During the reigns of Christian IV in Denmark and Christina in Sweden, the royal courts became known for elegant entertainment. Christian employed celebrated musicians, such as the Dane Mogens Pedersen and the German Heinrich Schütz. At the Swedish court, Georg Stiernhielm provided ballets and poems in honor of the queen. Scholars consider Stiernhielm to be the first great poet to write in Swedish.

In the early to mid-1600s, both Denmark and Sweden became involved in the THIRTY YEARS' WAR (1618–1648). Sweden won significant victories, but Denmark mostly met with disaster. By the time Christian IV died in 1648, the Danish state was bankrupt. Six years later, Sweden's queen Christina shocked the country by becoming a Catholic and giving up the throne. Nevertheless, both rulers made their mark, having encouraged the growth of art, literature, and learning in their kingdoms. (*See also* **Astronomy; Humanism; Literature; Music; Protestant Reformation.**)

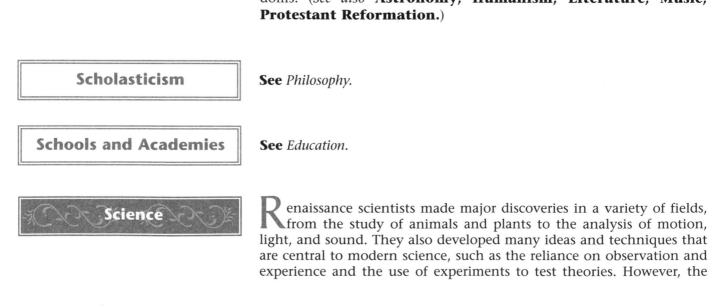

| **Scholasticism** | **See** *Philosophy.* |

| **Schools and Academies** | **See** *Education.* |

| **Science** | |

Renaissance scientists made major discoveries in a variety of fields, from the study of animals and plants to the analysis of motion, light, and sound. They also developed many ideas and techniques that are central to modern science, such as the reliance on observation and experience and the use of experiments to test theories. However, the

Astronomer Galileo Galilei published his *Dialogue Concerning the Two Chief World Systems* around 1630. In it he defended the views of Nicolaus Copernicus, who had created a model of the universe in which the Earth traveled around the Sun. This image from the title page of the book shows Copernicus, on the right, discussing his theory with the ancient scholars Aristotle and Ptolemy.

* **alchemy**   early science that sought to explain the nature of matter and to transform base metals, such as lead, into gold

* **astrology**   study of the supposed influences of the stars and planets on earthly events

term *science* had a much broader meaning in the Renaissance than it does today. The word could refer to several fields of study, such as alchemy*, astrology*, and magic, that the modern world does not regard as scientific.

THE MEANING OF SCIENCE

Renaissance thinkers based their concept of science on the writings of the ancient Greek philosopher ARISTOTLE, who defined science as knowledge that is certain and unchanging. Aristotle claimed that a person gained perfect knowledge of an object by knowing its cause. The cause of an object, he claimed, made it what it was, and made it impossible for it to be anything else. Thus, Aristotle saw scientific knowledge as fixed and not subject to change. For him, a scientific explanation had to involve a logical proof that one thing was the cause of another.

Since Aristotle's time, however, the concept of science had broadened to include less perfect types of knowledge. Over the course of the Middle Ages, and even more during the Renaissance, thinkers came to recognize that the kind of arguments Aristotle saw as "proof" always involved some amount of speculation. Thus, they began accepting theories that only identified the probable cause of a thing or event, rather than "proving" its cause. They also gave more credit to theories that could predict actual events, such as eclipses, without explaining why they occur.

Renaissance scholars divided science into two main types. The speculative sciences were concerned with knowledge for its own sake. The practical sciences, by contrast, focused on applying knowledge to everyday problems. Each of these broad categories included several more specific fields.

The speculative sciences covered three major areas: mathematics, metaphysics*, and natural philosophy. Of these three, only natural philosophy resembled the modern concept of science. This field, also known as natural science, dealt with the physical world. It included such disciplines as botany (the study of plants), geology (the study of the earth), and zoology (the study of animals). The speculative sciences also included some "mixed sciences" such as mathematical physics, which covered the same subjects as natural science, but examined them in terms of mathematical ideas.

While the speculative sciences dealt with what human beings could know, practical sciences dealt with what human beings could do or make. Renaissance thinkers saw the practical sciences as very close to the arts, and they viewed some fields, such as logic and medicine, as both arts and sciences. Practical sciences during the Renaissance included medicine, engineering, and the "moral sciences" of ethics* and politics.

NATURAL SCIENCES

The natural philosophy of the Renaissance was the basis of the disciplines now known as natural sciences. Several factors helped advance the study of natural philosophy. First, better translations of the classical* works on science became available. Scholars also rediscovered ancient sources that provided alternate views of nature. Perhaps the most important change, however, was the development of new ideas and new approaches in science.

Mathematicians had long relied on the use of suppositions, or hypotheses—ideas that they assumed to be true in order to test an argument. As mathematics and physics began to overlap more in the 1500s, scientists began using the same technique. The famous Italian scientist Galileo GALILEI (1564–1642) was one of the first to use experiments to test his proposed ideas. The use of hypotheses and experiments was a major breakthrough in the development of modern science.

* **metaphysics**   branch of philosophy concerned with the nature of reality and existence

* **ethics**   branch of philosophy concerned with questions of right and wrong

* **classical**   in the tradition of ancient Greece and Rome

See color
plate 6,
vol. 4

Botany. Since prehistoric times, humans had used plants for food, medicine, and other purposes. However, until the Renaissance, there were few attempts to study or describe plants in a systematic manner. The science of botany emerged in the 1400s as a result of several factors, including the revival of classical texts, the discovery of new plants, and the growth of printing, which made it much easier to reproduce pictures and descriptions of plants. Renaissance botany dealt mainly with the medical uses of plants and with identifying plants mentioned in ancient texts. In the later Renaissance, botanists focused more on classifying plants and describing their physical and chemical properties.

Two types of botany texts were widely available in the Renaissance. The first type, known as an herbal, was a list of plants—usually in alphabetical order—along with a brief description of each one, including its habitat and its medical uses. The only illustrations in the earliest printed herbals were woodcuts* based on drawings from medieval* texts, which barely resembled the actual plants. Some later herbals featured more realistic images drawn from life. The other common botany texts were new editions of ancient botanical works, such as *Natural History* by the Roman author Pliny the Elder and *On the Materials of Medicine* by the Greek physician Pedanius Dioscorides. The study of these classical texts raised suspicions among scholars that the ancients might not have known all the plants in the world.

In 1530 the scholar Otto Brunfels gave the illustrated herbal a distinctly Renaissance form with his *Living Images of Plants*. The woodcut illustrations, prepared from drawings made by a student of the famous German artist Albrecht DÜRER, were incredibly lifelike. Some pictures even showed the insect holes and withered leaves on individual plants. The text quoted new editions of classical authors and attacked medieval physicians' ignorance of plants.

Brunfels's success led others to follow in his footsteps. In 1542 Leonhard Fuchs, a German professor of medicine, published *Notable Commentaries on the History of Plants*. The simple line drawings in this volume could be printed at very small sizes while still showing each plant clearly, making them suitable for use in pocket-sized field manuals. Fuchs's text also included many New World plants not known to the ancients, such as maize (corn). In addition, it featured a glossary of old and new terms for the parts of plants.

By the late 1500s the number of known plants had grown to 6,000—ten times the number listed in Dioscorides' text. These newly discovered plants included many from beyond Europe, and specialized books began to appear about the plants of different lands. Scholars found it difficult to name and classify all these new plants. Over 200 different authorities existed, each with its own set of plant names. The confusion over names made it harder to classify plants. Some texts claimed to arrange plants according to similarities, but the guidelines for similarity—such as habitat, growth pattern, or visible features—differed from one book to the next.

Beginning in the 1530s, humanist* scholars reformed the teaching of medicine to reflect the advances in botany. Formal lectures on the

* **woodcut**   print made from a block of wood with an image carved into it

* **medieval**   referring to the Middle Ages, a period that began around A.D. 400 and ended around 1400 in Italy and 1500 in the rest of Europe

* **humanist**   referring to a Renaissance cultural movement promoting the study of the humanities (the languages, literature, and history of ancient Greece and Rome) as a guide to living

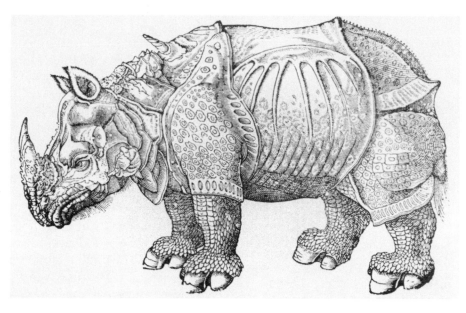

Renaissance artists such as Albrecht Dürer and Leonardo da Vinci helped promote the study of zoology with their lifelike portraits of animals. Dürer drew this picture of a rhinoceros in 1515.

medicinal uses of plants drew on new editions of texts by Dioscorides and the ancient Greek physician GALEN. Instructors also began to place more emphasis on direct, hands-on experience. Professors took students on botanical field trips and conducted demonstrations of plants in botanical gardens. An Italian teacher of botany developed a new type of study aid called an herbarium, which contained pressed and dried plants preserved on sheets of paper.

Zoology. During the Renaissance, the study of animals was based on texts and descriptions rather than on real-world experience. Universities emphasized the teachings of Aristotle, which inspired them to group living things into a value-based hierarchy*. Other classical authors, such as Pliny, focused on tales of animals rather than descriptions of them. These writers tended to include mythical creatures, such as unicorns, in their texts. They often assigned human traits to animals.

Like botany, zoology had strong ties to medicine. Most zoologists were physicians who studied stories of animals to seek ingredients for medical cures. Most of what scholars knew at the time about the structure and function of the human body was based on parallels drawn from dissecting* animals such as pigs and apes. Scientists also studied animals to learn more about their roles in transportation, nutrition, and sports.

Humanist activity encouraged the study of zoology as scholars restored the original versions of ancient texts. Works by Aristotle, Pliny, and other classical writers appeared in print in the late 1400s. Other factors promoted the growth of zoology as well. For example, Renaissance artists such as Albrecht DÜRER and LEONARDO DA VINCI created lifelike portraits of animals. The practice of letter writing also advanced the science by giving scholars a way to exchange information. World travelers brought back reports of new animals in other lands—though these reports were often false or exaggerated. Wealthy and powerful individu-

* **hierarchy** organization of a group into higher and lower levels

* **dissect** to cut open a body to examine its inner parts

als, such as popes, set up their own menageries (the forerunners of modern zoos) to display exotic creatures, such as monkeys and elephants.

During the 1500s scientists who wrote about nature relied mostly on evidence from books. In their eagerness to cover as many ancient sources as possible, they often discussed mythical creatures such as the phoenix that had been included in classical texts. Some of them also accepted as fact the claims of ancient authors that rotting wood could breed a certain type of geese. However, other scientists disproved the theories of ancient authors by dissecting actual animals. The Italian medical scholar Gabriele Falloppio, for instance, countered Aristotle's claim that lions have solid bones with no marrow in them. Similarly, Swiss physician Conrad Gesner disproved the belief that the liver of a mouse grows and shrinks with the phases of the moon.

While knowledge of animals increased, classifying them remained difficult. Scholars used a variety of methods for sorting animals into categories. Aristotle had grouped animals according to their structure, development, and habitat. Another common division involved several categories, including quadrupeds (four-footed creatures), birds, and fish. However, even these large groupings left room for confusion. For example, one text included a picture of a bat nursing, yet described the animal as a bird. Gesner suggested adding further branches to the four basic groups of animals, such as wild versus tame and hornless versus horned.

PHYSICS

During the Renaissance, the modern science of physics did not exist. The Renaissance concept of physics reflected the ideas outlined in Aristotle's *Physics,* which laid out a basic philosophy of nature. However, scientists of the time were studying many of the areas that make up modern physics, such as mechanics (the study of forces at work), optics (the study of light), and acoustics (the study of sound).

Mechanics. In its earliest form, the science of mechanics dealt with weights and the movement of heavy bodies. Renaissance scholars used a variety of sources to study mechanics. Two of the most important were Aristotle's *Physics* and another work called *Mechanics,* thought to be Aristotle's but actually written by one of his students. Scholars also relied on texts by ancient Greek mathematicians, such as Archimedes, Hero, and Pappus, and on treatises* about the medieval science of weights. The work of engineers who designed and built machines also contributed to the science of mechanics.

The earliest studies of mechanics occurred in the field now known as statics, which deals with the forces exerted by bodies at rest. The central idea of statics is the law of the balance, which tells how applying weights or forces at certain distances from a fulcrum, or balancing point, will bring the entire system to rest. The ancient Greeks had developed two ways to prove this law. The first, which involved calculating the ratios between the forces and distances involved, assumed that all the bodies were at rest. The other proof treated the bodies involved as if they

* **treatise** long, detailed essay

Plant Look-Alikes

Most botanists of the 1500s named, pictured, and described plants without attaching any special importance to their outward appearance. However, some held to the longstanding belief that God had made plants look like human organs to reveal their medical properties. The physician Paracelsus supported this view and proposed such remedies as the use of walnuts to treat brain ailments because a walnut resembles the brain.

were moving in a circle around the fulcrum. Renaissance mathematicians eventually came to favor the first proof, which led them emphasize the mathematical aspects of mechanics over its physical aspects.

In the 1300s scholars at Oxford University made advances in the study of bodies in motion. They developed laws more sophisticated than Aristotle's for analyzing the forces that move bodies and created rules for calculating the distances bodies travel in various periods of time. Scientists in Paris applied these new discoveries to the fields of physics and astronomy. In the mid-1500s the Spanish scholar Domingo de Soto sought, with limited success, to find common ground between Aristotle's laws of motion and those discovered at Oxford. De Soto also made a major contribution in 1551 when he suggested that the speed of a falling body changes steadily over time.

Galileo made the last great discoveries in Renaissance mechanics. His work in the field began in 1590, when he challenged one of Aristotle's laws of motion. Aristotle had claimed that the speed of a falling object depends on its weight and on the resistance it encounters. Galileo claimed that what mattered was not the absolute weight of the object, but its weight minus the weight of the volume of air, water, or some other medium that it displaced as it fell. Thus, two objects of unequal size made of the same material would fall at the same speed through a given medium.

Beginning around 1593 Galileo taught a course in mechanics at the University of Padua. In this course he used the law of balance to calculate the mechanical advantage of various simple machines, such as the screw and the lever. In the early 1600s Galileo performed a series of experiments with pendulums and inclined planes to study the properties of falling bodies. Eventually he determined that the speed of a falling object varies according to how long it has been falling, rather than on how far it has fallen. In a series of clever "tabletop" experiments, he succeeded in proving that the speed of a falling body increases steadily with time. After 1610 Galileo turned his attention to astronomy for many years. It was not until 1638 that he published *Two New Sciences,* which became the basis of modern mechanics.

Optics. The science of optics deals with the study of reflected and refracted (bent) light, as well as with the nature of light and theories of human vision. The most influential medieval work on this subject was *Optics,* by the Arab thinker known to the West as Alhazen. Drawing on anatomical, physical, and mathematical texts by ancient Greek scholars, Alhazen developed the idea that each point on the surface of an object gives off rays that strike the eye. About 1270 the Polish monk Witelo reworked Alhazen's ideas, along with those of various other authors, in a book titled *Perspective.* Early Renaissance scholars, however, largely ignored these medieval sources in favor of classical texts. For example, in 1486 the monk Gregorius Reisch published an encyclopedic work that drew on the ideas of ancient Stoic philosophers, who described vision in terms of a series of images that moves from the object to the eye of the viewer.

In 1572 scholar Friedrich Risner published his *Thesaurus of Optics*. This text combined *Optics* and *Perspective* in a single volume and was the first printed version of Alhazen's work. Risner prepared this book by comparing the texts of several different manuscripts. He also divided the book into sections, redrew the figures, and added references to link parts of Alhazen's work to that of Witelo. The book had a major influence on future studies of optics.

The work of German astronomer Johannes KEPLER laid the foundation for the modern science of optics. His *Supplement to Witelo*, published in 1604, explored such topics as reflection, refraction, the nature of light, and the relationship between light and color. Kepler also developed a theory of vision that stated that light rays enter the eye and create an upside-down image on the retina. He was the first to understand the role of the retina in vision.

One of the most important developments in optics during the Renaissance was the use of lenses to magnify the size of objects. This idea was not completely new. Eyeglasses had existed as early as 1313, and by 1500 the use of lenses to improve vision was common throughout Europe. However, making eyeglasses was the work of craftspeople, rather than scientists, and was not related to writings on optics. In 1593 the Italian humanist Giambattista della Porta published *On Refraction,* which described a series of experiments that combined convex lenses, which curve outward, with concave ones, which curve inward. By 1608 instrument makers in the Netherlands had put this idea to use, creating spyglasses that used two lenses to magnify images to three times their normal size.

Galileo began improving on the spyglass and developed an instrument that could magnify images 30 times. He used his new tool to study and describe the features of the moon's surface, the moons of Jupiter, and many new stars. In 1610 he published his discoveries in the book *Sidereal* Messenger.* The book stirred controversy about the value of the telescope. A critic in Florence attacked Galileo, denying that images seen through a telescope were real. Kepler responded by declaring his belief in the value of the telescope and the reality of Galileo's observations.

Acoustics. The science of acoustics deals with the physics of sound and the ways that humans hear sounds. For much of the 1400s, scholars and musicians based their understanding of sound on the book *Fundamentals of Music,* by the Roman scholar Anicius Boethius (480–524). This work combined the theories of various ancient Greek authorities in a single text. Boethius defined sound as a vibration of air that reaches a listening ear. Although a sound wave is actually a series of pulses, the ear senses it as a continuous tone, which is higher or lower depending on how fast the air is moving. Measuring the rate of the pulses, he argued, made it possible to assign a number to a pitch and compare it to the pitch of other notes.

Boethius agreed with the Greek author Pythagoras that only certain ratios between pitches would produce consonances—mixtures of high and low tones that were pleasing to the ear. He believed that simple

* **sidereal** relating to the stars

ratios, like 2:1 or 3:2, produced pleasing sounds. Because there was no way to measure the speed of the vibrations in the air directly, Boethius focused on the size of the objects that produced the sounds. He referred to a legend about Pythagoras hearing consonances coming from a blacksmith's shop and speculating that the combinations of pitches resulted from hammers of differing weights striking the anvil. Later scholars, however, proved that the weight of a hammer does not affect the pitch of the sound it produces.

While some parts of Boethius's work used Pythagorean ideas, in other sections he quoted authors who defined consonance and dissonance (a displeasing blend of tones) purely in terms of the listener's judgment. During the 1500s musical theorists argued over whether to define consonance in terms of mathematical ratios or listener reactions. Physicist Giovanni Benedetti analyzed the motion of strings and suggested that a consonance depended on having two vibrating strings pass through the central point of their vibration at exactly the same instant. The more often this happened, the more perfect the interval between the two notes would sound. For instance, if the two strings were tuned exactly one octave apart, then the lower string would be in its central position exactly half the time that the higher one was. Thus, the ear perceived the octave as a consonance.

Another major discovery of the 1500s had to do with sympathetic vibration. This occurs when the sound waves produced by one vibrating object, such as a string, set off vibrations in another object. Italian scholar Girolamo Fracastoro suggested that a vibrating string produces a sound by causing the air to compress and decompress in a series of pulses. When these waves of compressed air hit another string, they will cause it to vibrate if it is tuned to the same pitch as the first object. If the second string is tuned to a different note, it will interfere with the motion of the air and no sound will be produced.

CHEMISTRY

The modern science of chemistry arose out of the "chemical philosophy" of the Renaissance. This philosophy, in turn, grew out of the work of alchemists, especially the Swiss physician PARACELSUS (1493–1541). Chemical philosophers sought to identify the basic elements of which things were made. Some of them focused their attention on the study of metals and minerals. Others, such as Paracelsus, aimed to discover new medical uses for various substances. Some of their methods hinted at the techniques that would later be useful in the labs of modern chemists. However, most chemical philosophers did not make a distinction between their field and alchemy, which also contained magical and mystical* elements.

* **mystical**   based on a belief in the idea of a direct, personal union with the divine

Metallurgy.   Many early advances in chemistry occurred in the field of metallurgy (the study of metals). Italian scholar Vannoccio Biringuccio made several major discoveries in this field. Although he based his theories on the works of Aristotle, his methods were much more modern.

In *On Pyrotechnics,* published in 1540, he wrote at length about metallic ores and how to analyze them and prepare them for smelting. He also discussed alloys (blends of two or more metals) and "semiminerals" such as mercury and sulfur.

German scholars Georgius Agricola and Lazarus Ercker also published influential works on mining and metallurgy. Agricola's *On Metals* was a thorough survey of what Renaissance scholars knew about metals, including how to work with them. Ercker's *Description,* published in 1574, built on Agricola's work. It explained how to obtain and refine various metals and use them to produce acids, salts, and other compounds. Some consider this text the first manual of analytical and metallurgical chemistry.

Medical Chemistry. Paracelsus pioneered the field of medical chemistry. Unlike most doctors of his time, he favored the use of powerful drugs designed to treat specific diseases. He developed several new laboratory procedures to refine chemical substances for medical purposes, such as a method of concentrating alcohol by purifying and freezing it. He was also the first scientist to group chemicals according to how easy it was to perform certain chemical processes on them.

German scientists of the mid-1500s took the lead in expanding medical chemistry into a more complete field. Adam of Bodenstein edited and translated Paracelsus's works, focusing on the relationship between minerals and medicine. He also recommended the use of metallic compounds for treating disease. German scholar Andreas Libavius, by contrast, opposed the ideas of Paracelsus. The last edition of his book *Alchymia,* published in 1606, included plans for building a chemical laboratory. The text contained more than 200 designs and pictures of chemical glassware, furnaces, and devices. Many modern scholars view Libavius as the founder of chemical analysis. Another leading medical chemist in Germany was Oswald Croll, who performed experiments to determine the chemical properties of the drugs he used. His book *Chemical Edifice* (1609) described his preparations in detail and explained how to use them. It became the first textbook of medical chemistry, used for a course in the subject at the University of Marburg.

In France, scientist Guy de La Brosse combined his knowledge of botany with an interest in medicine and chemistry. De la Brosse admired Paracelsus because he had stressed the importance of experiments and direct experience and had opposed the ideas of ancient scholars such as Aristotle and Galen. In 1628 de la Brosse published a work on the nature of plants that he described as a "general treatise on chemistry." According to de la Brosse, the basic idea of chemistry is that everything can be broken down into the basic elements of which it is formed. Reducing a substance in this way, he argued, is the only way to understand it fully.

Belgian scientist Jan van Helmont (1579–1644) made several major discoveries in medicine and chemistry. He relied heavily on the use of experiments to test different substances. He analyzed smoke chemically and described it as a gas with specific properties based on the substance that produced it. Helmont identified several gases produced by burning

---

Living Rocks

During the Renaissance, scholars first began to suggest that fossils were not merely stones, but objects that had once been living beings. In 1547 the Italian scholar Girolamo Cardano argued that some fossils found on mountainsides had come from sea creatures. However, he rejected the suggestion that the great flood described in the Bible had deposited these fossils on land. In 1566 Conrad Gesner of Switzerland sorted fossils by shape, separating out specimens he felt resembled land and sea animals. His work was a first step toward the modern view of fossils as the remains of living creatures.

different substances, including carbon dioxide from charcoal and "explosive gas" from gunpowder. He also designed methods for preparing various acids from substances such as clay and salt.

While Helmont made many practical discoveries, Daniel Sennert of Germany was responsible for the most important advances in the theory of chemistry. He aimed to find common ground between the ideas of Paracelsus, Aristotle, Galen, and other ancient scholars. Sennert argued that all natural objects could be reduced to certain basic parts. He thought of these parts as very small particles, or *minima.* He viewed a chemical reaction as an object splitting into specific *minima,* which then moved around and reformed to create a new substance with its own properties. The *minima* themselves, he claimed, could never be created, destroyed, or changed. Sennert saw the science of chemistry not just as an aid to the practice of medicine, but as a separate field with the goal of breaking down natural substances and prepare them for other uses. (*See also* **Alchemy; Anatomy; Astronomy; Humanism; Magic and Astrology; Mathematics; Medicine; Mining and Metallurgy; Scientific Instruments; Scientific Method; Technology.**)

Scientific Instruments

Renaissance scientists used a variety of instruments for measuring, drawing, calculating, and so forth. Most of these tools had existed since ancient times and had been refined throughout the Middle Ages. Renaissance scientists improved the devices they had and invented several new ones.

Renaissance astronomers relied on three basic tools. The astrolabe and the quadrant were two devices used to measure the altitude of a heavenly body. An astrolabe was usually a small brass disk with markings that showed the positions of stars and a pointer in the center to indicate the angle between the user and a heavenly body. The quadrant was a simpler tool for measuring angles, composed of a quarter-circle marked off in degrees and equipped with a pointer. The third device, the armillary sphere, was a sphere made of rings that showed the supposed orbits of the heavenly bodies. Renaissance astronomers Bernard Walther (1430–1504) and Tycho BRAHE (1546–1601) built oversized versions of these tools that made remarkably accurate measurements.

The most important new astronomical device to appear during the Renaissance was the telescope. Zacharias Jansen, an eyeglass maker in the Netherlands, created the first telescope in 1608. Astronomer Thomas Harriot of England made the first recorded use of the telescope the following year. Italian scientist Galileo GALILEI made astonishing discoveries with this new tool. His *Sidereal* Messenger,* published in 1610, described the mountains on the Moon, the moons of Jupiter, and the stars of the Milky Way.

Sailors used some of these astronomical devices, including the astrolabe and the quadrant, as tools for estimating distances. They also used a variety of other instruments. The cross staff, a long wooden rod with one or more crosspieces, enabled sailors to measure the sun's altitude at midday or a star's height above the horizon. Magnetic compasses

* **sidereal** relating to the stars

Venetian physician Santorio Santorio invented several new medical tools. He used his weighing chair, shown here, to study the change that occurred in his body weight as a result of eating food and eliminating waste.

showed navigators their course. To measure speed sailors used a log—a weighted rectangular plate attached to a long cord. They threw the plate overboard and used a sandglass to measure the amount of time it took for the cord to unwind. This told them how fast the ship was moving. By the late 1500s, sailors had begun adding knots to the cord at regular intervals so that they could tell their speed by counting the knots. This practice gave rise to the term "knots" as a measure of nautical speed.

During the 1500s, artists and mathematicians used various types of compasses to compare the lengths of unequal lines and to divide straight lines and circles into parts. In the late 1590s, Galileo developed an improved compass that could aid a wide variety of mathematical tasks. English mathematician Thomas Hood invented a similar device, which he called a sector. Another new tool for calculating, the slide rule, appeared in the 1600s. Unlike the abacus, used by mathematicians and merchants of the early Renaissance, this device could help solve complex mathematical problems.

New tools for doctors also appeared during the Renaissance. Galileo experimented with several medical instruments, including a pulse watch and an early thermometer without a scale. The Venetian physician Santorio Santorio (1561–1636) developed the first clinical thermometer. The extreme points of its scale were the temperature of snow and that of a candle flame. He also invented a device to measure the pulse, an instrument for measuring humidity, a special syringe for extracting bladder stones, a bathing bed, and a weighing chair. The last major invention of the Renaissance was the microscope. By the middle of the 1600s, medical scholars had begun to make new discoveries with the help of this tool. (*See also* **Calendars; Clocks; Geography and Cartography; Mathematics; Medicine; Science; Weights and Measures.**)

Scientific Method

One of the most significant events in Renaissance science was the development of the scientific method. Modern scientists use this phrase to refer to a specific form of inquiry that involves forming a theory, or hypothesis, and using experiments to test it. The theory may change based on the results of the experiments. During the Renaissance, however, "scientific method" had a somewhat different meaning, which had its origins in the work of the ancient Greek philosopher ARISTOTLE.

Ancient scholars such as Aristotle and his teacher PLATO had used the term *method*—based on the Greek words *meta,* meaning "following," and *hodos,* meaning "way"—to refer to a process of rational inquiry. Plato described a method for investigating subjects in the area of the arts, and Aristotle extended the idea to all fields of knowledge. Later thinkers, such as the physician GALEN in the late 100s and the mathematician Pappus in the 300s, applied the concept of method to their own fields of study.

Italian scholars in the mid-1500s began to revive the ancient concept of method and to apply it to the study of science. Jacopo Zabarella of Padua drew a distinction between method and order. Order, as he defined it, meant simply learning one thing before another, while method involved using the knowledge of one concept to lead to understanding of another. Girolamo Borro, a teacher of Italian scientist Galileo GALILEI, described method as the quickest way to gain a particular knowledge or skill. Another of Galileo's teachers, Francesco Buonamici, also stressed the importance of method as a way to progress from one piece of knowledge to another.

* **treatise**   long, detailed essay

Galileo gave his own account of scientific method in his *Logical Treatises**, written around 1589. He defined method as a two-stage process. The first stage involved looking at an effect and reasoning backward to find its cause. For instance, a scientist might see a shadow on the ground and try to determine what type of object was casting it. Then, in the second stage, the thinker would reason forward from this cause to determine the effect—in this case, attempting to show that the object in question would indeed cast a shadow of that shape. However, Galileo, like Zabarella, believed that a third stage had to take place in between to prove that the cause in question was truly responsible for the effect. He proposed the use of logic and experiments to support the link between cause and effect. The idea of suggesting a probable cause for some fact, then testing it through experiments, forms the basis of the modern scientific method.

Other Renaissance thinkers also explored the idea of method, but they took a different approach to the concept from Galileo's. The French educator Petrus RAMUS, for example, developed a method of inquiry that he claimed was useful in all fields of knowledge. However, his method was geared more toward teaching a subject than making new discoveries. Ramus's efforts inspired the English philosopher Francis BACON, who set out to create a complete system of thought that would make use of experimentation and inductive* reasoning. He believed his method would enable humans to find the causes of everything that occurred in the world of nature. Although Bacon's method did not work as well as he claimed, his insistence on experimentation set a standard for later scientists in England. (*See also* **Logic; Science.**)

* **inductive**   proceeding from particular facts to a general conclusion

Scotland

* **Low Countries**   region bordering on the North Sea, made up of present-day Netherlands and Belgium

* **humanist**   referring to a Renaissance cultural movement promoting the study of the humanities (the languages, literature, and history of ancient Greece and Rome) as a guide to living

Though only a small and poor kingdom on the far edge of Europe, Scotland remained in close touch with Renaissance ideas and culture. This connection came in part from trade relations with France, the Low Countries*, and the Baltic states and in part from the readiness of Scots to travel and study abroad. Scottish political and cultural leaders worked hard to combat the popular image of Scots as ferocious barbarians constantly at war with one another. As a result of their efforts, Scotland became a center of humanist* learning and thought.

The Stuart Dynasty. Since 1371 the STUART DYNASTY had struggled to impose its authority over Scotland, a country divided geographically and politically into many small regions ruled by powerful local lords. However, by the late 1400s, after years of warfare the power of the regional lords was mostly broken. The Stuart monarchs then began to seek marriage alliances with foreign powers to increase their influence abroad. Perhaps the most significant of these marriages occurred in 1503, when James IV (ruled 1488–1513) wed Margaret Tudor, daughter of King HENRY VII of England. One hundred years later, Scotland's James VI would use this tie to claim the English throne as JAMES I and unite the two kingdoms.

Before the marriage of James IV and Margaret Tudor, Scotland and England had a long history of hostile relations. Defending Scotland against English aggression was considered one of the key roles of Scottish kings. Many Scots viewed the marriage as a betrayal of the crown's traditional loyalties. Nevertheless, Scotland remained allied with France, another long-time adversary of the English. The French king Louis XII called on James to fulfill the obligations of their alliance by invading England. James did so, but the invasion ended with his defeat and death at the battle of Flodden in 1513.

By this time, Scotland had established itself as a united kingdom under the control of the Stuart dynasty. James IV had expressed this supremacy by adding the arched "imperial" crown to his coat of arms*. The crown represented the idea of Roman law that "the king is emperor in his own kingdom." Scots thought of themselves as an imperial monarchy on an equal with any in Europe. James IV's elegant Renaissance court, and his own interests in architecture and medicine, reflected Scotland's self-confident view of itself and its monarchy.

Scottish Humanism. Scotland's familiarity with and acceptance of Renaissance culture and learning promoted such self-confidence. Since the mid-1400s, Scottish officials within and outside of the church had been collecting classical* literature as well as the works of Italian and French humanists. Under royal secretary Archibald Whitelaw, humanist rhetorical* skills were applied in government in the late 1400s.

Scottish universities also adapted to humanist ideas. A group of Scots who studied in Paris exercised enormous influence on university curricula after their return to Scotland. Led by the University of Aberdeen, Scottish universities gradually adopted a humanist course of study aimed at serving both the clergy and the lay* students. The emergence of a group of well-educated laypeople was one of the most significant cultural developments in this period of Scottish history. Many educated Scots went on to study and practice law, often in France or Italy.

James V, barely a year old, inherited the throne on his father's death in 1513. When James assumed control of the government in 1528, he made use of the lay lawyers to reassert the crown's powers. Scotland's influence with the Catholic powers of Europe increased after the English king HENRY VIII broke with the Roman Catholic Church in 1533. James V used this power to obtain money from the papacy* and to arrange marriage alliances between Scotland and France.

James invested the rewards of his diplomacy in the royal palaces of Stirling, Falkland, and Holyrood, creating some of the first and finest Renaissance buildings in Britain. However, his glittering court was torn by tensions between church officials and educated laypersons influenced

* **coat of arms**   set of symbols used to represent a noble family

* **classical**   in the tradition of ancient Greece and Rome

* **rhetorical**   related to the art of speaking or writing effectively

* **lay**   referring to people who are not members of the clergy

* **papacy**   office and authority of the pope

by humanism. James may have even considered following Henry's example in rejecting papal authority and establishing control of the church in Scotland. But the king died suddenly in 1542 at the age of 30.

The Reformation. Soon after James's death, his infant daughter MARY STUART was crowned queen of Scotland. Henry VIII forced the Scots to agree to a marriage between Mary and his heir Edward (died in 1553). Mary was secretly sent to France, where she became fluent in French and married Francis of Valois, the heir to the French throne. In 1561 Mary, a Catholic, returned to Scotland to claim the throne. She was overthrown six years later. Exiled and imprisoned in England, Mary continued to hope for the overthrow of Elizabeth, Queen of England, that would result in her becoming the Catholic queen of England. Mary's trial and execution in 1587 opened the way for her son James VI, the king of Scotland, to become next in line to the English throne.

James VI was baptized a Catholic but raised as a Protestant. His education was supervised by the humanist scholar George Buchanan, who attempted to teach his pupil respect for classical scholarship and the principles of limited monarchy. As a result of Buchanan's efforts, James developed a lifelong love of learning and literature. However, he failed to adopt Buchanan's political ideas. James developed his own theory of the "divine right of kings," based on the belief that a monarch's authority comes from God, not the people, and thus cannot be limited by the people.

The king's determination to maintain the crown's supremacy over church as well as state came partly from his concern for maintaining order in a land torn by years of political and religious turmoil. Although James tried to control religious matters by appointing his own bishops, he did not try to suppress the Catholic faith. In fact, many of the king's most trusted and influential counselors were Catholics.

James's reign was marked by a drive to establish law, order, and civility in Scotland. By 1600 the decline of political violence led many rural lords to abandon fortified castles for more luxurious country estates. Upon the death of Elizabeth I in 1603, James VI of Scotland took the English throne as JAMES I. This united the two crowns, but not the kingdoms. Although James I promoted a common "British" kingdom, Scotland remained a distinct political identity with its own culture. (*See also* **England.**)

* **relief**   type of sculpture in which figures are raised slightly from a flat surface

During the Renaissance, sculptors produced a remarkable range of works, from small carved figures and relief* images to massive public monuments and religious statues. In some parts of Europe, particularly Italy, the rise of humanism* led to an interest in the sculptural styles of ancient Greece and Rome. However, much of the sculpture produced in northern Europe during the Renaissance showed the influence of the Gothic* art of the Middle Ages.

Italy. The development of Italian Renaissance sculpture can be divided into three periods: 1250 to 1400, 1400 to 1500, and 1500 to 1600.

* **humanism**   Renaissance cultural movement promoting the study of the humanities (the languages, literature, and history of ancient Greece and Rome) as a guide to living

* **Gothic**   style of architecture characterized by pointed arches and high, thin walls supported by flying buttresses; also artistic style marked by bright colors, elongated proportions, and intricate detail

* **medieval**   referring to the Middle Ages, a period that began around A.D. 400 and ended around 1400 in Italy and 1500 in the rest of Europe

* **classical**   in the tradition of ancient Greece and Rome

* **perspective**   artistic technique for creating the illusion of three-dimensional space on a flat surface

* **allegory**   literary or artistic device in which characters, events, and settings represent abstract qualities and in which the author intends a different meaning to be read beneath the surface

* **Mannerism**   artistic style of the 1500s characterized by vivid colors and exaggeration, such as elongated figures in complex poses

During the first period Italian sculpture followed several different trends, such as the use of massive medieval* forms and the incorporation of Gothic realism. Another trend, which set the stage for the Renaissance, was the emerging awareness of ancient Roman art. In the 1200s the work of southern Italian sculptors such as Nicola Pisano showed some of these tendencies, reflecting both ancient Roman and French Gothic sources.

During the second period of Italian Renaissance sculpture—the 1400s—many outstanding sculptors worked in Italy, especially in FLORENCE. The start of this period is generally associated with a competition held in 1402 for the creation of bronze doors for the baptistery in the city. Several prominent sculptors, including DONATELLO, Filippo BRUNELLESCHI, and Lorenzo GHIBERTI submitted entries. Ghiberti (ca. 1378–1455) won the contest with a relief that displays remarkably realistic human anatomy in a classical* style.

Donatello (ca. 1386–1466), the most outstanding Italian sculptor of the 1400s, also worked in Florence. His earliest pieces show the influence of ancient Roman sculpture. Over the course of his career, Donatello's artistry ranged from powerfully dramatic figures, such as *Mary Magdalen,* to captivating images of youth and beauty, such as *David.* He experimented with perspective* and with various decorative effects. To add a sense of drama to his work, he sometimes created vast scenes filled with agitated figures, such as the bronze reliefs in the sanctuary of St. Anthony at Padua.

During this second period, portraits of individuals became more realistic. Most sculptures of women were still idealized, with perfect, youthful faces and figures. Likenesses of men, however, followed the ancient Roman custom of including the details of aging and other unflattering physical elements. Antonio Pollaiuolo (ca. 1431–1498) took this approach in the tomb of Pope Sixtus IV in the Vatican, which plainly shows the elderly features of its subject.

In the 1500s MICHELANGELO (1475–1564) dominated Italian Renaissance sculpture. Some critics, including the art historian Giorgio Vasari (1511–1574), view Michelangelo's work as the climax of Renaissance art. In a career that spanned more than 60 years, the artist created numerous images of the human body to express his artistic ideas.

For many viewers Michelangelo's famous statue of *David* represents the ideal Renaissance male nude. Its pose, facial expression, and large scale suggest a tremendous sense of power. Two figures of *Slaves* that he created for the tomb of pope JULIUS II have tense muscular poses and emotionless faces that suggest inner struggle. Michelangelo also explored the use of allegory*. For the MEDICI tomb in Florence, he produced portraits of Giuliano and Lorenzo de' Medici that represent thought and action. Overall, Michelangelo's depiction of the human body went beyond traditional realism and introduced an exaggerated style that became known as Mannerism*.

As the 1500s progressed, powerful rulers often used sculpture to create impressive public monuments. Major works, such as massive fountains, featured images from classical allegory. In Florence, Cosimo I de'

Donatello was the most admired Italian sculptor of the 1400s. This wooden statue of *Mary Magdalen,* carved around 1455, is one of his most moving and dramatic works.

---

* **Baroque** artistic style of the 1600s characterized by movement, drama, and grandness of scale

* **Flemish** relating to Flanders, a region along the coasts of present-day Belgium, France, and the Netherlands

* **Protestant Reformation** religious movement that began in the 1500s as a protest against certain practices of the Roman Catholic Church and eventually led to the establishment of a variety of Protestant churches

MEDICI hired the artist Benvenuto CELLINI (1500–1571) to produce a triumphant statue of the mythological hero Perseus. Sculptural decoration of buildings also became increasing important. The Venetian sculptor Jacopo Sansovino (1486–1570), for example, freely integrated sculpture with his architecture, giving it a luxurious appearance. Many of these elements were further developed in the Baroque* style of the 1600s.

Northern European Sculpture. During the late 1300s and early 1400s, artists in northern Europe created realistic sculptures with intricate detail. Their work had little connection with the classical style that developed in Italy. Instead, northern sculptors continued to use many of the artistic techniques found in the great Gothic cathedrals. They worked in a variety of styles and media, from large figures in wood and stone to exquisite ivory carvings. The pieces offer a broad range of emotional expression, from dramatic to sensitive.

By the end of the 1300s, northern European sculptors had developed a form of realism that was highly detailed. Sculptors began creating precise portraits of particular individuals. This realism reached a climax with the work of Flemish* sculptor Claus Sluter (ca. 1340–1406), whose images of biblical figures have animated expressions, a sense of movement, and include details such as signs of aging. Another characteristic of northern European work during this period is the use of paint on sculptured surfaces. Indeed, in the Netherlands, the development of painting and sculpture were closely connected.

In the 1400s sculpture in the realistic style appeared in Germany and Austria. The Dutch artist Nicolaus Gerhaert, who died in the 1470s, brought the style of Claus Sluter to the region. Notable German sculptural works of the late 1400s and early 1500s include monumental wooden altarpieces to decorate churches. Some of these pieces combine sculpture with painting, such as the Isenheim Altarpiece (1515), which features work by Matthias Grünewald and Nicholas of Hagenau.

In the 1500s the influence of the Italian Renaissance arrived in northern Europe. Flemish and German artists, such as Albrecht DÜRER (1471–1528), traveled to Italy and brought back Renaissance ideas and practices. In France and Spain, the monarchs were largely responsible for introducing Renaissance art. The rulers of both countries commissioned works from leading Italian masters. For example, in the 1540s the Italian artist Francesco Primaticcio adorned the French royal residence at Fontainebleau with elegant stucco nudes. In turn, many French and Spanish artists adopted Italian artistic techniques.

The rise of the Protestant Reformation* in German-speaking lands temporarily put an end to new religious sculpture. The more radical Protestant reformers were strongly opposed to the religious use of images, and some removed art from churches in the early 1500s. The followers of Martin LUTHER took a more moderate position, and their acceptance contributed to the re-emergence of religious sculpture in Germany in the late 1500s. (*See also* **Architecture; Art; Art in Britain; Art in Central Europe; Art in France; Art in Germany; Art in Italy; Art in the Netherlands; Art in Spain and Portugal; Baroque; Classical Antiquity; Decorative Arts; Tombs.**)

Servants

Servants made up a fairly large group in Renaissance society. Many households employed one or more servants, ranging from a sole farm worker to a staff of 100. By the early 1500s, a third of all families had live-in servants.

Although aristocratic households employed large staffs of servants of both sexes, a typical home had far fewer. Most people could afford only one or two servants, usually women or girls. Female servants made up 12 percent of the population of some European cities. The majority of these servants were unmarried women and girls, sometimes as young as seven or eight. They often worked as all-purpose maids, attending to various tasks such as cleaning bedchambers and helping in the kitchen. Employing male servants, which was less common, gave status to a household. English farmers employed servants of both sexes, one or two to a farm. In exchange for general tasks they received food, lodging, and a small wage when they left.

Many female servants who worked in cities moved there from the countryside. Often from poor families or from poverty-stricken regions, they came to the city hoping to work to save enough money for a dowry* to attract a husband. This could take many years, as wages were low, and some never reached their goal. Those who did marry almost always left service. Servants were typically single, either by custom or law, and a female servant who became pregnant could be dismissed.

Families found servants through word of mouth, local hiring fairs, or employment agencies. The conditions of their service varied greatly. All servants were entirely dependent upon their employers and could be punished or fired at will. They received little or no time off and worked long hours for little pay. Employers provided food and lodging, but quarters might be no more than a cupboard under the stairs or space on the kitchen floor. In addition, employers and servants lived close together, and female servants were at risk of sexual advances from men in the household. (*See also* **Social Status.**)

* **dowry** money or property that a woman brings to her marriage

Seville

See color plate 5, vol. 4

Located 70 miles from the Atlantic coast on the Guadalquivir River, the Spanish port of Seville controlled the burgeoning transatlantic trade that developed after Columbus's voyages. Between 1503 and 1717, the Spanish crown declared that all people and goods headed to America must be registered at Seville. The city became an international distribution point that attracted people from all over Europe. By 1600 its population had grown to at least 80,000, with some estimates as high as 130,000.

Two important institutions in Seville handled matters relating to Spanish America. The Casa de Contratación (House of Trade) had responsibility for the commerce, navigation, and movement of people between Spain and its overseas colonies. It also collected and studied maps and reports prepared by returning mariners. The Casa Lonja de Mercaderes (Merchant Hall) oversaw the traders and business transactions that provided supplies for the empire.

* **Jesuit**   belonging to a Roman Catholic religious order founded by St. Ignatius Loyola and approved in 1540

* **humanist**   referring to a Renaissance cultural movement promoting the study of the humanities (the languages, literature, and history of ancient Greece and Rome) as a guide to living

* **Spanish Inquisition**   court established by the Spanish monarchs that investigated Christians accused of straying from the official doctrine of the Roman Catholic Church, particularly during the period 1480–1530

* **plague**   highly contagious and often fatal disease that wiped out much of Europe's population in the mid-1300s and reappeared periodically over the next three centuries; also known as the Black Death

Sexuality and Gender

* **adultery**   sexual relationship outside of marriage

* **courtesan**   prostitute associated with wealthy men or men in attendance at a royal court

Seville grew into a cultural and intellectual center as well as a commercial capital. Spain's most active publishing city during the early 1500s, the city boasted a university and several schools founded by the Jesuits*. Columbus's son Hernando Colon collected humanist* texts that now form the core of a library at the Cathedral of Seville. The city also became a leading center of drama. Examples of Spanish Renaissance architecture in Seville include Merchant Hall, the Hospital de las Cinco Llagas (Hospital of the five wounds), and city hall. In the 1480s, the monarchs FERDINAND OF ARAGON and ISABELLA OF CASTILE launched the Spanish Inquisition* in Seville.

The 1600s marked a period of decline for Seville. Plague* struck the city in 1599–1601 and again in 1649. Also during this time, Madrid was gaining power as the seat of royal government, and the city of Cadiz took over much of the transatlantic shipping once handled by Seville. By 1717 the city had lost its control over trade with Spanish America. (*See also* **Americas; Art in Spain and Portugal; Spain.**)

Religion played a major role in Renaissance attitudes toward sex and gender. Both Roman Catholic and Protestant churches regarded sex as an activity that should occur only within marriage. Sexual behavior outside that framework—such as prostitution or homosexuality—was sometimes tolerated but rarely approved by either the church or society as a whole. The laws and customs that regulated sexual behavior tended to reinforce the inferior role of women in society. For example, women faced stricter penalties for adultery* than men did. On the other hand, men usually faced harsher punishment for homosexual acts. Sex between women went largely unnoticed.

Gender Roles. Men dominated both private and public life in the Renaissance. Most families were patriarchal, meaning that the male head of the household controlled the family's money and made all the important decisions. Both civil and church law supported this arrangement, which treated the family as a miniature version of the state in which the ruler held the place of father to his subjects.

A few women did manage to gain some degree of independence. Nuns, for example, could largely escape the control of men by removing themselves completely from male society. It was also possible for a woman whose husband had died to inherit his money, which would give her both economic power and social standing. For most widows, however, the death of a husband brought financial hardship rather than gain. Likewise, the life of a prostitute was usually a hard one, but for the upper-class courtesans* of Italy it offered economic and social power. These women offered refined companionship, as well as sexual services, to their clients. Writers and painters honored famous French and Italian courtesans for their glamour and elegance. A few women sought to escape their social boundaries by passing themselves off as men. Dressed in male clothing, these "passing women" could gain access to places open only to men.

* **theology**   study of the nature of God and of religion

Attitudes Toward Sex. During the Middle Ages, most of Europe based its attitudes about sexual desire on theology*. Religious thinkers such as AUGUSTINE OF HIPPO had seen desire as a force that could either draw individuals toward God or lure them away from the path of virtue and into the sins of the flesh. The Roman Catholic Church placed a higher value on virginity and celibacy (the state of being unmarried) than on sexual activity. It believed that sex should take place only within marriage, with the goal of producing children.

The Renaissance brought a shift in the church's attitude toward marriage and family. It began to focus more on love and companionship as a part of marriage. As a result, it became acceptable for married people to enjoy—in moderation—sexual pleasure that was not directly related to producing children. Although society did not openly approve of birth control, the practice was fairly common.

Society continued to recognize a variety of offenses relating to marriage. Fornication, or sex between unmarried persons, was officially a crime but seldom carried a severe punishment. Instead, it often served as a step toward marriage. A more serious offense was adultery, or sex between a married person and someone other than his or her spouse. Penalties for adultery varied, and men often faced less severe punishment than women. Social status also played a role in determining the penalties for this crime. For example, a married aristocrat who had sex with his female servants was unlikely to be charged with adultery at all.

Although Renaissance society recognized rape as a crime, the punishments for it depended on the age and social rank of the people involved. To a certain extent, society saw male desire as naturally violent. Literature, for example, often dealt with cases of a young man forcing himself on a woman. Thus, the penalties for rape were usually less harsh than those for homosexuality. Rape carried a severe penalty only if it involved very young girls—or if it involved a breach of social station, as in the case of a peasant attacking a noblewoman.

Prostitution. Prostitution was widespread during the Renaissance, especially in cities. Society appears to have viewed it as a necessary evil for coping with young men's sexual desires, which might otherwise pose a danger to honorable girls and women. In Italian cities, some people regarded prostitution as a way of encouraging young men to have sex with women rather than with other men.

The elegant courtesans of Italy and France were the exceptions rather than the rule. Most prostitutes were poor women who often suffered from violence and disease. Some women combined prostitution with other forms of labor, such as sewing, laundering clothes, or selling food and drink, moving from town to town with other members of the working poor. The few accounts left by these women suggest that they regarded prostitution primarily as work that paid relatively well. In most cases, it seems, their neighbors did not shun them because of their occupation.

The status of urban prostitutes changed significantly over the course of the Renaissance. During the 1300s and 1400s many cities and towns

Women in Love?

It is difficult to determine to what extent sexual relations between women occurred during the Renaissance. The concept of "lesbianism" did not exist at the time, and there is very little surviving evidence about such activities. Thus, scholars can only guess. For example, some suggest that Queen Christina of Sweden (ruled 1644–1654) was a lesbian because she refused to marry. Other scholars believe that, like Elizabeth I of England, Christina may have rejected marriage because she did not want to share power with anyone, not even a husband.

The courtesans of the Renaissance offered refined companionship, as well as sexual favors, to their upper-class clients. Artists often celebrated the glamour and elegance of these women, as in the French painting *The Prodigal Son with Courtesans*.

* **brothel**   house of prostitution

throughout Europe opened official brothels* or set aside certain districts where prostitution was allowed. Laws regulating the brothels tried to protect both prostitutes and their clients by such measures as forbidding weapons, banning the sale of women, and checking the prostitutes for disease. In this era, prostitutes—at least those who lived in the city-run brothels—were an accepted part of urban society. They appeared as a group at city festivals and openly welcomed important visitors to the city.

In the later 1400s, however, many cities—especially in northern Europe—placed greater restrictions on prostitutes. They had to wear clothing that distinguished them from "honorable" women and stay in the brothels at all times. Those who lived outside the official brothel or district faced harsh penalties, such as banishment or mutilation (having parts of their bodies cut off). German cities closed their brothels altogether in the 1500s, and Spanish cities did the same in the early 1600s. Major Italian cities did not outlaw prostitution entirely, but they regulated it more strictly.

Scholars once believed that this shift toward tighter control of prostitution was due to the appearance of syphilis, a sexually transmitted disease. Today, however, most believe that the main cause was the new moral strictness brought about by the religious reform movements of

* Protestant Reformation religious movement that began in the 1500s as a protest against certain practices of the Roman Catholic Church and eventually led to the establishment of a variety of Protestant churches

the era. Martin LUTHER, a leader of the Protestant Reformation*, called prostitutes tools of the devil and accused them of bewitching single men. Catholic reformers of the time attacked prostitution in equally vicious terms.

Homosexuality. Since the Middle Ages, European societies had defined sodomy, or same-sex relations, as both a sin and a crime. Nonetheless, such activities were widespread in Renaissance society. Both men and women engaged in sexual activities with others of the same sex, but male homosexuality attracted much more attention. It occurred at all levels of society, from kings and nobles to priests, merchants, and sailors. Most relationships between men involved an older man, often one who was married, and an adolescent. Society viewed the older man as the more active partner and imposed stricter penalties on him. Among women, same-sex relations sometimes involved "passing women," who sometimes carried their male role so far as to "marry" other women.

Modern scholars disagree about the nature of homosexuality in the Renaissance. Most believe that Renaissance culture did not recognize the concept of "being" homosexual. According to this view, homosexuality was an act rather than an identity—a sin into which anyone might fall at some point. A few scholars, however, argue that the Renaissance gave rise to the first inklings of an idea of "homosexuals" as a group. They note that the cultures of ancient Greece and Rome, so widely admired by humanists*, had recognized and accepted sex acts between men. Humanists such as Marsilio FICINO of Italy penned defenses of male love. (*See also* **Family and Kinship; Feminism; Love and Marriage; Women.**)

* humanist Renaissance expert in the humanities (the languages, literature, history, and speech writing techniques of ancient Greece and Rome)

Shakespeare, William

1564–1616
English writer

English playwright William Shakespeare is known throughout the world as one of the greatest writers who ever lived. His plays cover a wide range of dramatic forms, including comedy, tragedy, and history. One of Shakespeare's greatest skills was his ability to portray every possible emotional state. His works deal with the essential elements of human life, such as love, friendship, growing old, and facing the approach of death.

SHAKESPEARE'S LIFE

Shakespeare was born in Stratford-upon-Avon, a market town in central England. His father, John, kept a large home from which he ran a business manufacturing gloves and other leather goods. As a man of wealth and social position, he held several positions in local government. Later in life, however, Shakespeare's father seems to have lost much of his fortune. Some scholars believe his troubles sprang from his unwillingness to abandon the Catholic faith when England became a Protestant nation.

SHAKESPEARE, WILLIAM

Widely regarded as one of the greatest writers who ever lived, William Shakespeare produced dozens of plays during his lengthy career in the theater. His plays and poems have influenced a host of writers over the last five centuries.

William probably attended the King's New School in Stratford, which emphasized the study of Latin. As a student there Shakespeare would have read the works of such ancient Roman authors as VIRGIL, Ovid, and Seneca. The influence of these writers appears in several of Shakespeare's plays. At the age of 18, Shakespeare married Anne Hathaway, who was eight years older than himself. Their first child was born about six months later, and within two years, the couple had three children. Scholars are unsure how he supported his family for the next eight years. However, they do know that by 1592 Shakespeare had moved to London, apparently leaving his wife and children behind in Stratford, and taken up a career as an actor and a playwright. An angry review by an older playwright offers the first clear record of Shakespeare's presence in London.

Shakespeare achieved his first dramatic success with his history play *The First Part of King Henry the Sixth,* perhaps as early as 1589. He also wrote poetry during his early years in London. His two major non-

* **patron** supporter or financial sponsor of an artist or writer

dramatic poems, *Venus and Adonis* and *The Rape of Lucrece,* appeared in print in 1593 and 1594. The author dedicated both of these works to the Earl of Southampton, who may have been an important patron* for the young poet.

Shakespeare arrived in London during a bright period in English theater. A new form of drama was taking shape that mixed the native drama of England with the classical style of ancient Greece and Rome. English playwrights began to borrow characters from classical sources, such as young lovers, old misers, and boastful soldiers. The blend of classical and English traditions gave new life and versatility to English theater. Drama also took its place at the center of national debate, as both Catholics and Protestants made it a weapon in their battles of words.

Records show that in 1594 Shakespeare joined the Lord Chamberlain's Men, an acting company that performed mostly at a London playhouse known simply as the Theatre. The building was probably in the shape of an octagon and could seat about 3,000 spectators. At one end stood a large rectangular stage with a trap door, partially covered by a roof supported by two pillars. This building was eventually taken apart and rebuilt on the south side of the Thames River as the famous Globe Theater, the one most associated with Shakespeare's name.

SHAKESPEARE'S WORKS

Shakespeare spent at least 19 years writing for the theater. In that time he produced dozens of plays, along with a variety of long and short poems. His works remain popular centuries after his death, providing enjoyment for viewers and readers, as well as inspiration for writers, around the world.

* **convention** established practice, custom

* **ballad** narrative poem, often of folk origin and intended to be sung, consisting of simple stanzas and usually having a recurrent refrain

Comedies. Shakespeare's early comedies show strong signs of classical influence. For example, *The Comedy of Errors* follows the conventions* of ancient drama by taking place entirely in one city over the course of a single day. Shakespeare based this play loosely on an ancient Roman work by Plautus called *The Twins.* Shakespeare's comedy *The Taming of the Shrew* also borrows from Plautus. Its secondary plot features several classical character types, including the young lovers, the anxious father, and the clever servant. However, the play's main plot, about a sharp-tongued woman and the husband who "tames" her, comes from an old English ballad*. This play illustrates the blend of classical and English influences popular in the drama of this period.

Shakespeare began to break away from the classical style in his comedy *The Two Gentlemen of Verona.* The plot centers on two young lovers who face a series of obstacles to their union—the opposition of their parents, separation, rivalry, misunderstandings, narrow escapes, and sudden changes of heart—plot elements that are hardly typical of classical drama. Shakespeare's next romantic comedy, *Love's Labor's Lost,* also steers away from classical conventions in its plot about courtship and misunderstanding between the sexes.

Shakespeare's distinctive comic form emerged in the late 1590s, beginning with *A Midsummer Night's Dream*. He completely abandoned the classical mode by weaving together several plots: the troubles of four lovers who seek shelter in the forest, the quarrels of the king and queen of the fairies, and the antics of a group of laborers preparing to stage a play for the wedding of their duke. Through this mixture of stories, Shakespeare examined the experience of love from several different angles. The play is also anti-classical in its blend of human characters and otherworldly spirits.

Shakespeare gave his comedy a darker note in *The Merchant of Venice*. The central figure in the play is Shylock, a Jewish moneylender who threatens the life of a Christian merchant. This comedy narrowly escapes turning into a tragedy thanks to the cleverness of the heroine, Portia. Yet this play also features more traditional comic elements in its secondary plot, a love story about the courtship of Portia and her husband, Bassanio. This blend of straightforward comedy and the threat of tragedy appears again in *Much Ado About Nothing*. The first plot features a misunderstanding between two lovers that nearly destroys the heroine; the other is a joyful comedy about a man and a woman whose bitter rivalry masks a deep affection.

Several of Shakespeare's comedies feature a woman in male disguise. This device was particularly amusing in Shakespeare's time, when all actors were male, and thus the woman dressed as a man was really a boy dressed as a woman. Such "breeches parts" play an important role in two of Shakespeare's most famous comedies, *As You Like It* and *Twelfth Night*. Disguised as men, the heroines of these two plays become friends with the young men with whom they eventually fall in love. Thus, their marriages are founded on a basis of deep friendship and trust.

* **genre** literary form

Histories. The English history play was a fairly new genre* in Shakespeare's time, and Shakespeare did more than any other writer to give it a distinct form. His first four history plays—the three parts of *Henry VI*, followed by *Richard III*—revolve around a prolonged civil war that divided England in the 1400s. Shakespeare's play cycle reveals the brutal chaos of civil war, yet it ends in triumph with the crowning of Henry VII, the grandfather of ELIZABETH I. This work helped establish the history play as a truly English form of drama that owed nothing to the classical tradition.

* **depose** to remove from high office, often by force

Shakespeare produced another series of major history plays in the late 1590s. This time, he dealt with an earlier conflict in English history, in which Henry Bolingbroke deposed* Richard II in 1399 and took the throne as Henry IV. The play *Richard II* centers on this transfer of power, but the next three plays—*Henry IV, Parts 1* and *2*, and *Henry V*—focus on the figure of King Henry's son, Prince Hal, who will later rule as Henry V. While Henry IV struggles with military and political rivals, he must also face his growing concern about his wayward son. The prince spends most of his time in the tavern with his friend John Falstaff, a drunken, thieving old knight who is hardly a fitting companion for a prince. Torn between this friendship and his duty to his stern father, Hal must eventually abandon his careless ways and take his rightful place as England's king. In the cycle's final play, *Henry V,* the new king triumphs over his political enemies and leads the British to victory against the French at the famous battle of Agincourt (1415).

Tragedies. Shakespeare did little work in the tragedy genre during the 1590s. His famous *Romeo and Juliet* (ca. 1595), though tragic, resembles a comedy in many ways, with its focus on comic wooing in the first half. In 1599, however, Shakespeare began work on a series of tragedies that have earned a place among the greatest plays ever written in the English language. In his four major tragedies—*Hamlet, Othello, King Lear,* and *Macbeth*—Shakespeare focused on the darkest human emotions: sexual jealousy, conflict within marriage, and the fears that come with old age.

Hamlet is a "revenge play" about a prince whose murdered father returns as a ghost to demand that his son avenge his death. The focus of the play is not the act of revenge, but the effect his father's command has on the prince's mind. He questions the ghost's reality, his own strength, and the concept of human happiness. The play ends with a stage littered with corpses, a reminder of the harsh struggle Hamlet leaves behind.

The title character of *Othello* is a tragic hero in the classical sense: a good man with one fatal flaw that drives him into a destructive action. As a black man living in European society, Othello appears to doubt that his young, beautiful, white wife truly loves him. The villain, Iago, plays on the hero's jealous insecurity. His cunning lies about the unfaithfulness of Othello's wife lure the hero into murder.

In *King Lear,* the lead character is a king driven into madness by his two ungrateful daughters. To an extent, he is also a tragic hero whose fatal flaw is insecurity. His obsessive need for assurances of love leads him to banish his one faithful daughter, Cordelia. The cruelty he suffers at the hands of his other children leads him to understand the injustice in the world, hinting at the idea that true wisdom comes about only through pain and despair.

Shakespeare's *Macbeth* involves the murder of a king and the unnatural forces it releases. Macbeth is tempted into his terrible crime by his own ambition, his wife's challenges that he prove his manhood, and the twisted prophecies of three witches who promise that he will one day be king. Their prediction unleashes Macbeth's darker nature and leads him toward his inevitable doom.

While he was producing these famous plays, Shakespeare also created several tragedies set in ancient Greece and Rome. In *Julius Caesar, Coriolanus,* and *Antony and Cleopatra,* Shakespeare examined the themes of honor and duty, political struggle, and just rule through the lens of Roman history. In *Timon of Athens* he portrayed a generous man who becomes bitter and angry when his friends desert him after he loses his fortune.

Problem Plays and Romances. Between 1601 and 1605 began to experiment with dramatic forms, producing three plays scholars refer to as the "problem" plays. While these pieces appear to be comedies, they also contain darker elements more suitable to tragedy. Within their trou-

The Authorship Question

Over the centuries, many readers have wondered whether a middle-class writer with no university training could have produced such great works as Shakespeare's. Some have suggested that his plays were actually the work of a nobleman who used Shakespeare's name to conceal his identity. Several people have been suggested as the true author, including Sir Frances Bacon and Edward de Vere, the earl of Oxford. However, other readers point out that for the "real" Shakespeare to hide his identity would have required a truly massive cover-up. They see the desire to assign Shakespeare's works to a noble author as a matter of simple snobbery.

* **sonnet** poem of 14 lines with a fixed pattern of meter and rhyme

bled world, morality is unclear and happiness uncertain. For example, in *Measure for Measure,* a judge seeks to abuse his position to seduce a woman in exchange for sparing her brother's life. He then attempts to cover up his action by killing her brother anyway. Even the supposedly good characters in this play are curiously flawed. The sister, who is about to become a nun, agrees to trick the wicked judge by sending another woman to take her place in his bed.

A similar "bed trick" occurs in *All's Well that Ends Well,* which features a young gentleman so eager to avoid marriage that he runs away from his wife. She wins him back only by sneaking into his bed. These twisted stories, with their unclear moral standards, clearly test the boundaries of comedy. The third problem play, *Troilus and Cressida,* actually crosses the line into tragedy. Cressida proves unfaithful to her lover, Troilus, and Troilus's brother Hector dies a brutal death at the hands of an enemy soldier.

In his final years of writing (1606–1613), Shakespeare turned to a new form, the romance. Like his problem plays, these pieces blend sorrow and joy, but their overall mood is one of hope and wonder. The first two romances, *Pericles* and *Cymbeline,* focus on the joyous reunion of a father and daughter after a long separation. The father-daughter bond also plays a strong role in Shakespeare's other romances, which add an element of fantasy and magic. *The Winter's Tale* concerns a king who wrongly accuses his wife of being unfaithful. His jealousy leads to her apparent death and to the loss of his infant daughter, whom he orders banished because he believes she is not his child. Yet these characters reappear miraculously in the play's second half.

The Tempest, commonly seen as Shakespeare's last complete play, focuses on the strong bond between an aging magician, Prospero, and his daughter Miranda, a girl on the edge of womanhood. Cast away on an island with no other humans, the two have lived for years in the company of two supernatural creatures—the beastlike Caliban and the delicate Ariel—whom Prospero has enslaved. This plot hints at a variety of issues, from the justice of colonial rule to the burden of artistic creation.

Other Works. Along with his plays, Shakespeare created a great number of poems. In addition to his longer verses, he wrote more than 150 sonnets*. These short poems deal largely with two major relationships in the poet's life. The first is his friendship with a young man, whose forgetfulness and ungratefulness are a source of pain for the author. The other is a love-hate affair with a mysterious woman known as the Dark Lady, who is as unfaithful to the poet as she is to her own husband. The sonnets also discuss other emotions the author has faced: jealousy of other writers, concerns about aging, the desire for fame, and the fear of losing his skill with words.

For centuries Shakespeare's insights and words have influenced other important writers, from the late Renaissance poet John MILTON to the modern American author William Faulkner. His works have spread throughout the globe, and his famous phrases have also found their way into the everyday speech of countless generations of readers. As the

English playwright George Bernard Shaw once observed: Shakespeare has a word for everything. (*See also* **Drama; Drama, English; English Language and Literature.**)

Ships and Shipbuilding

The main difference among various types of Renaissance ships concerned the way they were powered—by oars or by sails. The most famous oared ship, the galley, was a long vessel with oarsmen on both sides of the hull. These ships carried passengers and goods, particularly luxury items, and also found service in warfare. Galleys used oars when entering or leaving port, during combat, or whenever they needed a burst of speed. The sails were hoisted for long-distance cruising. Though fast, galleys had a limited capacity. For transporting larger cargoes, people relied on sailing ships.

During the Middle Ages the sailing ships of northern Europe differed in style from those of the Mediterranean. The early northern ships featured a rudder in the rear and a single square sail. Southern ships adopted the triangular lateen sails of Muslim vessels. In the 1400s the two traditions merged to produce the model followed by all later oceangoing vessels. The new ship had a rear rudder, two masts with square sails and a third mast in the rear of the vessel with a lateen sail. It was balanced and maneuverable in a variety of conditions. The largest of these vessels were known as carracks (or some variation of that name). The ships that carried Columbus on his first voyage across the Atlantic were smaller versions called *nao, nef,* or *nau.*

Carracks and similar multi-masted ships had a variety of functions. Large vessels might be used for trade and transportation, warfare, fishing, or whaling. Smaller craft found service in coastal trade, small-scale fishing, exploration, and piracy. Often the same ship had several roles

See color plate 7, vol. 4

The galleon was the most advanced ship of the Renaissance period. The Elizabethan galleon shown here features the four masts, crescent profile, and low front deck typical of such ships.

during its career. Shipbuilders developed numerous variations on the carrack with different numbers of masts or types of sails. Each seafaring country had its own fleet of sailing ships, similar to but not exactly the same as that of its neighbor.

The galleons, sailing ships used widely in the late 1500s and early 1600s, appeared in numerous versions but shared certain common features. Marked by a crescent profile, galleons generally had three or four masts, a low deck in front called the forecastle, and two full decks above the waterline on which to mount artillery. The ship's hull was sturdy enough to withstand rough seas and the hazards of combat. The ocean-going galleons were the most advanced vessels of the age, combining technology from fields such as forestry and metallurgy (the science of metals). (*See also* **Economy and Trade; Exploration; Transportation and Communication.**)

Sicily

For most of the Renaissance, the Mediterranean island of Sicily (now part of Italy) was part of the political world of Spain. The island's main distinction during this time came from its role in ancient Greek and Roman history. The few Sicilian scholars and artists of note sought fame elsewhere.

Sicily was linked to the mainland kingdom of NAPLES until 1282, when it revolted against Charles of Anjou, the French ruler of the two kingdoms. Sicily then came under the control of the Spanish kingdom of Aragon. It remained in Spanish hands for more than 400 years, except for a few years in the mid-1400s, when it was temporarily reunited with Naples. Sicily's monarchs usually ruled from afar, and powerful local barons and their followers had considerable influence. The feudal* nobility generally supported the monarchs, to whom their privileges were tied. But the nobles' resistance to urban growth and Aragonese fiscal policy revealed their power. Sicily passed to the Spanish HABSBURGS in 1516.

Before the 1300s the island's economy was dominated by the western part of Sicily and the city of Palermo, which produced grain and wine. Later, economic power shifted to the east and the city of Messina, which had silk, sugar, wine, and oil. The founding of universities in Catania (1445) and Messina (1590s) reveal the increasing importance of Sicily's eastern region. The overall trend during the Renaissance, however, was toward greater poverty and outlawry in Sicily.

The island appears in a few literary works of the Renaissance. MACHIAVELLI's *The Prince* (1513) mentions Sicily only in connection with an ancient story of the king of Syracuse (in Sicily). SHAKESPEARE set his comedy *Much Ado about Nothing* (1600) in the court of an Aragonese prince in Messina, and scenes of his play *A Winter's Tale* also take place in Sicily. In addition, the island produced several notable figures, including the scholar Marineo Siculo (ca. 1444–1536), who established a humanist* school in Spain, and the painter Antonello da Messina (ca. 1430–1479), who worked in Naples and northern Italy. (*See also* **Naples; Spain.**)

* **feudal**   referring to an economic and political system in which individuals gave service to a lord in return for protection and use of the land

* **humanist**   referring to a Renaissance cultural movement promoting the study of the humanities (the languages, literature, and history of ancient Greece and Rome) as a guide to living

Sickness and Disease

* **elite**   privileged group; upper class

D uring the Renaissance, disease was a common part of life for all social classes. However, illness took a much harsher toll on the poor than it did on the rich. Members of the elite* might live to an advanced age, managing their chronic ailments with the help of physicians. The poor, by contrast, had limited access to medical help. Any disease could pose a threat to their lives by endangering their ability to earn a living.

Types of Sickness. Perhaps the most feared disease during the Renaissance was PLAGUE. This highly contagious illness swept across Europe in the mid-1300s, killing as much as a third of the continent's population. After that, it returned at least once in every generation. Other diseases also struck rich and poor alike. These included cancer, fevers, tuberculosis, and painful joint ailments such as rheumatism and gout.

Renaissance physicians had to treat a variety of previously unknown medical problems, such as gunshot wounds and new illneses. Chief among these was the sexually transmitted disease syphilis. Renaissance people called this illness the "great pox" to distinguish it from smallpox, which became a serious epidemic in the late 1500s. Epidemics of typhus, a severe fever spread by body lice, appeared suddenly during the wars of the early 1500s. Long sea voyages and the colonization of tropical regions introduced Renaissance Europeans to scurvy (a disease caused by lack of vitamins) and yellow fever (a tropical illness spread by mosquitoes). Another mosquito-carried illness was malaria, which causes severe chills and fever. A few diseases were work-related, such as those suffered by miners in the Alps and in the silver mines of the Americas.

Disease and Social Class. To some extent, the upper classes could escape disease epidemics by retreating to country estates, away from crowded urban centers of infection. When they did become sick, they could afford to treat themselves with special diets, imported wines, costly medicines, and visits to hot springs or baths thought to have healing powers. The great majority of people, however, lacked the means to pay for such treatments.

Physicians came to associate some diseases, such as plague, with the lower classes. Cities introduced public-health rules to keep the poor masses away from members of the elite during epidemics. However, physicians believed that the upper classes were particularly subject to a few illnesses. In the mid-1500s the Italian scientist Girolamo Fracastoro wrote about a disease he called lenticular fever that tended to attack "those who are rather delicate and less robust." This ailment, Fracastoro noted, had less effect on the hearty peasant classes "because they exert themselves strenuously [vigorously] and their diet is more frugal [thrifty]." An English disease called "sweating sickness" also tended to strike the wealthy.

The experience of sickness undoubtedly varied according to social and economic class, but some problems cut across class lines. One example was infant death. A quarter of all babies, whether born into wealth

One of the most feared diseases of the Renaissance was the plague. Highly contagious and often deadly, it struck repeatedly throughout the period, wiping out large parts of Europe's population. This painting of plague sufferers shows the large swellings, or buboes, caused by the disease.

or poverty, died before their second birthdays. Infectious diseases may have been more common among the poor, but they could still torment the rich and famous. Many members of Italy's powerful MEDICI family, for example, struggled with tuberculosis, and England's King HENRY VIII suffered from ulcers—painful and ugly sores—on his legs that refused to heal. People who underwent surgery, whether for toothache, bone fractures, or even complications of childbirth, might experience persistent sores as a result.

Illness posed a great threat to rural and urban day laborers, who depended upon wages from daily work. Sickness, like any other disaster, could plunge a family into deeper poverty. Hospitals and traditional charities rarely helped families cope with this challenge. As a result, the gap between rich and poor grew wider during the late Renaissance. The effects of disease were only one of the many ways in which the contrast between social classes became more visible at this time. (*See also* **Death; Medicine.**)

Sidney, Philip

1554–1586
English poet

Philip Sidney was one of the leading poets of Renaissance England. His work had a major influence on the flowering of English literature, arts, and music in the late 1500s and early 1600s. A member of the nobility, Sidney held a place in the inner circle of writers, artists, scientists, and men of action at the court of ELIZABETH I. His death while fighting Spanish soldiers in the Netherlands turned Sidney into a national hero.

Life and Times. Although relatively poor by noble standards, Sidney's family had connections among the wealthiest and most powerful figures in England. His mother, Mary Dudley, was a lady-in-waiting to Queen Elizabeth; she tended the queen when she came down with smallpox (and caught the disease herself as a result). His uncle, Robert Dudley, was one of Elizabeth's favorite courtiers and, according to rumors, her lover. Sidney himself was named after the Spanish king PHILIP II, who attended his christening and referred to him as "my godson." Other members of Sidney's family were famous as traitors. Several of his relatives lost their heads for their involvement in a plot—which succeeded briefly—to place Sidney's aunt, Lady Jane GREY, on the English throne.

At the age of 13, Sidney entered Oxford University. There he received an excellent education centered on the Bible and on Latin and Greek literature. When he was 22, Sidney took a three-year grand tour of continental Europe. During his years abroad he mastered a number of languages and met with many of the leading artists, scientists, and scholars of his day. He also witnessed the St. Bartholomew's Day Massacre in France in 1572, in which Catholics murdered thousands of Huguenots. This event may have influenced Sidney's writings, which contain many descriptions of mass violence.

After returning to England, Sidney became a favorite at the royal court and was knighted in 1583. A year later he signed on with Sir Francis DRAKE to explore the New World. When Queen Elizabeth discovered his plans, however, she put a stop to them by sending Sidney to the Netherlands as the new governor of the town of Flushing. At the time England controlled this town as part of an agreement to assist the Dutch, who were involved in a struggle against Catholic Spain. In 1586 Sidney died of injuries suffered during an attack on Spanish supply lines.

Literary Achievements. Sidney's literary reputation rests chiefly on three major works. The first is his *Defence of Poetry,* one of the Renaissance's greatest critical writings. In this influential text, Sidney praised poetry as an art form with more power to cure the soul than either history or philosophy. He argued that poetry—a term he used to refer to all forms of imaginative writing—made the bitter truths of philosophy more acceptable by hiding them under the sweet coating of an appealing story. A poetic work, Sidney claimed, inspired its readers to improve themselves morally by making them identify with the heroes and heroines who face moral conflicts in the story. He saw the world of the imagination as superior to the natural world, since the poet is free to describe things that never were real but that might have been or even should have been. Sidney's work also reviewed the course of English literature and challenged his fellow writers to imitate, in English, the great achievements of the ancient Greek and Roman poets.

Scholars have described Sidney's second major work, *Arcadia,* as the first English novel. The modern writer Virginia Woolf claimed that Sidney's romance* contained "all the seeds of English fiction." It blended a variety of styles, including letters, stories within stories, and tales told from both the first-person and the third-person viewpoint. It also established certain themes that became standard in later English novels, such as escapes from drowning, crowd scenes, and events set in courts

* **romance** adventure story of the Middle Ages, the forerunner of the modern novel

* **sonnet**   poem of 14 lines with a fixed pattern of meter and rhyme

of law and in royal courts. Sidney's work also portrayed female characters with unusual skill and sensitivity.

Sidney's third notable work was *Astrophel and Stella* (1581), a series of love sonnets* about a brilliant, yet self-deceiving young man who pursues the charming Stella, a young woman unhappily married to another man. *Astrophel and Stella* offers a marvelous psychological study of the foolishness of human desire, the joy of poetic ambition, and the sorrows of love. Throughout the work Sidney mocks his own use of such concepts as the notion of the ideal and the lasting power of love.

Sidney's other works include a short, humorous drama, another collection of sonnets, and part of a translation of the biblical Book of Psalms. Sidney's sister Mary completed this work after his death. (*See also* **English Language and Literature; France; Netherlands; Poetry, English.**)

* **republic**   form of Renaissance government dominated by leading merchants with limited participation by others

* **Black Death**   epidemic of the plague, a highly contagious and often fatal disease, which spread throughout Europe from 1348 to 1350

* **Holy Roman Emperor**   ruler of the Holy Roman Empire, a political body in central Europe composed of several states that existed until 1806

* **siege**   prolonged effort to force a surrender by surrounding a fortress or town with armed troops, cutting the area off from aid

Siena, an independent republic* in northern Italy, was an important center of commerce and learning during the Middle Ages. The city-state gained its wealth from banking, commerce, and wool manufacturing. Before the Black Death*, Siena ranked as one of the largest cities in Italy with about 65,000 people. The plague reduced the population to about 15,000, a decline from which the city recovered very slowly.

Like other republics of the region, Siena had a complicated political structure. From 1285 to 1355 its Government of the Nine, dominated by merchants, brought relative stability to the city. However, during the late 1300s and the 1400s, sharp divisions between ancient noble families, nobles from the countryside, and wealthy merchants characterized political life in Siena. Governments favoring tradesmen and shopkeepers alternated with those serving the interests of the nobles. After a period of economic decline and political unrest, noble families gained the upper hand in the city in the mid-1400s. Pandolfo Petrucci, a prominent Sienese nobleman, took personal control of Siena in 1487, and he and his heirs ruled the city until 1523.

Siena lost its independence during the Wars of Italy (1494–1559). Florence had long wanted to gain control over Siena. In 1530 the Holy Roman Emperor* Charles V (Charles I of Spain) forced Siena to accept his protection and a Spanish garrison. The Sienese threw the Spanish troops out in 1552, which led to a three-year siege* of the city. After Siena finally surrendered in 1555, the Spanish gave the city to its ally, Cosimo I de' Medici, the ruler of Florence.

Culturally, Siena was renowned for its university, which emphasized law and attracted students from many countries during the Renaissance. Pope Pius II, St. Catherine of Siena, and St. Bernardino of Siena are among the best-known people of this time from the city. Various Sienese artists made significant contributions to Renaissance painting and sculpture. (*See also* **Art in Italy; Florence.**)

Sixtus IV

See *Popes and Papacy.*

Slavery

* **artisan**   skilled worker or craftsperson

* **Black Death**   epidemic of the plague, a highly contagious and often fatal disease, which spread throughout Europe from 1348 to 1350

By the time of the Renaissance, Italy was one of the few European countries where slavery still existed. This engraving from the 1500s shows a Venetian galley slave in ankle chains.

Slavery existed in Europe in ancient times and continued in some regions for centuries. By the time of the Renaissance, it could still be found in Italy, Spain, and Portugal but was uncommon in the rest of Europe. Slavery also existed in the Muslim world, and contact with Muslim communities reinforced the practice in Europe. In the 1500s the slave trade spread to the Americas. Europeans carried great numbers of African slaves across the ocean to work in colonies in the New World.

Conditions of Slavery. Ancient Roman law included a set of rules governing the ownership and treatment of slaves. During the Renaissance, interest in ancient cultures strengthened the influence of Roman law on European society. Although all slaves had the same or similar status under the law, their circumstances varied.

Slavery was different in rural and urban areas. Most rural slaves labored on farms, though some worked in manufacturing on country estates. Most urban slaves served as servants, guards, or sexual partners. Those owned by artisans* often worked in their masters' workshops. Other slaves provided labor in city ports, factories, warehouses, or markets. In both Europe and the Muslim world, slavery took place on a small scale. Artisans bought one or two slaves and wealthy families had a few more. Large-scale or gang slavery, as practiced in ancient Rome and the Americas, did not exist in Europe.

In Renaissance Europe slaves were either born into slavery or captured in a war or raid. Masters had legal control over slaves and could sell or transfer them as they pleased. Still, the law allowed slaves to become free in several ways. Masters could set them free, and slaves who had been captured might be ransomed or exchanged for other prisoners. In addition, slaves could purchase their freedom. Although former slaves never had the full legal standing of those born into freedom, their children were completely free under the law.

Slavery increased in Italy, Spain, and Portugal in the late 1300s. This was partly due to the Black Death*, which swept across Europe and killed as much as one-third of the population. The loss of large numbers of workers created a labor shortage that allowed individuals who might have become servants to find better jobs. People were needed to take over the lowest level of work. Meanwhile, some well-to-do survivors were able to hire more workers or purchase slaves with riches inherited from deceased relatives. These two factors produced a demand for slaves.

Italy. In 1363 the Italian city of Florence allowed residents to import slaves, as long as the slaves were not Christians. Venice, Genoa, and other Italian cities also permitted slave trading. Although Venice banned slave auctions in 1366, citizens could still buy slaves privately.

Slaves in Italy came from a variety of racial and ethnic groups, such as Russians or other peoples from the region around the Black Sea. They also included Muslims purchased from North Africa, Spain, or Portugal. Black slaves were fairly common in Sicily and southern Italy but rare in the northern Italian cities.

Spain and Portugal. Spain and Portugal were close to the Muslim lands of North Africa, which served as a source of non-Christians who could be captured or enslaved. This ready supply of slaves meant that slavery gained a stronger hold in Spain and Portugal than elsewhere.

Portugal and Spain were the first European nations to become involved in the slave trade in black Africans. Some Africans were taken to islands in the Atlantic and others to the Americas. Blacks had been present in Europe in small numbers since ancient times, and since the 800s Muslim traders had brought black slaves across the Sahara desert for sale in Mediterranean ports. Still, during the Renaissance blacks remained rare in Europe outside of Spain, Portugal, and Italy.

The Portuguese were the main slave traders of Europe in the late 1400s and early 1500s. In the capital city of Lisbon, the crown administered the slave trade. By the mid-1500s black slaves and former slaves made up 2.5 to 3 percent of the total population of Portugal. In southern Portugal and Lisbon, the figure was as high as 10 percent.

The Spanish city of Seville was also noted for its many black and Muslim slaves—7.4 percent of the city's inhabitants in 1565. During much of the Middle Ages, large areas of Spain—including Seville—were under Muslim rule. The population at that time included large numbers of slaves. Later, the Christians fought to regain control of Spain, and many Muslims were captured and enslaved. (*See also* **Agriculture; Economy and Trade; Servants; Social Status.**)

Social Status

* **hierarchy** organization of a group into higher and lower levels

Renaissance society recognized many different degrees of social rank. Since the Middle Ages, the social hierarchy* had contained three broad groups: the CLERGY (known as the First Estate), the nobility (the Second Estate), and the commoners or workers (the Third Estate). Within each estate were many ranks that sometimes overlapped. However, not everyone fit neatly into this structure. Beginning in the late Middle Ages, a new category—the middle class—had emerged and grown to include many levels of its own. Also, certain groups of people were outsiders, with no fixed position on the social ladder.

The First Estate: Clergy. Members of the clergy had high status in Renaissance society, which saw their spiritual activities as vital to the public welfare. The highest-ranking clergy members—popes, cardinals, patriarchs, and bishops—were mostly of noble birth. Urban and rural priests occupied a much lower place on the social scale. They generally fell far below the high-ranking prelates* in terms of wealth and education.

* **prelate** high-ranking member of the clergy, such as a bishop

The clergy also included members of RELIGIOUS ORDERS: monks and nuns who lived apart from the everyday world. The leaders of these orders usually came from the ranks of the nobility. Some orders ranked higher on the social scale than others and tended to attract people from wealthy noble families.

The Second Estate: Nobility. Originally, membership in the nobility depended on birth and family background. By the 1500s, however, more individuals were gaining noble rank either by buying land and titles or by earning distinction in battle. Three factors affected the status of a noble: birth, political power, and wealth. People valued land above other forms of wealth and looked down on money gained through trade or manufacturing. Thus, stark differences of rank existed within the noble classes. Some families controlled large estates with authority over many peasants, while others had fallen in fortune and had little left to them but their titles.

The highest-ranking members of the nobility, such as dukes and barons, often associated themselves with the royal courts. The lesser nobles and the gentry stood one rung below them on the social ladder. These social categories were not always clearly defined. Their members came from varied backgrounds and drew their status from many sources: military service, government offices, success in business, or marriage into higher-ranking families. The lesser nobles and gentry worked to increase their prestige by acquiring land and making desirable marriages. Some eventually created their own coats of arms* as a symbol of their rank.

The Third Estate: Commoners. The Third Estate was the most complex and changeable part of society. Originally defined simply as the working class, by the Renaissance it included high-ranking professionals and the entire, growing middle class. Moreover, the makeup of the Third Estate varied across rural and urban settings.

Most Europeans lived in the countryside. The highest classes of commoners in rural areas were the landlords who leased land from members of the clergy or nobility and rented it out. Below them were small farmers and peasants who rented the land they worked. Next came landless laborers who moved about in search of jobs. During the Middle Ages, most rural laborers were serfs, tied by law to the lands that they worked. By the time of the Renaissance, serfdom had fallen into decline in western Europe, but in eastern regions it expanded, and many peasants fell to the status of serfs.

Those who lived in Renaissance cities tended to look down on country dwellers, except for those who owned large amounts of land. In addition to these social boundaries between city and country, deep divisions existed within urban society. In many areas, for example, the citizens of a city or town enjoyed special status and privileges that the rest of the city's residents did not share. In northern Italy and parts of Germany, Spain, and the Netherlands, only citizens could hold public office. These citizen elites* overlapped with the ranks of the gentry and lesser nobility.

The urban middle class covered a broad range of social rank, based on such factors as education, profession, and wealth. Lawyers and judges, with their high levels of education and positions of social power, held the highest positions in urban society—sometimes even higher than the lesser nobles. Government officials, physicians, and intellectuals also stood high in the middle-class social order. Just below them in status were merchants and artisans*, especially those who belonged to local guilds*. Guild membership set artisans apart from low-ranking laborers,

* **coat of arms** set of symbols used to represent a noble family

* **elite** privileged group; upper class

* **artisan** skilled worker or craftsperson

* **guild** association of craft or trade owners and workers that set standards for and represented the interests of its members

who were usually poor and enjoyed few legal rights. Even within this class, however, differences in status existed based on working skills. Laborers whose work required more strength than skill fell nearly at the bottom of the social scale. Only household servants had lower status.

Outsiders. Some groups, such as Muslims, JEWS, gypsies, and slaves, existed outside the structure of the three estates. Usually poor, they had limited legal rights and often lived apart from the rest of society.

Women were also a group apart. A woman held no social rank in her own right, but shared that of her father and later, if she married, her husband. Aside from these relations, her status depended to a large degree on her "honor"—that is, on her observance of a strict social code that prohibited sex and childbirth outside marriage. (*See also* **Aristocracy; Bourgeoisie; Cities and Urban Life; Family and Kinship; Peasantry; Servants; Slavery; Women.**)

* **Iberian Peninsula**   part of western Europe occupied by present-day Spain and Portugal

In the 1400s the Iberian Peninsula* contained five separate kingdoms—Aragon, Castile, Navarre, PORTUGAL, and Granada. The first four kingdoms were Christian, but Muslims from North Africa—known as Moors—ruled the southern kingdom of Granada. Many Europeans used the term *Spain* to refer either to Castile or to the whole Iberian Peninsula except Portugal. Eventually, the Christians drove the Moors out of the region and established a unified kingdom. During the 1500s, Spain emerged as a major European power and empire with territories around the world.

HISTORY

During the Renaissance a series of strong monarchs succeeded in unifying Spain and increasing its political power. Spain became part of the Holy Roman Empire* and established a network of colonies that helped spread Spanish culture to other lands.

* **Holy Roman Empire**   political body in central Europe composed of several states; existed until 1806

Moorish Spain. In the 1400s the population of the Iberian Peninsula was mostly Catholic, but it also included large numbers of Muslims and Jews. Muslims had first arrived in the early 700s from North Africa. The Moors conquered most of the peninsula and built a brilliant civilization there. Spain became an important part of the Islamic world.

The Muslims failed to conquer all of Iberia. Small Christian strongholds remained in the mountainous north and became the basis for the Christian kingdoms. From the 700s on, the Christians fought to regain control of Spain. Throughout this effort, known as the Reconquest, episodes of warfare between Christians and Muslims alternated with periods of relative peace. The Christians learned a great deal from the Moorish culture and also benefited economically. Nevertheless, as the Reconquest moved south, tensions between the two groups increased. By the 1400s relations had become hostile.

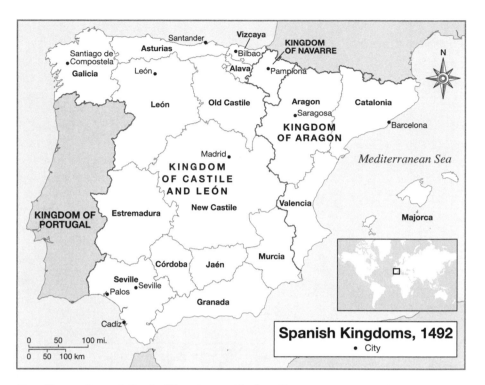

Ferdinand and Isabella. In 1469 the Christian monarchs FERDINAND OF ARAGON and ISABELLA OF CASTILE were married, technically uniting their two kingdoms. In reality, the various kingdoms of Spain remained divided as a result of geography and history. The kingdom of Castile dominated the center of the Iberian Peninsula. The kingdom of Aragon, to the east, consisted of three distinct areas: Aragon, Catalonia, and Valencia. The kings of Aragon also ruled a Mediterranean empire that included SICILY, Sardinia, and the kingdom of NAPLES. Surrounding the united kingdoms were Navarre in the north, Granada in the south, and Portugal in the west.

In 1492 Ferdinand and Isabella conquered Granada, the last remaining Moorish region in Europe. Determined to create an entirely Christian kingdom, the two monarchs ordered Jews in Spain to convert to Christianity or leave the country. About half the Jewish population left, settling mainly in North Africa and Portugal. The rest converted. In 1500 the king and queen gave the Muslims the same choice—either adopt Christianity or leave. Most chose to convert and remain.

By the early 1500s, there were two significant minority groups in Spain: the *conversos* (Christians of Jewish origin) and the Moriscos (Christians of Muslim origin). Old Christians resented and feared the converts, viewing them as poor Christians and a threat to religious unity. The Spanish Inquisition* addressed the problem by attempting to enforce Christian beliefs and practice among the converts.

Ferdinand and Isabella also focused on foreign policy. They built alliances through marriages with members of the HABSBURG DYNASTY and the royal families of England and Portugal. Ferdinand ended revolts in Aragon and consolidated his power there. Meanwhile, Isabella increased

* **Spanish Inquisition** court established by the Spanish monarchs that investigated Christians accused of straying from the official doctrine of the Roman Catholic Church, particularly during the period 1480–1530

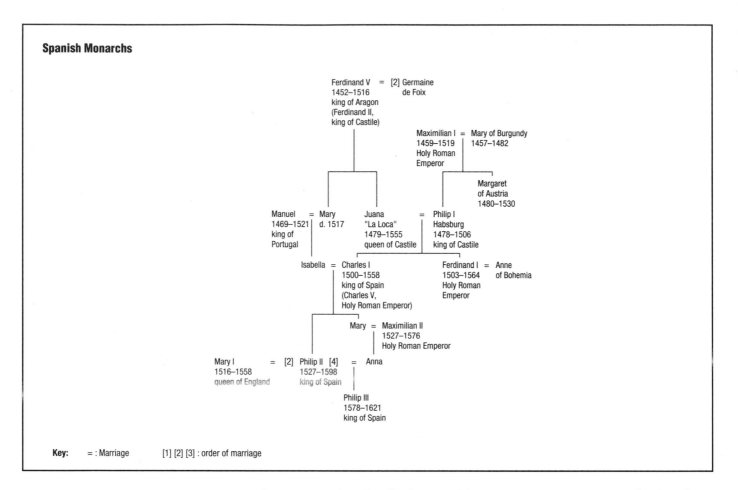

Spanish Monarchs

Ferdinand V
1452–1516
king of Aragon
(Ferdinand II,
king of Castile)
= [2] Germaine
de Foix

Maximilian I = Mary of Burgundy
1459–1519   1457–1482
Holy Roman
Emperor

Margaret
of Austria
1480–1530

Manuel = Mary
1469–1521 d. 1517
king of
Portugal

Juana
"La Loca"
1479–1555
queen of Castile

= Philip I
Habsburg
1478–1506
king of Castile

Isabella = Charles I
1500–1558
king of Spain
(Charles V,
Holy Roman Emperor)

Ferdinand I = Anne
1503–1564   of Bohemia
Holy Roman
Emperor

Mary = Maximilian II
1527–1576
Holy Roman Emperor

Mary I
1516–1558
queen of England
= [2] Philip II [4]
1527–1598
king of Spain
= Anna

Philip III
1578–1621
king of Spain

Key: = : Marriage   [1] [2] [3] : order of marriage

Defending Christianity

Some Spanish nobles and clergy belonged to religious military orders, which were founded in the 1100s to help with the Reconquest of the Iberian peninsula. These orders received huge grants of land, authority over about a million people, and the right to bestow the title of *caballero* (knight). The religious military orders provided positions of respect and influence for members of noble families. But the wealth and power of the orders also made them threats to the crown, and Spanish monarchs took steps to control the religious military orders more closely.

her power in Castile by working out arrangements with Castilian nobles. Gradually, the two rulers unified much of Spain. In addition, they sponsored the voyages of Christopher COLUMBUS, who searched for a westward route to Asia and, in the process, claimed land in the AMERICAS for Spain. After Isabella's death in 1504, Ferdinand married Germaine de Foix, heir to the throne of Navarre. Their marriage led to the incorporation of much of Navarre into Castile.

Charles I. When Ferdinand died in 1516, his grandson Charles took the throne as Charles I, ruling a territory that corresponded roughly to modern Spain. Three years later Charles was elected Holy Roman Emperor, succeeding his Habsburg grandfather, MAXIMILIAN I, and became CHARLES V. With these legacies, Charles controlled the largest empire in Europe. In addition to Spain, his territories included much of central Europe, the NETHERLANDS, lands in the Mediterranean, and colonies in the Americas.

Born and raised in the Netherlands, Charles was considered a foreigner by many of his Spanish subjects. Spanish discontent led to a series of revolts in Castile and Valencia in the 1520s. However, the revolts failed, leaving Charles with peace in Spain. Elsewhere, Spanish forces took control of territories in North Africa and Italy. Charles, who viewed himself as a protector of Catholicism, also spent considerable

* **Ottoman Turks** Turkish followers of Islam who founded the Ottoman Empire in the 1300s; the empire eventually included large areas of eastern Europe, the Middle East, and northern Africa

effort fighting the Ottoman Turks* in the Mediterranean and Protestantism in Germany.

In 1556 Charles I gave up his crowns and retired to a monastery. Before stepping down, he divided his empire. Charles's younger brother Ferdinand assumed the position of Holy Roman Emperor; his son Philip became king of Spain, the Netherlands, part of Italy, and the colonies in the Americas.

The reign of PHILIP II (1556–1598) was a mixture of successes and failures. In Spain, uprisings in Granada (1566–1571) and Aragon (1591, 1592) threatened the peace. However, both were put down. In the Netherlands, opponents of Spanish rule rebelled in 1566, and the revolt led to the loss of the northern Dutch provinces. In 1571 a Christian force led by Spain won a great victory over the Turks at the battle of Lepanto, temporarily halting Ottoman advances. Nine years later, Philip won the throne of Portugal, adding the Portuguese possessions in Africa, South America, and Asia to the Spanish Empire. Then, in 1588, the great Spanish Armada (naval fleet) failed in its attempt to attack England. The defeat dealt a serious blow to Spain's prestige and marked the beginning of a period of decline.

* **plague** highly contagious and often fatal disease that wiped out much of Europe's population in the mid-1300s and reappeared periodically over the next three centuries; also known as the Black Death

In the 1590s, the Spanish monarchy faced a series of difficulties, including bankruptcy and widespread plague* and famine. Philip III took the throne in 1598. During his reign, Spain began adjusting to its status as a secondary power in Europe.

SOCIETY AND ECONOMY

Spain's historical circumstances led to the development of a distinct Spanish culture during the Renaissance. The Roman Catholic Church played a major role in the kingdom, and the church and local traditions shaped Spanish society. At the same time, a vigorous economy based on agriculture and trade helped support the growing Spanish Empire.

The Catholic Church. Throughout the Renaissance, the Catholic Church had enormous power in Spain. Members of the church enjoyed certain rights and privileges as well as wealth and status according to a well defined hierarchy*. Various monastic* orders occupied a prominent place in Spanish society, and some groups, such as the Jesuits*, conducted important educational and missionary activities. According to estimates, the Spanish clergy in the late 1500s included about 91,000 members, slightly more than 1 percent of the total population.

* **hierarchy** organization of a group into higher and lower levels

* **monastic** relating to monasteries, monks, or nuns

* **Jesuit** refers to a Roman Catholic religious order founded by St. Ignatius Loyola and approved in 1540

The church had always had a close relationship with the Spanish crown. In 1478 at the request of Ferdinand and Isabella it launched the Inquisition. The governing council of the Inquisition was part of the royal administration, and the crown appointed all members of the Inquisition courts. Besides punishing those who practiced Judaism, Islam, or Protestantism, the courts also reviewed the religious ancestry of candidates for high office and censored works.

With the conquest of Granada, Ferdinand and Isabella won the right to name candidates for the office of bishop there. This gave them con-

The Spanish city of Seville, shown here, was a major center of trade in Europe. In the 1400s it became home to many Italian merchants, whose banking activities helped fund the voyages of Christopher Columbus.

trol over the direction of church policy. The right of naming candidates was later extended to other church offices in all Spanish lands. From the church, the monarchy also acquired important sources of revenue.

Society. The militant Christianity of the Middle Ages continued into the Renaissance in Spain. The Reconquest encouraged the view among some Spaniards that wealth could be gained from the armed conquest of alien peoples and that the survival of Christian society depended on unity and a militant defense of the faith. Still, the social structure and occupations of the Spanish people were similar to those of other European peoples.

Spanish society was overwhelmingly rural—four out of every five people worked on the land. The majority did not have property or animals of their own and worked for others. Some hired out on a day-to-day basis; others had labor contracts for a season or a year. Most of the agricultural workers lived in small villages or towns and traveled back and forth to labor in the fields and pastures.

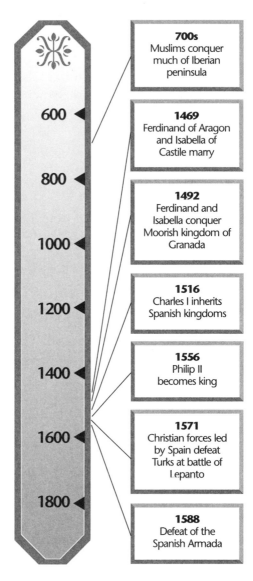

700s
Muslims conquer much of Iberian peninsula

1469
Ferdinand of Aragon and Isabella of Castile marry

1492
Ferdinand and Isabella conquer Moorish kingdom of Granada

1516
Charles I inherits Spanish kingdoms

1556
Philip II becomes king

1571
Christian forces led by Spain defeat Turks at battle of Lepanto

1588
Defeat of the Spanish Armada

At the upper end of society was the nobility, whose ancestors had received land and status, usually for military service to the monarchy. The nobility was divided into three groups. The *hidalgos,* the lowest group, could claim a certain amount of local prestige and exemption from some taxes. The *señores,* in the middle, controlled small territories. The top level consisted of titled nobles, often called the *títulos* or *grandes.* These individuals possessed great wealth and power, and vast landholdings—sometimes even including towns.

The nobles of Castile tended to live in towns and cities and to dominate local government. The highest-ranking nobles followed the royal court, seeking to gain control over important offices and to influence foreign commerce. Political power brought Spanish nobles greater wealth and social status. By the mid-1400s, a small group of noble families had amassed great amounts of land, titles, wealth, and government positions.

The legal system of Renaissance Spain was based on ancient Roman law. It developed from a code adopted by King Alfonso X of Castile in the mid-1200s. In the 1500s Spanish monarchs sought to impose royal law throughout the various kingdoms, but local traditions limited what they could do. In addition, some provinces preferred law codes from the Middle Ages that offered protection against the abuse of royal power.

Economy. Beginning in the late 1400s, the Spanish economy expanded, especially in terms of long-distance trade. The largest and most important economic activity was agriculture, ranging from cereals and livestock in Castile to rice, vegetables, and fruits in Granada, Valencia, and Aragon. Although the Spanish consumed most of their farm products, they exported large quantities of wine, olive oil, fruits, and other items.

Spain also developed successful industries, including the production of woolen cloth and shipbuilding. By the 1400s the kingdom of Castile had become one of western Europe's main suppliers of high quality wool. Cities such as Barcelona and Bilbao were important shipbuilding centers.

Trade played a vital role in the Spanish economy. Since the 1200s Spanish merchants had developed strong trading networks in the Mediterranean. Later, trade routes connected Spain to England, France, and the rest of northern Europe. In Castile, foreign trade increased along with religious pilgrimages. The route of the Way of St. James pilgrimage drew large numbers of Europeans across northern Spain to the shrine of St. James in the city of Santiago de Compostela. During the 1400s busy trade fairs in Castile brought merchants together. The most important fair, in the town of Medina del Campo, attracted traders from all over Europe. By the 1500s the town had become the financial center of Castile.

Spain's strong trading network encouraged interest in overseas exploration. It also helped develop the organizational skills and business techniques that were used to manage the country's vast overseas empire. In 1436 Castile created a convoy system, which involved sending armed ships with merchant vessels to protect them against piracy and other threats. This type of convoy system was later used to protect ships traveling to Spain from the Americas.

Many Italian merchants settled in Spain and married into the local nobility. By the 1400s Italians from GENOA were prospering as bankers in SEVILLE. Merchants such as these helped finance the voyages of Christopher Columbus, and later expanded their trading operations in Spain's American empire.

EUROPEAN TIES

Spain maintained close relations with the rest of Europe during the Renaissance. Like other Catholic countries, it had strong ties with Rome. Spanish clergy lived in Rome and played a significant role in church affairs. Many Spanish students traveled abroad to study. Similarly, foreign students attended Spanish institutions such as the prestigious University of Salamanca.

Artists came to Spain from various parts of Europe, especially the Netherlands, and Spanish monarchs, nobles, and clergy collected Netherlandish art. Italian artists also found patrons* at the Spanish court. Scholars from across Europe worked in Spain, and Spanish became a common second language among the upper classes in France, Italy, and the Netherlands.

* **patron** supporter or financial sponsor of an artist or writer

Spain's vast European and overseas empire helped make it the world's first superpower. However, maintaining this empire was very costly. As a result, Spain entered a period of decline in the 1600s. Although it kept its American empire, it gradually lost influence in Europe as other nations took the lead. (*See also* **Armada, Spanish; Art in Spain and Portugal; Catholic Reformation and Counter-Reformation; Cortés, Hernán; Drama, Spanish; Exploration; Madrid; Spanish Language and Literature; Toledo; Universities.**)

Spain and Portugal, Art in

See *Art in Spain and Portugal.*

Spanish Language and Literature

* **classical** in the tradition of ancient Greece and Rome

* **Iberian Peninsula** part of western Europe occupied by present-day Spain and Portugal

Spain, like other parts of Europe, was influenced by the revival of classical* languages and culture during the Renaissance. While scholars in other regions sought to restore the Latin of ancient Rome, in Spain the Renaissance focused mainly on the use of classical forms and styles in Spanish. During this period, the Spanish language took on a standard form that gradually replaced the local dialects used in different parts of the Iberian Peninsula*. Spanish authors published works in a variety of literary forms, including poetry, drama, and religious writing. In addition, several Spanish writers, most notably Miguel de CERVANTES SAAVEDRA, played a major role in the development of the novel.

DEVELOPMENT OF THE SPANISH LANGUAGE

In the early Middle Ages the inhabitants of Iberia spoke a variety of different dialects. Beginning in the 700s, soldiers from the northern kingdom of Castile gradually gained control of much of the peninsula, slowly driving out the Moors*. As the Castilians moved south, they spread their language. In the 1200s Alfonso X, king of Castile and León, used Castilian Spanish, rather than Latin, to conduct official business. He also ordered translations of works from Arabic and Latin into Spanish. These actions helped standardize the Spanish language.

In the 1400s the culture of the Italian Renaissance began to influence the Spanish tongue. Words borrowed from Italian and Latin came into use, sometimes replacing words borrowed from Arabic. Antonio de Nebrija, the first major Spanish humanist*, studied in Italy and learned classical Latin. In 1481 he published the first Latin textbook in Spain. Eleven years later, Nebrija published a Spanish grammar—the first grammar textbook in any modern European language. This text established Castilian as the language of Spain.

Spanish continued to evolve during the 1500s. Pronunciation began to change, taking on the forms now part of modern Spanish. New patterns of speech also developed. In 1611 Sebastián de Covarrubias y Orozco compiled a dictionary called *Treasury of the Castilian or Spanish Language,* which set forth the rich vocabulary of Renaissance Spanish. All these changes in vocabulary and language structure affected the development of new styles in literature.

SPANISH LITERATURE IN THE RENAISSANCE

Some scholars have described the 1500s and 1600s as a golden age of Spanish literature. A variety of new literary forms emerged during this period. Classical studies, religious reforms, and medieval* styles all played a role in shaping the literature of this time.

Poetry. During the 1400s, Spanish poets began to adopt the styles of classical Latin and Renaissance Italian verse. At the beginning of the century, many Spanish poets were writing love poems in a style borrowed from the popular songs from the Middle Ages, which had short lines of about eight syllables. Juan de Mena broke away from this style, developing a poetic form with longer lines, based on ancient Latin verse. Around 1450 the Marquis de Santillana produced a collection of sonnets* in the Italian style.

Italian forms continued to influence the development of Spanish poetry in the 1500s. At a royal wedding in 1526, a number of Spanish authors met Italian humanists and discussed writing with them. This meeting inspired two of the Spanish writers, Juan Boscán and Garcilaso de la Vega, to experiment with various forms of verse. Their work, published jointly in 1543, introduced distinctive new styles into Spanish poetry.

Garcilaso wrote few poems, yet his pieces set new standards for verse writing in Spain. He did most of his work in NAPLES and often followed

The poems of Garcilaso de la Vega set new standards for verse writing in Spain. Inspired by the work of Italian humanists, he introduced a variety of new forms into Spanish poetry.

* **Moor** Muslim from North Africa; Moorish invaders conquered much of Spain during the Middle Ages

* **humanist** Renaissance expert in the humanities (the languages, literature, history, and speech and writing techniques of ancient Greece and Rome)

* **medieval** referring to the Middle Ages, a period that began around A.D. 400 and ended around 1400 in Italy and 1500 in the rest of Europe

* **sonnet** poem of 14 lines with a fixed pattern of meter and rhyme

* **elegy**   type of poem often used to express sorrow for one who has died

* **pastoral**   relating to the countryside; often used to draw a contrast between the innocence and serenity of rural life and the corruption and extravagance of court life

* **ode**   poem with a lofty style and complex structure

* **Spanish Inquisition**   court established by the Spanish monarchs that investigated Christians accused of straying from the official doctrine of the Roman Catholic Church, particularly during the period 1480–1530

* **epic**   long poem about the adventures of a hero

* **mystical**   based on a belief in the idea of a direct, personal union with the divine

* **theology**   study of the nature of God and of religion

* **elite**   privileged group; upper class

* **romance**   adventure story of the Middle Ages, the forerunner of the modern novel

* **chivalry**   rules and customs of medieval knighthood

the examples of Italian writers such as Jacopo SANNAZARO and Bernardo Tasso. Garcilaso's poems include sonnets, elegies*, pastoral* love poems, and an ode*. Scholarly editions of his work, published between 1570 and 1580, helped establish him as a leading Renaissance poet.

Luis de León (1527–1591), another notable poet, taught at the University of Salamanca and became the leader of a group of humanist writers and translators. A member of a Catholic religious order, he was descended from *conversos* (Christian converts from Judaism) and specialized in the study of the Hebrew Bible. Because of these connections with Judaism, he was imprisoned and tried by the Spanish Inquisition*. León wrote a number of poems modeled on those of Garcilaso. Some explore Christian themes and others tell pastoral stories. A few describe the injustices León received at the hands of the Inquisition. Circulated in manuscript form, León's poems gained a wide readership.

Spanish writers published more than 50 epic* poems in the 1500s. The main model for these works was the *Aeneid,* by the ancient Roman poet Virgil. Some of the best Spanish epic poems dealt with religious subjects. However, the greatest Spanish epic, *La Araucana* by Alonso de Ercilla y Zúñiga (1533—1594), tells the story of the conquest of Chile.

Religious Works.   During the Renaissance, religion in Spain focused increasingly on the inner life of the spirit. Religious reformers such as TERESA OF ÁVILA helped promote this tend through their writings. Teresa, a Carmelite nun, became the most important writer of spiritual literature in Renaissance Spain. Her autobiographical *Book of Her Life,* written in the 1560s, described her own spiritual journey. In *Interior Castle* (1588), she analyzed the different forms of religious experience. Another religious reformer who played a role in literature was Juan de Yepes, also known as St. John of the Cross. His superb mystical* poetry used erotic images to describe intense religious experience. He also wrote commentaries explaining the theology* behind his poems.

One major form of religious writing in Spain was the sermon. In Spain, as in the rest of Europe, sermons provided an important link between the "high" culture of the Latin-speaking elite* and the popular culture of the masses. The sermons people heard each Sunday focused on moral, theological, and political themes. Their authors drew on a variety of sources, including the Bible, humanist writings, traditional tales, and medieval bestiaries (books about animals whose behavior offered moral lessons). A few of the many sermons delivered during this period became available in either manuscript or print form for study.

Fiction.   During the 1500s, many types of fiction appeared in Spain. In the first part of the century, romances* in the tradition of chivalry* were extremely popular. These works combined tales of skill and courage with scenes of courtly love. They often portrayed knights as models of Christian virtue. Nevertheless, some preachers disapproved of romances because of their love scenes.

Pastoral romances told stories about characters living in peaceful, rural settings. Often echoing Renaissance theories of love, they appealed to more sophisticated readers than chivalric romances. The first pastoral romance in Spanish, *Diana* (1559) by Jorge de Montemayor, dealt with the lives and loves of a group of shepherds and shepherdesses. Other writers, including Gaspar Gil Polo and Miguel de Cervantes, based romances on Montemayor's model.

A more realistic form known as the picaresque novel focused on the adventures of a *pícaro* (rascal). The earliest known example is *The Life of Lazarillo de Tormes,* written by an unknown author in 1554. A later work, *Guzmán de Alfarache* (1599–1602) describes the life of a man who has had a religious conversion. After each episode, the narrator explains what he learned from his experience.

Spanish Renaissance fiction reached its peak with the novel *Don Quixote* by Miguel de Cervantes. Part 1, published in 1605, met with immediate success. Part 2 appeared ten years later, shortly before the author's death. Widely hailed as the world's first modern novel, it tells the story of a minor nobleman who sets out as a wandering knight to right the wrongs of the world. The complex treatment of character, plot, and themes in *Don Quixote* has had a lasting impact on the development of the novel. Cervantes's *Exemplary Novellas* (1613) also explored new ground. A collection of experimental short novels, it combines elements from romances, the picaresque* novel, and Italian fiction, told from various points of view.

Drama, History, and Other Forms. Spanish drama developed slowly during the Renaissance. The first significant drama of the period, *Celestina* by Fernando de Rojas, appeared in 1499. However, it was not written for the stage, but rather as a novel in dialogue form. Toward the end of the 1500s Spanish writers began to experiment with plays intended for the theater. By the 1600s, playwrights such as Lope Félix de VEGA CARPIO had established drama as a lively art form in Spain.

Another popular prose form in Spain was history. Several Spanish historians recorded the events surrounding their country's conquests in the AMERICAS. They based their works on various ancient and medieval traditions. In the early 1500s some Spanish authors produced works that mixed different forms of writing, including information, advice, and fiction. Antonio de Guevara's *Dial of Princes; or, Golden Book of the Emperor Marcus Aurelius* (1529) combines fictional letters by the Roman emperor with fables and other lore. Guevara's *Familiar Epistles,* written about ten years later, contains fictional letters along with advice, sermons, and short novels. (*See also* **Biography and Autobiography; Conversos; Drama, Spanish; History, Writing of; Humanism; Inquisition; Literature; Pastoral; Poetry; Religious Literature; Spain.**)

The Moorish Novel

Although Spain drove the last of the Moors out of its territory in 1492, they remained a presence in the nation's literature. A type of fiction called the Moorish novel described the relations among Christian and Islamic knights and ladies in highly idealized form. The most successful work of this type was *The Civil Wars of Granada,* by Ginés Pérez de Hita, published in two parts (1595 and 1619). Viewed as the first historical novel in Spain, it later became the basis for *The Alhambra,* a collection of stories and essays written in 1832 by American author Washington Irving.

---

* **picaresque** refers to a type of fiction dealing with the adventures of a rogue or rascal

---

Spenser, Edmund

ca. 1552–1599
English poet

Born a commoner in London, Edmund Spenser became both a gentleman and the leading English poet of his day. Scholars view him as one of four authors whose work forms the foundation of English literature, along with medieval* author Geoffrey Chaucer, William SHAKESPEARE, and John MILTON. Spenser produced memorable and dis-

* **medieval**   referring to the Middle Ages, a period that began around A.D. 400 and ended around 1400 in Italy and 1500 in the rest of Europe

* **humanist**   referring to a Renaissance cultural movement promoting the study of the humanities (the languages, literature, and history of ancient Greece and Rome) as a guide to living

* **patron**   supporter or financial sponsor of an artist or writer

* **pastoral**   relating to the countryside; often used to draw a contrast between the innocence and serenity of rural life and the corruption and extravagance of court life

* **woodcut**   print made from a block of wood with an image carved into it

* **epic**   long poem about the adventures of a hero

* **allegory**   literary or artistic device in which characters, events, and settings represent abstract qualities, and in which the author intends a different meaning to be read beneath the surface

tinctive verse in every major form and invented a variety of new verse and stanza forms. He also developed the idea of poetry as a noble calling, which inspired many later writers.

Spenser's Life. Scholars know little about Spenser's early life. Some evidence indicates that his father was a poor cloth maker. As a boy Spenser attended the Merchant Taylors' School, which promoted the humanist* ideals of scholarship and public service. After receiving his bachelor's and master's degrees from Cambridge University, Spenser became secretary to Dr. John Young, the bishop of Rochester. He later entered the service of the earl of Leicester, who became his patron* and introduced him to several other poets. In 1579 Spenser married Machabyas Chylde, who bore him two children.

A year later Spenser became private secretary to Lord Grey of Wilton, the new lord deputy of IRELAND, then a colonial possession of England. Spenser moved with Lord Grey to Ireland and lived there for the rest of his life. He did, however, return to England several times to deliver messages to the queen and to oversee the publication of his books. In the late 1580s Spenser acquired Kilcolman Castle in Ireland, along with 3,000 acres of surrounding land.

In 1594 Spenser, whose first wife had died, married Elizabeth Boyle. A year later he lost his estate when an uprising broke out in Ireland and rebels looted and burned Kilcolman. In December 1598 Spenser made his last trip to England, where he died the following month. Many of England's noted poets attended his funeral, held in London's Westminster Abbey, and the queen, ELIZABETH I, ordered a memorial for him (although none was ever actually built).

Spenser's Works. Spenser's first major work, *The Shepheardes Calender,* appeared in 1579. The book contains a dozen poems in the pastoral* style, one for each month of the year. The 12 sections tell the story of Colin Clout, a lovesick shepherd-poet who represents the author. This character later reappeared in *The Faerie Queene* and in a minor work called *Colin Clout's Come Home Againe.* Each verse begins with a woodcut* illustration and a brief summary of its content and ends with a motto, followed by scholarly notes. These notes, together with an introduction in which the poet praises his work, make the entire collection look like an edited classic. He dedicated *The Shepheardes Calender* to his friend, the poet Philip SIDNEY.

In 1590 Spenser gained literary fame for his publication of *The Faerie Queene,* an epic* about the growth of the English nation. Spenser did not deal directly with the military and political struggles of his time in this work, but instead created a lengthy allegory* set in a mythical Faeryland. Each section of the poem follows the adventures of a wandering knight or knights who represent a particular virtue, such as holiness, justice, or purity. These knights battle fantastic creatures that stand for various vices. Spenser links these tales together through the character of the legendary King Arthur. Arthur appears in this work not as England's national hero but as a youthful wanderer on a quest to find Gloriana, the queen of the fairies, who has appeared to him in a dream.

* **romance** adventure story of the Middle Ages, the forerunner of the modern novel

* **sonnet** poem of 14 lines with a fixed pattern of meter and rhyme

* **stanza** section of a poem; specifically, a grouping of lines into a recurring pattern determined by meter or rhyme scheme

The Faerie Queene blends together many literary forms, including folklore, romance*, and political theory.

Throughout the 1590s Spenser produced a variety of shorter poems. He described his *Complaints,* published in 1591, as "sundrie [assorted] small poemes of the worlds vanitie." His next collection, *Amoretti and Epithalamion,* is a series of sonnets* celebrating his courtship of and marriage to Elizabeth Boyle. He later produced another "marriage poem," entitled *Prothalamion,* in honor of the weddings of four English nobles.

Spenser's works influenced many generations of poets. The nine-line stanza* he created for *The Faerie Queene,* for example, was copied by several major English poets, including John Keats and Alfred, Lord Tennyson. Spenser's portraits of feminine experience strongly influenced the late-Renaissance poet John MILTON in his own portrayals of female characters, such as Eve in the epic *Paradise Lost.* For more than two centuries, Spenser's most original creation—his mythical Faeryland—became English literature's chief symbol for the poetic imagination. For authors of the Renaissance and later periods, Spenser became a model of the poet as a spokesman for his culture's lasting values. (*See also* **English Language and Literature; Pastoral; Poetry; Poetry, English.**)

Sports

* **medieval** referring to the Middle Ages, a period that began around A.D. 400 and ended around 1400 in Italy and 1500 in the rest of Europe

* **elite** privileged group; upper class

* **Holy Roman Emperor** ruler of the Holy Roman Empire, a political body in central Europe composed of several states that existed until 1806

During the Renaissance, people of all social classes engaged in sports, many of which had medieval* origins. Some of these sports, such as tournament jousting, are no longer common. However, Renaissance Europeans also played tennis and a variety of ball games that were much like modern football or soccer.

Jousting tournaments were mock battles in which mounted warriors tried to knock each other from their horses using long lances. Originally a pastime of medieval knights and lords, they remained popular among Renaissance nobles. Courtiers also practiced other military sports, including archery, swordplay, and horse racing.

One of the most popular sports among the upper classes of the Renaissance was tennis. This game originated in medieval France, and as it spread across Europe, regional variations developed. In 1555 a monk standardized the sport by setting forth rules and a scoring system. Another sport of the elite* was golf, an ancient Scottish game revived by James VI of Scotland. Although elite men sometimes competed against members of the lower classes, Baldassare CASTIGLIONE advised in *The Book of the Courtier* that they do so only when they were certain to win. He declared that "it is too sad and shocking, and quite undignified, when a gentleman is seen to be beaten by a peasant."

The sports played among the elite varied little throughout Europe. Monarchs set the tone for sport, and royalty from different countries sometimes met to compete. For example, in 1523 HENRY VIII of England joined Holy Roman Emperor* CHARLES V in a doubles match of tennis against the princes of Orange and Brandenburg. Few noble women engaged in sports during the Renaissance. Though MARY STUART, the mother of James VI, enjoyed golf, sports were generally seen as an activ-

Renaissance Europeans played a variety of ball sports similar to modern football and soccer. This wall painting by Jan van der Straet, dating from 1555, shows ball players in a public square in Florence.

* **humanist** Renaissance expert in the humanities (the languages, literature, history, and speech and writing techniques of ancient Greece and Rome)

ity for men. Castiglione wrote that a court lady's role in sports was to stand by and cheer for her man.

The sports of the lower classes varied by region. In France, men played games such as *la soule,* a ball game in which opposing teams tried to drive a ball forward and past a goalpost with the foot, the hand, or a stick. The English game of football, or soccer, may have been based on *la soule*—although a popular myth claimed that the game had originated in the 1000s when Englishmen kicked around the severed head of a Danish foe. Another English game, stool ball, is said to have begun among milkmaids who tried to knock over their milking stools by throwing balls at them. By the Renaissance, stool ball was associated with courtship and the Easter season. It later developed into the modern games of cricket and rounders. In Italy, the Easter season brought games to public squares throughout the country, where noblemen kicked and hurled a leather ball filled with animal hair while spectators cheered.

Many humanists* of the early Renaissance regarded athletic ability as a necessary skill for an educated man to have. They approved of any sport that had been practiced in ancient Greece, such as swimming, running, or wrestling. However, athletic events also had their critics.

Authorities worried about the problems that accompanied sports, such as violence, gambling, and dice games. Some people considered sports "devilish pastimes," especially when people played them on Sunday. Various Protestant states or communities banned or strictly limited sporting activities, considering them signs of the sin of idleness. (*See also* **Tournaments.**)

Strozzi, Alessandra Macinghi

ca.1407–1471
Florentine letter writer

* **plague**   highly contagious and often fatal disease that wiped out much of Europe's population in the mid-1300s and reappeared periodically over the next three centuries; also known as the Black Death

Alessandra Macinghi Strozzi of Florence wrote an extensive and unique collection of letters to her sons during the mid-1400s. These letters provide a firsthand account of the life of a Renaissance woman, as well as a glimpse of the social and political climate of Florence during that time.

Born into an upper-class Florentine family, Alessandra received the basic education common for women of her standing. In 1422 she married a merchant named Matteo Strozzi. After 12 years of marriage and several children, her husband was exiled to the Italian city of Pesaro for being a political opponent of the ruling MEDICI family. His family followed him into exile, and soon afterward Matteo and three of the couple's children died of the plague*. Alessandra returned to Florence a few months later. She never remarried, and she spent a great deal of her time trying to arrange good marriages for her children and to establish her sons in business.

Seventy-three of Alessandra's letters to her sons in other cities survive today. A keen observer, Alessandra reported on current political events and circumstances. She also offered ordinary details such as food prices and the family's financial situation. Alessandra's letters show that she was a devoted mother, though like most Renaissance mothers, she was closer to her sons than to her daughters. As one of few large collections of correspondence written by a woman, these letters provide an intimate look into the life of a Florentine family that few other sources can offer.   (*See also* **Medici, House of; Women.**)

Stuart Dynasty

The Stuart dynasty—a succession of rulers from the same line of descent—occupied the thrones of Scotland and England during the Renaissance. Its turbulent history included civil wars, international intrigues, religious controversies, and the death by violence of six Stuart monarchs.

The family originated in Scotland as the Stewarts, who rose to power after half a century of Scottish civil war. The man who became King Robert II of Scotland in 1371 was the founder of the dynasty. Although some disputed his claim to the throne, many of his 21 children became nobles or married into noble families. By the time Robert's son was crowned King James I of Scotland in 1406, the dynasty's hold on the throne was secure. Ruling Scotland was, however, a dangerous occupation. James I was murdered, the next three kings (all Jameses) died in battle; and two Stuart monarchs were executed for treason.

Artist Paul van Somer created this portrait of the man who ruled Scotland as James VI and England as James I. The son of the Scottish queen Mary Stuart, James became the first Stuart monarch of England in 1603.

Stuart Monarchs

James IV
ruled Scotland 1488–1513

James V
ruled Scotland 1513–1542

Mary Stuart
ruled Scotland 1542–1587

James VI
ruled Scotland 1587–1625, ruled England 1603–1625 as James I

Charles I
ruled Scotland and England 1625–1649

The fortunes of Scotland and England were joined in 1503 when James IV of Scotland wed the daughter of King HENRY VII of England. The marriage was designed to seal a peace treaty between the two kingdoms. For a hundred years the Stuarts (as they now spelled their name) continued to rule their northern kingdom. Scotland was far smaller than England in both size and population, and its political and economic systems were less developed than those of England. Despite the peace treaty, the Scots felt threatened by their larger and more powerful neighbor to the south. To protect their country from England, the Stuarts built relationships with other nations by marrying into European ruling families. They also formed military alliances with France. As a result, in 1513 and 1542 Scotland became involved in conflicts between France and England, and it launched failed attacks on northern England.

These disasters forced Scots to consider the long-term future of their country. Some saw Scotland as a province of England, others as a colony of France. This difference turned into a religious divide. England became officially Protestant in 1559, and the Scots who favored England also became Protestants. But although Scotland adopted Protestantism as the official religion in 1560, those who sided with France—including the Stuarts—remained Roman Catholic.

Meanwhile, the English throne passed to HENRY VIII (ruled 1509–1547) and eventually to Henry's daughter, ELIZABETH I (ruled 1558–1603). During Elizabeth's reign, MARY STUART inherited the Scottish throne. Mary spent many years in France before returning to Scotland to rule in 1561. But six years later her controversial actions led to an uprising and the loss of her throne. She fled to England, where her cousin Elizabeth imprisoned her and in 1587 authorized her execution. Elizabeth later died childless. The closest heir was James VI of Scotland, Mary Stuart's son. While remaining king of Scotland, he became JAMES I of England in 1603.

James's son, CHARLES I, believed that it was his god-given right as king to rule with absolute authority, without regard to Parliament. He was also determined to reverse some aspects of the PROTESTANT REFORMATION in England. These policies plunged the kingdoms into civil war and led to Charles's trial and execution. The Scots, however, crowned his son Charles II as their king in 1651. Nine years later the monarchy and the Stuart dynasty were restored in England when Charles II came to the English throne. Charles died without an heir, and his brother became King James II.

A Catholic, James wanted to change England's constitution to guarantee civil and religious rights for Catholics. This policy alarmed the majority of the English, who wanted a Protestant king and kingdom. William of Orange, a Protestant ruler from Europe, was James's nephew and son-in-law, which gave him a claim on the throne. After a son was born to the elderly James in 1688, William arrived in England with an army to protect that claim. James fled, and William and his wife, Mary, became monarchs. For 20 years, James and later his son and his grandson (known respectively as the Old Pretender and the Young Pretender)

tried to reclaim the thrones of England and Scotland. Despite support in the Scottish Highlands and parts of Ireland, and encouragement from France and other enemies of England, they failed, and the Stuart dynasty came to an end. (*See also* **Scotland.**)

1494–1566
Turkish sultan

* **Ottoman Turks**   Turkish followers of Islam who founded the Ottoman Empire in the 1300s; the empire eventually included large areas of eastern Europe, the Middle East, and northern Africa

* **Holy Roman Empire**   political body in central Europe composed of several states; existed until 1806

* **Protestant Reformation**   religious movement that began in the 1500s as a protest against certain practices of the Roman Catholic Church and eventually led to the establishment of a variety of Protestant churches

Known as "the Magnificent" and "the lawgiver," Süleyman I was one of the most famous rulers of the Ottoman Turks*. Through military victories, he greatly expanded the boundaries of the Ottoman Empire. He also waged a jihad (holy war) in Europe at a time when the Holy Roman Empire* under the HABSBURG DYNASTY was expanding rapidly and battling the spread of Protestantism.

Süleyman I, the son of Selim I, took power in 1520. During the early years of his reign, he defeated the armies of Louis II of HUNGARY in the battle of Mohács (1526). His numerous military expeditions into that country led to the conquest of central Hungary and control over Transylvania in present-day Romania. After the Ottomans took the Mediterranean island of Rhodes in 1522, the Turkish fleet led by the famous pirate Barbarossa (Khayr ad-Din) conducted constant raids on ships and coastal areas.

Süleyman's military successes had a substantial impact on the Protestant Reformation* in Germany. In 1536 Süleyman formed an alliance with the French king FRANCIS I against the Habsburg emperor CHARLES V. Protestant princes in Germany took advantage of Charles's military engagements with Süleyman and the French to advance their goal of establishing the Lutheran church in Germany.

Süleyman's reputation as a lawgiver is based on laws to eliminate corruption and restore the basic principles of Ottoman legislation handed down by MEHMED II in the 1400s. Süleyman's greatest achievement was in maintaining and enlarging the Islamic empire. After his death, however, internal and external forces worked to undermine the stability and power of the Ottoman rulers, leading to a period of decline. (*See also* **Holy Roman Empire; Ottoman Empire; Piracy.**)

The modern nation of Switzerland began to take shape during the Renaissance. In 1386 several independent cantons (states) came together to form the Swiss Confederation. By 1513 the confederation included 13 cantons, along with allies and subject territories. During the late 1400s and 1500s Switzerland fought wars with Burgundy and the HABSBURG DYNASTY. The confederation also participated in the WARS OF ITALY (1494–1559), which brought it Italian-speaking territories and the attention of Europe. The Swiss War of 1499 began the process of Switzerland's separation from the Holy Roman Empire, which was not completed until 1648.

During this period Europeans began to take notice of Switzerland. The country appeared on maps as a distinct geographical region with the ancient Roman names of Helvetia and Rhaetia. Church COUNCILS

* **mercenary**   hired soldier

* **humanism**   referring to a Renaissance cultural movement promoting the study of the humanities (the languages, literature, and history of ancient Greece and Rome) as a guide to living

* **Protestant Reformation**   religious movement that began in the 1500s as a protest against certain practices of the Roman Catholic Church and eventually led to the establishment of a variety of Protestant churches

* **Gothic**   artistic style marked by bright colors, elongated proportions, and intricate detail

held in the Swiss cities of Constance (1414–1418) and BASEL (1431–1449) brought additional attention to Switzerland. The country also became known for its mercenaries*, who gained a reputation as fierce and effective soldiers. Various European observers commented on the Swiss political systems. The Italian political writer Niccolò MACHIAVELLI praised Switzerland's republican government and its soldiers, while French author Jean BODIN used the confederation as an example of how popular government leads to anarchy.

The influence of humanism* began to be felt in Switzerland in the late 1400s. Swiss humanists wrote national histories, some praising their system of government, others criticizing it for overthrowing the power of nobles. The city of Basel became the center of Swiss humanism in the 1500s thanks to its publishing industry, university, and trade links to Italy and other centers of Renaissance thought. The great Dutch humanist Desiderius ERASMUS made his home in Basel. After 1520, however, the Protestant Reformation* brought religious conflict to Switzerland. Thinkers had to choose between Catholicism and Protestantism, dividing the humanist community. Basel joined the Protestant camp, and Erasmus left the city.

The areas of Switzerland south of the Alps were much more open to Renaissance ideas in art than were the alpine regions. Swiss churches and palaces in the south were decorated in versions of Renaissance style, while those in the north generally remained faithful to Gothic* design. Basel was the only city strongly influenced by Italian art. Hans HOLBEIN the Younger, the famous German Renaissance painter, worked in Basel for about 12 years. On the whole, though, the artistic ideas of the Renaissance appear in Switzerland more as features of individual works than as a widespread movement. (*See also* **Humanism; Protestant Reformation.**)

Tasso, Torquato

1544–1595
Italian poet and dramatist

* **epic**   long poem about the adventures of a hero

* **Spanish Inquisition**   court established by the Spanish monarchs that investigated Christians accused of straying from the official doctrine of the Roman Catholic Church, particularly during the period 1480–1530

Torquato Tasso was the last major poet of the Italian Renaissance. His artistic style combines intense emotion with a serious moral tone. In his most famous work, the epic* *Jerusalem Delivered,* he explored the themes of love and heroism, providing a rich and complex account of the tensions between the two. This work made Torquato famous as one of the greatest poets of his day.

Tasso's Life.   Tasso was born in Sorrento, in southern Italy. His father, Bernardo, was a court poet in the city of NAPLES, which at the time belonged to Spain. In 1547 Bernardo Tasso became involved in a resistance movement against the introduction of the Spanish Inquisition* into Naples. He eventually had to flee the city, along with his son. Tasso spent the 1550s moving from court to court in central and northern Italy. In the course of his travels, he acquired an excellent education and became familiar with the literary culture of Italian courts.

Tasso studied at both the University of Padua and the University of Bologna, but he never received a degree. Instead he traveled to Ferrara

* **patronage** support or financial
sponsorship

and became a member of the household of Cardinal Luigi d'ESTE. He also enjoyed the patronage* of the cardinal's brother, Alfonso II, the duke of Ferrara. In 1575 Tasso completed the first draft of his epic *Jerusalem Delivered.* Before publishing it, he sought comments from five noted critics, hoping that their approval would protect him from later attacks on its political and religious views. Instead, the critics attacked his work so vigorously that the strain of defending it caused Tasso to have a nervous breakdown. He became suspicious of the court and all those around him. In the summer of 1577 he tried to stab a servant whom he accused of spying on him. Placed under strict guard for this crime, he managed to escape and fled south to Sorrento—leaving behind the precious manuscript of his epic.

When Tasso returned to Ferrara in 1579, he could not get his manuscript back. In a fit of anger he publicly attacked Alfonso II and his court. Tasso was taken to a nearby hospital, declared insane, and imprisoned for seven years. During this period, he recovered the text of *Jerusalem Delivered* and completed the poem, which appeared in 1581. After his release, Tasso spent the rest of his life wandering restlessly around Italy, producing various works of poetry and prose. He died in Rome.

Major Works. Like other Renaissance writers, Tasso aimed to master as many different literary forms as possible. He worked in the pastoral*, epic, lyric*, tragedy, and a variety of other forms. Tasso's great pastoral drama, *Aminta* (1573), relates the love of Aminta, a young shepherd-poet, for Silvia, a woman who at first rejects his advances. Aminta's love leads him into despair and attempted suicide before the two lovers finally unite. Tasso sets his work in an ancient golden age, a common Renaissance theme. However, his tone clearly shows that this idealized world is a fantasy as unrealistic as it is beautiful.

* **pastoral** relating to the countryside;
often used to draw a contrast between
the innocence and serenity of rural life
and the corruption and extravagance of
court life

* **lyric** refers to a type of verse that
expresses feelings and thoughts rather
than telling a story

* **classical** in the tradition of ancient
Greece and Rome

Renaissance authors viewed the epic as the highest form of poetry. In *Jerusalem Delivered,* Tasso attempted to live up to the classical* ideal that an epic should both delight and instruct. The poem, set during the period of the First Crusade (1096–1099), presents a contrast between the ideas of love and honor. In two different episodes, a hero must resist the temptations of a love that runs counter to his duty. Like other classical and Renaissance epics, *Jerusalem Delivered* contains many battle scenes, and Tasso combined the violent action of the battles with powerful emotional experience. Tasso's work expresses both the sorrows of war and the glory of military heroism, both pagan* and Christian.

* **pagan** referring to ancient religions
that worshiped many gods, or more
generally, to any non-Christian religion

Aside from these two famous works, Tasso is best known for his lyric poetry, which focuses on such typical Renaissance themes as love, religion, and the glory of his patrons. He also produced a tragic drama, a lengthy religious poem about the creation of the world, dialogues on a variety of topics, and works of literary criticism. These works earned Tasso a lasting reputation as one of the greatest poets of the Renaissance. Although his reputation declined during the 1900s, he remains a significant figure in the history of Renaissance literature. (*See also* **Chivalry; Italian Language and Literature.**)

Taxation and Public Finance

Financing the activities of the state was the greatest challenge faced by Renaissance rulers. Increasing costs, especially those associated with warfare, forced rulers to find new ways to raise money from their subjects. Their efforts produced solutions that had a significant impact on both finance and politics.

Taxation. All rulers raised money through taxes. They taxed merchandise, exports and imports, salaries, property, land, and other items. In the 1400s northern and central Italian cities had the most sophisticated tax schemes. Many charged a tax called the *gabelle* on certain goods and services, wages, and criminal proceedings. A major source of revenue was the state salt monopoly* called the *dogana.* Government control of salt involved both the amount available and the price. During times of emergency, rulers raised the price of salt and forced citizens to buy a certain quantity. In 1427 FLORENCE instituted the *catasto,* a tax based on wealth.

French citizens demonstrated a greater resistance to paying taxes than the Italians. The French tended to see taxes as temporary measures that could be used in emergencies but were not needed in times of peace. In the late 1300s public pressure led the French king to cancel taxes temporarily. Such measures decreased revenues. To make up for the shortage, French monarchs often resorted to debasing the currency (reducing the amount of precious metal in the coins). In the late 1400s a land tax called the *taille* became the major source of revenue. The French king Louis XI (ruled 1461—1483) raised two-thirds of his government's income from the *taille.* Other taxable items included wine and salt, although in France the salt tax brought in only a fraction of the money that it did in Italy.

Rulers needed the consent of the people to raise taxes. For this reason, monarchs and representative assemblies often struggled over the issue of taxation. Even when the public approved taxes, they were not easy to collect. Many Italian cities employed tax farmers, who received a fixed fee in exchange for the right to collect taxes. This was helpful in times of war, when rulers needed money as soon as possible. Tax farming also occurred in France and England. Tax farmers were often charged with unfair practices, such as collecting more money than citizens owed.

Borrowing and Debt. Taxes rarely covered all of a state's expenses, and most governments raised money by borrowing money from the clergy and from banks. Sometimes public officials forced citizens to lend money to the state at a fixed rate of interest. Occasionally, governments offered a higher rate of interest to citizens who agreed to make voluntary loans.

In times of crisis, many citizens avoided loaning money to the state for fear that it would not be repaid. In such cases public officials often sought loans from Jews, threatening them with imprisonment or expulsion if they refused to cooperate. In Italy, lending by Jews rose sharply in the 1400s.

* **monopoly** exclusive right to engage in a particular type of business

Repaying large loans was difficult since the amount borrowed was often far more than a state could collect through taxation. Several states addressed this problem by consolidating their loans into a single debt, called a *monte* (mountain) in Italy. In many places citizens were able to invest in the state's debt, buying shares that paid interest and could be freely sold. In the 1400s almost every prosperous family in Florence had some of its wealth invested in the public debt.

The funding of public debt was just one of the new financial practices that evolved during the Renaissance. Over time, these practices led to the idea of a national budget. In addition, the growing reliance of rulers on wealthy individuals for revenue created common interests between the two. This bond was an important condition for the growth of the modern state. (*See also* **Accounting; Economy and Trade; Mercantilism; Money and Banking.**)

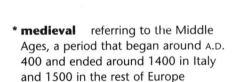

Technology

The Renaissance period witnessed many advances in the "mechanical arts," a broad field that covered activities ranging from craft production to the design and operation of machines. However, most new developments built on earlier advances that had taken place during the Middle Ages. Traditional methods in such areas as farming, cloth making, and carpentry remained common throughout the Renaissance, and changes in these fields usually came about gradually.

Agriculture and Water Use. In most regions, agricultural practices changed little during the Renaissance. One of the most important problems in farming was controlling the water supply to irrigate dry fields or drain marshy ground. Medieval* techniques involving irrigation canals, wells, and dams remained in use, but some new methods emerged as well. English farmers, for example, flooded entire fields periodically to produce "floating meadows." This technique protected the fields from frost and deposited fresh layers of silt (river mud).

In the Netherlands, elaborate techniques existed for draining marshlands. Since the 1000s farmers had built dikes to protect land from the sea. Construction methods varied from place to place, but the basic dike had an earth core covered by clay and straw, seaweed, or bundles of reeds. By the 1500s, engineers in the Netherlands were draining small lakes to make more land available for farming. The process involved building an earthen bank around the lake, then cutting a channel around the bank and pumping the lake water into it. These large projects led to the invention of many new types of pumps and other drainage devices such as the drainage mill, which operated by wind power.

In Italy, large-scale projects focused on controlling river flooding, digging canals for transportation, and draining swamps. Engineers built stone walls, dikes, and various other structures to hold back the flood-prone rivers. The canals designed to carry away floodwaters also became useful for transportation. The ruling Sforza family in Milan built the first navigable canals in Italy in the late 1400s. Around the same time, engi-

* **medieval** referring to the Middle Ages, a period that began around A.D. 400 and ended around 1400 in Italy and 1500 in the rest of Europe

Brunelleschi's Dome

The dome of the cathedral of Santa Maria del Fiore in Florence is one of the period's greatest technical achievements. The space beneath the dome was too vast for a traditional wooden supporting structure, so architect Filippo Brunelleschi distributed the dome's weight on several stone ribs that met at the top of the dome. He built the dome as a smaller inner shell surrounded by a larger outer shell, with a stairway between the two leading to the lantern atop the dome. The bricks in each shell were laid in a pattern that enabled them to support themselves during construction.

* **classical** in the tradition of ancient Greece and Rome

neers explored ways to drain the huge, malaria-ridden Pontine Marshes near Rome. A solution came from artist and scientist LEONARDO DA VINCI, who suggested reopening an ancient Roman canal and building another canal at a right angle to it to carry away water flowing down the nearby Lepini Mountains. However, work on this project did not begin until many years after Leonardo's death. Major drainage projects also took place in France and England.

Construction. Building techniques in the Renaissance remained much the same as they had been during the Middle Ages. Building styles, by contrast, changed substantially as classical* designs became popular. Renaissance Europe experienced a building boom as the upper classes demanded spacious, comfortable homes that displayed their wealth. Construction projects fueled a demand for brick, stone, timber, gravel, and lime (used in mortar).

Bridge construction required advanced techniques to lay foundations in riverbeds. One method involved sinking large wicker containers of rubble in the river to create an island on which stone piers could be built. Another way to create these islands involved driving columns, known as piles, into the riverbed to form an underwater enclosure and filling the enclosure with rubble. In other cases, engineers would sink the foundations directly into the ground below the riverbed. This method required diverting or draining the river temporarily, often by building a watertight enclosure in one area of the river and pumping out the water.

Crafts. The manufacture of cloth was a basic part of the Renaissance economy, employing people in a wide range of skilled and unskilled occupations. Techniques varied based on the kind of fiber used. Making woolen cloth involved at least ten separate processes, from shearing the sheep and cleaning the wool to dyeing, stretching, and finishing the fabric.

Spinning was often hired out to peasant women in what was known as the putting-out system. During the Renaissance, the use of spinning wheels replaced hand spinning. The spinning wheel had appeared in Europe in the 1200s, but early models required two separate actions to spin the fibers and wind the yarn. A device called the flyer, invented around 1480, combined these two processes. Another improvement, the treadle, appeared in the early 1500s. This was a foot pedal that allowed a seated spinner to turn the wheel with her feet while using her hands to work the yarn.

Other tasks associated with textile manufacture occurred on a larger scale. Master weavers and their assistants, working in central locations, wove the yarn on looms. The fulling process—beating woolen cloth with a mixture of water and other substances to thicken and strengthen it—usually took place in mills located near fast-flowing rivers. Waterwheels powered the hammers that beat the cloth.

Aside from cloth, most craft goods in the Renaissance were still produced by hand in the shops of artisans*. Carpenters and smiths made

* **artisan** skilled worker or craftsperson

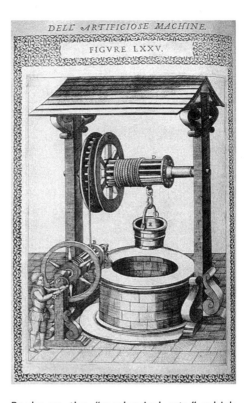

DELL ARTIFICIOSE MACHINE.

FIGVRE LXXV.

Books on the "mechanical arts," which ranged from craft making to machine design, began spreading throughout Europe in the early 1400s. Many of these texts featured stunning illustrations. This image of a mechanical well appeared in *Various and Ingenious Machines,* published in 1588 by Italian engineer Agostino Ramelli.

farm implements, as well as the tools used by more specialized craft workers, such as wheelwrights (wheel makers) and coopers (barrel makers). Potters created plates and bowls, while glassmakers produced vases, windows, drinking glasses, and many other glass items. Glassmaking was a complex industry, involving many specialized processes that varied from one place to another. The most famous and sought-after glassware came from Venice, and the city's glassmakers guarded their trade secrets closely.

Tools and Machines. Instrument making became a specialized craft during the 1400s. Instrument makers produced various devices to aid in navigation, such as the quadrant and the cross staff, which helped sailors establish their position at sea by measuring the location of heavenly objects. Versions of these tools were useful to surveyors and astronomers as well. Instrument makers also constructed timekeepers, such as sundials and clocks, as well as tools for military purposes. Optical instruments, such as the telescope, became important near the end of the Renaissance period.

The Renaissance brought significant improvements to various types of machines, including mills, pumps, and cranes. Mills served a variety of purposes, including grinding grain, making paper, and fulling cloth. Many of these machines were human- or animal-powered, using either a horse turning a mill or a human walking on a treadmill. Mills could also be powered by waterwheels or by wind. The expansion of the mining industry led to improvements in suction pumps, which drew water out of deep mine shafts. Other inventions in the field of mining included the blast furnace, which used waterwheels to power the huge bellows that supplied air for the fire, and wheeled vehicles on rails to carry ore.

Some improvements to machines centered on specific parts, such as gears and screws. Machines that used the screw, such as the lathe (a cutting device), improved significantly during the Renaissance. An old technology called the screw press found new functions during this period in stamping coins and, even more importantly, in printing books.

Writings on Mechanical Arts. Starting in the early 1400s, books on crafts and mechanical arts spread throughout Europe. Their subjects included machines, engineering, architecture, military technology, painting, sculpture, and navigation. Most of these texts were not primarily how-to manuals on mechanical arts. Instead, they served to feed the popular interest in skilled craftwork and how it was produced. They also represented the power and glory of the princes who sponsored the works. The texts reflected a pride in fine craftsmanship and helped to raise the status of the mechanical arts in the eyes of the public.

Some scholars have suggested that the artisans of the Renaissance made a significant contribution to the development of modern science. At the outset of the Renaissance, a sharp distinction existed between the mechanical arts and natural science, a form of philosophy. By the 1600s, however, scientists were relying heavily on physical instruments to test their theories about the natural world. As a result, an alliance between science and technology emerged that has lasted for centuries. (*See also*

Agriculture; Artisans; Clocks; Fortifications; Industry; Mining and Metallurgy; Printing and Publishing; Science; Scientific Instruments; Transportation and Communication; Warfare.)

Teresa of Ávila

**1515–1582
Spanish mystical writer**

* **mystic**   believer in the idea of a direct, personal union with the divine

Teresa of Ávila was a noted mystic* religious reformer of the 1500s. Born Teresa Sánchez in the city of Ávila in central Spain, she received no formal education, although she read a great deal as a child. In 1535 Teresa entered the religious order of Our Lady of Mount Carmel (known as the Carmelites). Around age 40 Teresa began to hear voices and see visions. At first the Carmelite priests were concerned about these experiences, but in time they came to agree with her view of them as evidence of a connection with God.

In 1562 Teresa founded a small convent called Saint Joseph's of Ávila. There she introduced such reforms as a simple lifestyle, devotion to inward prayer, and the rejection of racial prejudice. In 1567 she met the Carmelite priest who would later become St. John of the Cross. A great poet and mystic, he helped Teresa spread her religious reforms to other Carmelite institutions. By the time of her death in 1582, Teresa had founded 17 convents. Forty years later the Catholic Church declared her a saint. In 1970 she became the first woman to receive the title of Doctor of the Church, an honor granted to a select group of religious writers.

* **allegory**   literary or artistic device in which characters, events, and settings represent abstract qualities and in which the author intends a different meaning to be read beneath the surface

Scholars have viewed Teresa both as a model of womanly obedience and as a feminist who challenged the exclusion of women from positions of power in the church. Her three most famous works are her autobiography, entitled *Book of Her Life;* an allegory* called *The Interior Castle;* and *The Way of Perfection,* a guidebook to mental prayer. This text offered a strong defense of women's right to pursue a mystical path. (*See also* **Religious Literature.**)

Theaters

Few permanent theaters existed in Europe during the Middle Ages. Even in the Renaissance, many dramatic performances took place in temporary theaters set up in inns, public buildings, or private houses. Often, troupes of traveling actors moved from town to town presenting their work in a variety of spaces. However, by the 1500s permanent theaters with stages, dressing rooms for the actors, and seating for the audience began to appear in Italy, Spain, and England.

Temporary Theaters. Many Renaissance theaters could be set up for a particular occasion and then taken apart and stored until the next event. Temporary theaters in royal courts tended to be more elaborate than those in inns and town halls. The Great Hall at Whitehall Palace near London was equipped with moveable bleacher-like seats and possibly a stage. Around 1620 the English architect Inigo JONES built a new Banqueting House at Whitehall. It included moveable theater equipment such as a broad stage, seven rows of stepped seating, and a

The Teatro Olimpico in Vicenza, Italy, is one of the few surviving Renaissance theaters. Designed by Andrea Palladio in the 1500s, the structure features columns and statues in a classical style.

gallery—a raised seating area projecting over the main floor. The queen's palace in Somerset House also featured a portable theater setup, known as a "frame."

In England, Oxford and Cambridge colleges held performances of plays in their halls. A theater built in 1605 for the hall at Christ Church, Oxford, had scenes designed by Inigo Jones and an auditorium inspired by Sebastiano Serlio, an Italian architect. Serlio's designs adapted many of the elements of ancient Roman theaters to fit them into a Renaissance courtyard or hall.

Italy and Spain. Many of the ruling families of Italy, such as the dukes of FERRARA, set up temporary theaters at their palaces. Italian academies (informal groups of scholars) also staged plays in their halls. By the late 1500s permanent theaters began to appear in towns such as Vicenza, Sabbioneta, Piacenza, and Parma. In 1588 the Italian architects Andrea PALLADIO and Vincenzo Scamozzi built a theater for an academy in Vicenza. Scamozzi also built the Teatro Olimpico at Sabbioneta between 1588 and 1590. This theater featured a semicircular auditorium with stepped seating and classical* columns and statues. Part of this building still stands today.

Charitable organizations built some of the most important theaters in Spain as a way to raise funds for hospitals. Two major theaters in MADRID, the Corral de la Cruz and the Corral del Principe, began as simple courtyard auditoriums in the late 1570s and early 1580s. Over a period of decades, they developed into complex playhouses with roofs and galleries, including a special screened gallery where women sat apart from men. Theaters of the early 1600s, such as the Coliseo in SEVILLE, feature designs that blend different styles of architecture.

* **classical** in the tradition of ancient Greece and Rome

England. The first public theaters in England opened up around London in the mid- to late-1500s. The Red Lion (1567) consisted of a set of galleries erected in a yard behind a farmhouse. The galleries surrounded a stage with a tall structure in the center that may have served as a dressing room and an upper acting area. Nine years later, the owner of the Red Lion opened another establishment—known as the Theater—north of the city, with galleries on three levels, a raised stage, and formal entrance doors for the actors. This design, inspired by ancient Roman theaters, became the model for English playhouses.

Other important London theaters included the Curtain, built near the Theater, and the Rose, located on the south side of the Thames River. A 14-sided timber-frame structure, the Rose measured 74 feet across. The stage was open to the sky, but a thatch roof protected the galleries. In 1592 Philip Henslowe, the owner of the Rose, pulled down its stage and rebuilt it a few feet farther back, changing the theater's outline to a D-shape with the stage at the flat end. He also added a roof over the stage, supported by columns at the corners. The Rose is no longer standing, but in 1989 workers unearthed its remains, revealing details of its design.

In 1599 the owners of the Theater dismantled their building and took it across the river to a site near the Rose. There they rebuilt it and renamed it the Globe. This theater would become famous as the place where many of William SHAKESPEARE's plays first appeared on stage. Both the galleries and the stage of the Globe had thatched roofs. In 1613 one of these roofs caught fire and the Globe burned down. It was promptly rebuilt, this time with a tile roof.

Shortly after the new Globe opened, the actor Edward Alleyn financed a new theater north of London, the Fortune. Like the rebuilt Globe, the Fortune featured a tile roof. Nevertheless, in 1621 the Fortune burned down, and the owners replaced it with a brick theater, probably round in shape.

In addition to the public theaters, London also developed private playhouses. Fully enclosed and lit by candles, these theaters were smaller than the public ones and charged more for seating. Unlike the public houses, which allowed some spectators to stand in the open space in front of the stage, private theaters provided seating for all and served a more exclusive audience. London's most important private theater, the Blackfriars, had a U-shaped auditorium of two or three galleries, a balcony, and a raised stage with a trap door. In 1609 it became the winter home of the King's Men, Shakespeare's acting company. (*See also* **Architecture; Drama; Drama, English; Drama, French; Drama, Spanish.**)

Theology

See *Religious Thought.*

New Frontiers

Plate 1
The Renaissance was a period of tremendous growth and discovery. Scholars not only learned more about their world but turned their attention to the rest of the universe as well. Nicolaus Copernicus, Tycho Brahe, and others brought about a revolution in astronomy by challenging long-established ideas about the nature of the universe. Copernicus claimed that the Sun, rather than the Earth, stood at the center of the universe. Tycho rejected this theory but agreed with Copernicus that the other planets of the solar system traveled around the Sun and not around the Earth. This illustration of Tycho's theory appeared in a Renaissance guide to the heavens.

Plate 2: Left
In 1497–1498 Portuguese explorer Vasco da Gama sailed around Africa and found a sea route to India. Europeans wanted spices and silks from Asia, but the overland trade route to the east was long and difficult. Da Gama's voyage opened the way for profitable trade in these luxury goods and for a Portuguese empire in East Africa and Asia.

Plate 3: Below
During the 1500s Europeans began to establish settlements in North America. The French built a fort on the northeast coast of present-day Florida in 1564, but the fort was soon taken over by Spanish forces based in St. Augustine. The illustrations of Flemish artist Theodore de Bry, such as this one of French colonists and Indians in Florida, provided Europeans with some of their first images of the New World.

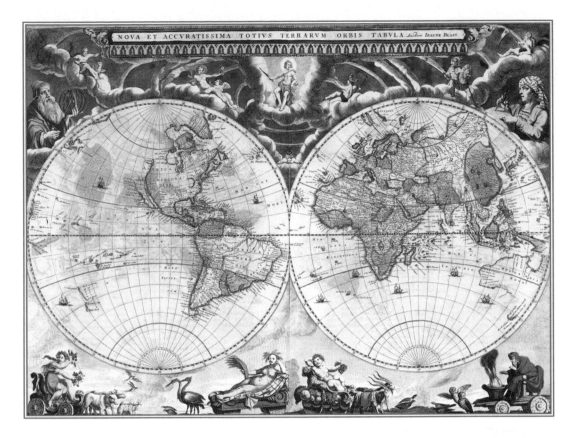

Plate 4: Above
Willem and Jan Blaeu were leading map-makers in Holland in the 1600s, and they published impressive multivolume atlases. This world map by Jan shows European knowledge of the world about 1630. Blaeu's maps often have illustrations of figures, animals, and places around the outer edges.

Plate 5: Right
In the 1500s the Spanish city of Seville emerged as a lively center of international exploration and trade. In 1519 Portuguese navigator Ferdinand Magellan set off from Seville with a fleet of five ships on what was to be the first complete voyage around the world.

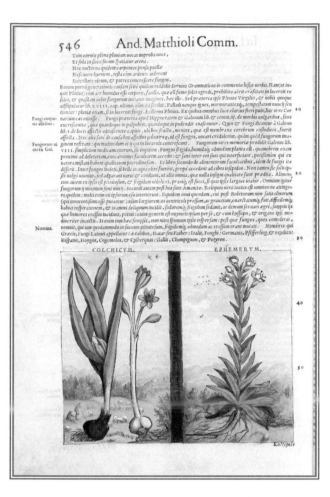

Plate 6: Left
Renaissance scholars took great interest in natural science, including botany. The revival of ancient texts, the discovery of new plants, and the growth of printing all contributed to the development of botany as a science. There were major efforts to study, describe, and classify plants and to publish illustrated texts. This detailed print of Colchicum (a crocus-like plant) and Ephemerum (a hyacinth-like plant) appeared in a famous book of plants by Pietro Andrea Mattioli, first published in 1554.

Plate 7: Below
By the late 1400s European shipbuilders had developed a new three-masted vessel that had a rear rudder and both square and triangular sails. The larger ships of these new ships, usually called carracks, could carry enormous loads of cargo and found service primarily in trade. This painting (ca. 1521) by Flemish artist Joachim Patinir provides a glimpse of Portuguese carracks at sea.

Plate 8: Left
Leonardo da Vinci of Italy was a man of great curiosity and imagination. Some of his ideas were far ahead of his times. As an artist he explored new techniques for using light and arranging figures in paintings. As a scientist he probed the fields of anatomy, geology, and engineering. Leonardo left many notebooks filled with sketches of ingenious devices and machines of the future. The modern model of the aerial screw, shown here, was based on one of his sketches.

Plate 9: Below
Renaissance medicine made great strides in explaining the structure of the human body. Scholars began to focus on observation rather than theory, and the practice of dissection became an important tool for learning about human anatomy. This illustration from a manuscript of the 1400s shows a dissection in progress.

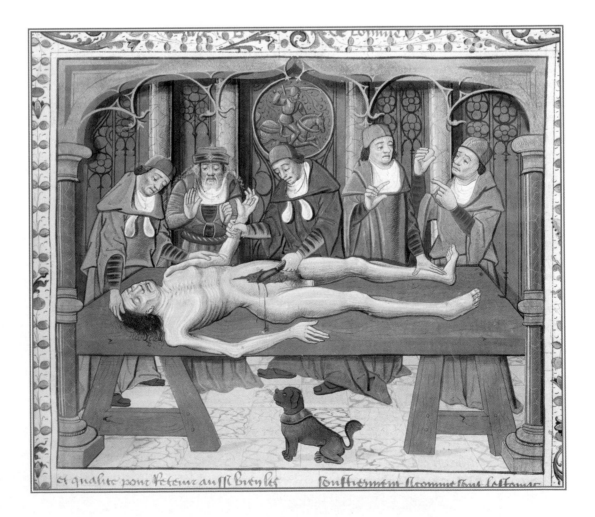

Plate 10: Left
The Fugger family of Germany built a financial empire and acquired substantial economic and political influence in Renaissance Europe. The family lent money to rulers for wars and foreign expeditions and took silver and copper mines as security. Christoph Fugger, shown here, played a key role in the election of the Holy Roman Emperor Charles V in 1519.

Plate 11: Below
Weapons and methods of warfare changed considerably during the Renaissance. Primitive pistols packed with gunpowder and bullets appeared in the early 1300s. The invention of firing mechanisms in the 1400s made firearms more reliable and easier to use. Heavy cannons that fired large stones or iron balls came into use around the same time. By the late 1400s smaller cannons emerged that could be mounted on wheels and transported, even on ships. Cannons were produced in foundries, such as the one in this illustration.

Plate 12: Left

Martin Luther set off the Protestant Reformation with his Ninety-five Theses (1517), a document attacking practices of the Roman Catholic Church. German artist Lucas Cranach, a friend and supporter, created a group portrait of Luther with some of his supporters and colleagues in 1530. Luther is on the right; Philip Melanchthon stands on the left.

Plate 13: Below

The empire of Philip II, king of Spain, included Portugal, the Netherlands, and colonies in the New World. Philip's brief marriage to Mary I, queen of England, also made him co-ruler of England from 1554 to 1558. However, the cost of running this huge empire drained the Spanish treasury. Flemish artist Peter Paul Rubens portrayed the king as a commanding figure on horseback.

Plate 14: Left

The Renaissance brought new ideas and innovations in many fields, including art. One major advance during this period was a better understanding of perspective, an artistic technique for creating the illusion of three-dimensional space on a flat surface. Artists achieved this illusion by using lines that appeared to lead toward a distant "vanishing point," as shown in the painting *Nuptials of the Virgin* by Raphael.

Plate 15: Below

Many advances occurred in music as well, including the development of new instruments and improvements in older ones. One of the most important new instruments was the violin, which has survived into the modern era with almost no change. This detail from *The Sense of Hearing*, painted around 1617 by Jan Brueghel the Elder, features the violin and a variety of other Renaissance instruments.

Thirty Years' War

* **Holy Roman Emperor**   ruler of the Holy Roman Empire, a political body in central Europe composed of several states that existed until 1806

* **prince**   Renaissance term for the ruler of an independent state

* **sovereignty**   supreme power or authority

The Thirty Years' War (1618–1648) was an extended conflict between the Holy Roman Emperor* and the princes* of individual territories within the empire. It began as a struggle over the crown of BOHEMIA but eventually developed into a political and religious war that raged over much of central Europe and involved most of the major powers of Europe. The war also marked the political end of the Renaissance.

Progress of the War. The central issue of the war was sovereignty*. Who had ultimate authority in the states that made up the Holy Roman Empire—the emperor or the prince of each state? The war had its roots in a religious and political crisis in Bohemia, where an angry mob of Protestant nobles tossed two ministers of the Catholic King Ferdinand out of Prague Castle. From there, the conflict gradually expanded, playing itself out in several stages. The first phase, which ended in 1621, saw the Protestant nobles defeated. During the next two phases, which lasted until 1629, the Holy Roman Emperor strengthened his control over the German states.

From 1629 to 1632 the Swedish King Gustavus Adolphus turned the tide in favor of the Protestants. However, his death at the battle of Lützen in 1632 caused Sweden's German allies to abandon the fight. A brief peace was signed at Prague in 1635, but soon after the French entered the conflict. The French minister Cardinal Richelieu hoped to use the war to attack and weaken his Spanish and Austrian enemies. The final phase of the war lasted until 1648, by which time exhaustion had set in and everyone wanted to end the fighting.

Several factors drove the participants of the war, including religious differences, the rights of sovereign states, and defense of traditional systems. In addition, many international interests became entangled in the war. This combination of factors meant that victory in one area of the war might have unexpected consequences in another. As a result, military victories did not prove decisive. The conflict was finally settled at the negotiating table, not on the battlefield. The Peace of Westphalia ended the Thirty Years' War in 1648.

Aftermath of the War. The Thirty Years' War was bitterly fought and terribly destructive. Its impact left deep and lasting scars on both political leaders and the public. A strong feeling that no clear winner had emerged from this devastating event helped promote a more peaceful mood after the war.

Several trends that had begun in the 1500s accelerated as a result of the Thirty Years' War. The conflict between the emperor and the rulers of individual states helped define the nature of sovereign state authority. At first the war strengthened ties between church and state, but the long period of indecisive warfare ultimately weakened those links. In addition, the war marked the end of a long period of economic expansion and prosperity. Finally, the war was concluded by a peace treaty that set the model for international relations in the post-Renaissance era. Because of these developments, many historians regard 1648 as a dividing line that marks the beginning of modern Europe. (*See also* **Holy Roman Empire; Palatinate; Saxony.**)

1518–1594
Venetian painter

* **narrative** storytelling

* **apprentice** person bound by legal agreement to work for another for a specified period of time in return for instruction in a trade or craft

* **confraternity** religious and social organization of Roman Catholics who were not members of the clergy

* **patronage** support or financial sponsorship

One of the major Venetian artists of the Italian Renaissance, Tintoretto was known for his bold brushwork, startling lighting effects, and dramatic treatment of narrative* scenes. His works cover a range of subjects, with particular emphasis on biblical, mythological, and historical themes. Tintoretto had great admiration for both TITIAN and MICHELANGELO—Titian for his use of color and Michelangelo for his skill in drawing. Tintoretto often used Michelangelo's work as models for his own drawing and adapted these models in his compositions.

Born Jacopo Robusti in Venice, Tintoretto got his name (which means "little dyer") from his father's occupation as a cloth dyer. Information about the artist's training is sketchy, but according to one tradition Tintoretto served briefly as an apprentice* to Titian. His earliest paintings suggest the influence of a number of other Italian painters, including Bonifazio de' Pitati. Whatever his training, by 1539, Tintoretto was working as an independent artist.

In 1548 Tintoretto attracted much attention with his painting for the meeting hall of the Scuola Grande di San Marco (St. Mark), an important confraternity* in his native Venice. The work, *St. Mark Rescuing a Slave,* caused a sensation and was initially rejected by the members of the organization. It featured a dynamic use of space and human figures that were shorter than normal, which gave the illusion of depth. Tintoretto's style differed from traditional Venetian mural painting, which had a flat, one-dimensional quality. The work also caused controversy because it had been painted so quickly, with rapid brushwork that made it seem unfinished to many people. Between 1562 and 1566 Tintoretto produced three more paintings of scenes from the life of St. Mark, the patron saint of Venice, for the Scuola di San Marco.

Although many continued to find fault with Tintoretto, he enjoyed considerable success. In 1564 the artist was hired to create a painting for the ceiling of a meeting room in the Scuola Grande di San Rocco. Instead of submitting a small model for approval, the customary procedure, Tintoretto presented the finished painting as a gift. While criticized for not following the usual practices, Tintoretto continued to create other pieces for the room. Among these is a huge *Crucifixion,* generally considered his grandest painting. Tintoretto became a member of the Scuola di San Rocco and arranged to continue his decorative work. In 1575–1576, he painted the central scene on the ceiling of the organization's large meeting hall, as well as a series of painting on the walls below that illustrate scenes from the life of Christ (1579–1581).

Tintoretto's main patronage* came from within Venice. In addition to his work for San Marco and San Rocco, he played a major role in the redecoration of Venice's Ducal Palace and worked extensively for the city's lesser confraternities. For these groups he painted a number of versions of the *Last Supper* of Christ, which featured figures and scenes in a humble style. Tintoretto's paintings of the Last Supper differ considerably in this respect from those of Paolo VERONESE, another Venetian artist of the time. Various assistants contributed to Tintoretto's later works. His son Domenico, his chief assistant, continued to run the family workshop after Tintoretto's death. (*See also* **Art in Italy; Confraternities.**)

Titian

ca. 1488–1576
Italian painter

* **patron**   sponsor or financial supporter of an artist or writer

* **apprentice**   person bound by legal agreement to work for another for a specified period of time in return for instruction in a trade or craft

* **fresco**   mural painted on a plaster wall

* **plague**   highly contagious and often fatal disease that wiped out much of Europe's population in the mid-1300s and reappeared periodically over the next three centuries; also known as the Black Death

* **altarpiece**   work of art that decorates the altar of a church

Tiziano Vecellio, called Titian, was the leading Venetian painter of the 1500s. He achieved great fame and success in his lifetime, serving as the official painter of VENICE and accepting commissions from powerful patrons* throughout Italy and Europe. Titian also transformed the art of oil painting with new techniques that changed the way that Renaissance artists used paints.

Artistic Training. Much of what is known about Titian's life comes from Lodovico Dolce's *Dialogue on Painting* (1557). According to Dolce, Titian was born into a prominent family in a small town in northern Italy and moved to Venice at the age of nine. The boy served as apprentice* to a local artist, who recognized Titian's extraordinary talent and sent him to the workshop of Gentile BELLINI. After studying briefly with Gentile's brother, Giovanni, Titian became an assistant to GIORGIONE, a Venetian artist known for experimenting with techniques.

From Giorgione, Titian learned a new method of handling oil paints. Venetian artists had begun to work on canvas because the high humidity of the island city damaged fresco* paintings. Accordingly, Giorgione developed his technique to suit the canvas surface. Before, oil paints had been applied in the form of glazes that allowed the underlying layers to show through. This technique created a luminous effect. Giorgione, however, began mixing additional pigment into his paints, making them more densely colored. Artists who used this technique could cover earlier work or scrape off paint. Painting became looser and less polished—but more vibrant and personal.

In 1508 Titian assisted Giorgione on a major assignment, decorating a warehouse in Venice's commercial center. Dolce wrote that the young Titian received more praise than the master painter for this project. Titian's rise to fame had begun.

Early Career. In 1510 Titan moved to the Italian city of Padua, perhaps to escape an outbreak of plague*. There he produced his first large-scale designs, three murals representing the life and works of St. Anthony, the city's patron saint. Returning to Venice, Titian offered to paint one of the halls in the ducal palace. Through this work he hoped to be chosen to succeed Giovanni Bellini as the official state painter. In 1516 Bellini died, and Titian won the position.

Meanwhile, Titian painted a number of significant landscapes, continuing a Venetian tradition of depicting outdoor scenes. In these works he often used forms from nature in a symbolic manner. In *Sacred and Profane Love* (1514), for example, a hilly, wooded landscape on one side of the picture (representing earthly concerns) is contrasted with a spacious, open scene on the other (representing the spiritual world). Titian also created altarpieces*, including the massive *Assumption of the Virgin* (1518) in the church of Santa Maria Gloriosa dei Frari in Venice. More than 22 feet high, it fills the space above the high altar. Another remarkable altarpiece, *The Martyrdom of St. Peter Martyr* (completed 1530, destroyed by fire 1867), showed angels descending in a blaze of glory to the murdered saint, while a terrified companion flees.

Many of Titian's works used scenes from nature in a symbolic manner. In *Sacred and Profane Love*, shown here, the hilly, wooded landscape at left represents earthly concerns, while the spacious, open scene on the right represents the spiritual world.

---

* **naturalistic**   realistic, showing the world as it is without idealization

* **classical**   in the tradition of ancient Greece and Rome

* **antiquity**   era of the ancient Mediterranean cultures of Greece and Rome, ending around A.D. 400

* **Holy Roman Emperor**   ruler of the Holy Roman Empire, a political body in central Europe that was composed of several states that existed until 1806

See color plate 7, vol. 1

Having achieved fame in Venice, Titian went on to establish a reputation in the rest of Italy. At the courts of various ruling families, such as the ESTE in Ferrara and the GONZAGA in Mantua, he produced portraits of princes with their wives and mistresses. Painted in a naturalistic* style, the works make elements such as flesh, fur, cloth, and armor seem real.

Like many Renaissance artists, Titian became interested in classical* culture and sought to revive it. Often, he tried to recreate works from antiquity* by following descriptions in ancient texts. Like other artists of the time, he also sought to surpass the accomplishments of the great Greek and Roman artists. Titian painted a series of mythological scenes, including *Bacchus and Ariadne* (1523), for Alfonso d'Este.

Later Works. In the 1530s Titian began to work for prominent patrons outside Italy. He painted several portraits of the Holy Roman Emperor* CHARLES V, receiving in return substantial sums of money as well as the title "Count Palatine and Knight of the Golden Spur." In one portrait Titian showed the emperor after an important victory, recording every detail of the triumphant leader's armor and horse. Painted in the style of certain classical portraits, the picture became a model for later artists.

Titian also worked for Charles's son, PHILIP II, king of Spain and ruler of the Netherlands. He painted a portrait of Philip around 1550. Then he sent Philip a series of paintings that he called *poesie*, celebrations of the nude female body in mythological scenes. Titian expanded Philip's understanding of Renaissance art and benefited from the king's patronage.

With his titles, privileges, and wealth, Titian enjoyed very high status for an artist. He continued to run a family workshop in Venice with his son Orazio, but as time passed he distanced himself from the world in which most artists moved. He purchased a grand house on the northern edge of Venice and took for his motto the Latin phrase *Natura Potentior Ars* ("art more powerful than nature").

By the mid-1500s critics considered Titian and MICHELANGELO to represent the two main styles of Italian art. Titian and the Venetian school emphasized color and created natural appearances through broad and open brushwork. Michelangelo and the central Italian painters emphasized form, precise drawing, and clear outlines. According to Giorgio Vasari, who wrote biographies of many Renaissance artists, Michelangelo visited Titian's studio and declared that, although no one was better than Titian at imitating nature through coloring, it was a pity that Venetian artists never learned to draw. For centuries, art critics continued to discuss the characteristics of these two styles of painting.

In the 1540s Titian visited Rome. The trip exposed him to many examples of ancient art and allowed him to study the works of painters such as Michelangelo and RAPHAEL. At the time, Titian was moving toward larger and more complex arrangements of figures in his own work. The influence of the Roman painters and ancient pieces is clear in his later works.

Meanwhile Titian continued to develop his skill as a portrait artist. In Rome he painted Pope Paul III, showing the aged pope with his two grandsons. Although unfinished, the moving scene fully exhibits Titian's ability to portray the personalities of his subjects.

Some of Titian's late works, including *The Flaying of Marsyas*, reveal the touch of the painter's hand. In his final years the artist sometimes abandoned the brush and applied paint to the canvas with his fingers. Critics remarked on the development of a new quality in his work. In 1566 Vasari noted that Titian's later pieces "are carried out in bold strokes … in such a manner that they cannot be looked at closely but from a distance appear perfect."

Shortly before his death, Titian painted a pietà* that he intended for his own tomb. Within the painting is a smaller picture of two kneeling figures—Titian and his son Orazio. Although the cause of Titian's death is unknown, he died during a plague that later claimed Orazio. But Titian's influence remained strong on the young artists of his own day and on the great masters of the next century—Rembrandt, RUBENS, and Velázquez. (*See also* **Art in Italy.**)

A New Way of Seeing the World

One of Titian's friends and admirers was the Italian writer Pietro Aretino, whose published letters contain accounts of gatherings at the painter's home. In a 1544 letter, Aretino relates how Renaissance painters were teaching people to view the world around them with the eyes of an artist. Describing a sunset over Venice's Grand Canal, Aretino says, "Oh with what beautiful strokes of nature's brush was the atmosphere pushed back, clearing it away from the palaces, just as Titian does in painting landscapes!"

* **pietà**   image of the Virgin Mary holding the lifeless body of Christ

Toledo

One of the foremost cities of Spain during the Renaissance, Toledo was a major commercial, cultural, and religious center. It served as the headquarters of the Spanish church and the site of various church COUNCILS. By 1571 Toledo had become the country's second largest city after Seville. However, after King PHILIP II (1527–1598) established Madrid as his capital, Toledo lost prestige and began a period of decline. Between 1571 and 1639, its population shrank from about 60,000 to 24,000.

Before this decline, Toledo was a dynamic and varied place. From 1519 to 1522 it emerged as the center of resistance to the new HABSBURG rulers. Many of Toledo's residents worked in the manufacture of wool and silk cloth. Almost 20 percent were *conversos*—Jews who had converted to Christianity because of the Spanish Inquisition*—and they dominated the city's economy.

* **Spanish Inquisition**   court established by the Spanish monarchs that investigated Christians accused of straying from the official doctrine of the Roman Catholic Church, particularly during the period 1480–1530

The University of Toledo, founded in the mid-1500s by a family of *converso* origin, was only one example of the city's cultural vitality. Toledo also had several important printing presses as well as prominent literary circles and groups of reformers. The most famous artist of Renaissance Toledo was the Greek-born painter Domenikos Theotokopoulos, better known as EL GRECO. He painted scenes of the city and some of its prominent citizens. (*See also* **Madrid; Spain.**)

Tombs

* **classical**   in the tradition of ancient Greece and Rome

* **Gothic**   style of architecture characterized by pointed arches and high, thin walls supported by flying buttresses; also, artistic style marked by bright colors, elongated proportions, and intricate detail

* **coat of arms**   set of symbols used to represent a noble family

* **effigy**   representation of a person

The tradition of building memorial tombs to honor prominent individuals continued from the Middle Ages into the Renaissance. Sculptors created thousands of tombs, mixing architectural elements with carved human images and decorations. Many of these works feature classical* designs. However, Gothic* style tombs remained popular in Italy well into the 1400s and even later in northern Europe.

Renaissance tombs fall into three basic types: tomb slabs, wall tombs, and freestanding memorials. Tombs were often placed in churches, as close to the high altar as possible, depending on the wealth and importance of the person honored. Some are located in private chapels. Tombs mark the location of a body and have certain common features. They give the name of the deceased and usually the date of death. Some display a family coat of arms* and an inscription indicating the person's social status. Other inscriptions might describe the individual's virtues and accomplishments or appeal to God for the salvation of his or her soul.

The least expensive type of tomb marker in the Renaissance was a small plate set in the church floor. A large slab, about the size of the grave beneath it, was also popular. Made of marble or sometimes bronze, these tomb slabs usually contained only inscriptions and coats of arms, though some also had carved effigies*. In the 1420s the Italian sculptor DONATELLO designed a bronze tomb slab for Bishop Giovanni Pecci (Cathedral, Siena) that includes an effigy of the bishop. The use of tomb slabs decreased in the 1500s, as tastes changed and available floor space in churches became scarce.

Wall tombs, more expensive than slabs, consist of carvings and architectural structures placed against the walls of churches or other buildings. Some have a sarcophagus (stone coffin) in an arched recess raised on brackets. Relatively small and simple, these raised memorials were very popular in the late 1400s. Most Renaissance wall tombs, however, sit at floor level. They often contain classical-style arches and columns and feature delicate sculptural portraits and details. Variations of the wall tomb include multilevel structures with life-size, freestanding figures of the deceased along with saints, warriors, and other individuals. MICHELANGELO designed two famous wall tombs (1521–1534) for Giuliano and Lorenzo de' MEDICI, young princes of the ruling family of FLORENCE.

Freestanding tombs featuring a simple sarcophagus and effigy became popular in the Middle Ages in northern Europe. During the Renaissance, northern sculptors continued to produce them, usually in a Gothic

* **Holy Roman Emperor** ruler of the Holy Roman Empire, a political body in central Europe composed of several states that existed until 1806

style. The most important examples are memorials dedicated to German and French royalty. In Innsbruck, Austria, the tomb of the Holy Roman Emperor* MAXIMILIAN I is flanked by 28 life-size bronze figures, creating a moving scene. In France, the freestanding memorials of Louis XII, FRANCIS I, and Henry II and their queens (in the church of St. Denis) include traditional French elements, such as kneeling figures at prayer. In Italy, Michelangelo designed a massive freestanding tomb for Pope JULIUS II in 1505. The plan called for a three-level structure with some 40 oversized figures. However, the design was abandoned and replaced by a wall tomb incorporating some of Michelangelo's sculpture, including the famous figure of Moses. (*See also* **Art; Death; Sculpture.**)

Tournaments

See color plate 12, vol. 2

Exhibitions of military skill, known as tournaments, began in Europe some time after A.D. 1000. They continued to be held during the Renaissance, though their form and purpose changed considerably over the years. Early tournaments often featured a *mêlée*, a combat between groups of men. The fighting was generally conducted in deadly earnest and resulted in numerous casualties. Eventually *mêlées* were replaced by the joust, which involved two mounted knights who charged at one another with lances. The introduction of blunted weapons and a tilt (barrier) to prevent the horses from colliding made jousting safer. However, jousting could still be a dangerous affair, as shown by the death of France's King Henry II in Paris in 1559 as a result of a wound suffered in a joust.

Banned at times by church or state officials, tournaments remained extremely popular throughout the Renaissance. They were valued as training in martial arts, as a sport, and as a grand spectacle. Tournaments often took place to celebrate occasions of state, such as royal births and weddings or visits by foreign dignitaries. Participants wore elaborate armor and costumes, and special parades might be held before the tournament to show them off. In time the pageantry of the tournament came to be more important than the fighting.

* **classical** in the tradition of ancient Greece and Rome

* **chivalric** referring to the rules and customs of medieval knighthood

Many Renaissance tournaments adopted themes from classical* or chivalric* literature. A tournament held at the Spanish city of León in 1434 was centered on the theme of a knight supposedly trying to free himself from enslavement to a lady. In other cases, knights would imitate heroic literature by declaring their intention to defend a certain place against all challengers. Around 1460 René of Anjou wrote a detailed, illustrated text describing how tournaments should be staged, and many similar works appeared in the later years of the Renaissance.

By the 1500s it was common for tournaments to have a fictional framework or storyline. For example, a tournament held to celebrate the birth of an heir to King HENRY VIII of England featured a challenge from four "visiting" knights of the mythical land of Ceure Noble. One of the knights was played by the king himself. The outcome of many combats in these themed tournaments was decided beforehand. A tournament held for England's Queen ELIZABETH I included the staged failure of four knights to capture the Fortress of Perfect Beautie, which represented the

The Renaissance tournament combined military training, sport, and spectacle. Most tournaments featured jousting, in which two mounted knights charged each other with lances, as shown here.

Queen's virginity and moral integrity. These late Renaissance tournaments were usually staged to celebrate the reigning dynasty, and those who took part were more like actors than combatants. The tournaments eventually came to include music and displays of horsemanship and may have played a role in the early development of OPERA. (*See also* **Arms and Armor; Chivalry; Duel; Honor; Parades and Pageants.**)

Translation

* **humanist** Renaissance expert in the humanities (the languages, literature, history, and speech and writing techniques of ancient Greece and Rome)

* **vernacular** native language or dialect of a region or country

* **Ottoman Turks** Turkish followers of Islam who founded the Ottoman Empire in the 1300s; the empire eventually included large areas of eastern Europe, the Middle East, and northern Africa

* **medieval** referring to the Middle Ages, a period that began around A.D. 400 and ended around 1400 in Italy and 1500 in the rest of Europe

Translation made both ancient and modern works available to a much wider audience during the Renaissance. Although many humanists* stressed the need to read ancient Greek and Roman works in their original languages, translations opened up these texts to the large number of readers who did not know those languages. Scholars translated many volumes from Greek to Latin and from both Greek and Latin into vernacular* tongues. At the same time, translations from one vernacular language to another brought books to readers in different parts of Europe.

From Greek to Latin. Few Europeans knew ancient Greek before 1397. In that year, the Greek scholar Manuel Chrysoloras arrived in Italy. Other learned Greeks followed, especially after 1453, when the city of Constantinople, a center of Greek culture, fell to the Ottoman Turks*. These scholars helped spread knowledge of the language and literature of ancient Greece.

Italian humanists learned to read Greek texts and began to translate them into Latin. They also produced improved versions of texts translated during the Middle Ages. Renaissance scholars pointed out many mistakes in medieval* versions of ancient works. Most of these were word-for-word translations, which simply replaced each word in one language with its nearest equivalent in the other. Humanists aimed to translate the true meaning of the text, even if it meant changing the wording.

During the 1400s, some of the most important efforts in the field of translation involved works of philosophy. The Italian humanist Leonardo BRUNI, a leading translator of the early 1400s, created Latin versions of many Greek texts, including works by the philosopher PLATO. In the late 1400s another Italian scholar, Marsilio FICINO, produced the first translation of Plato's complete works. His translation made all of Plato's writings available for the first time in western Europe. Humanists also produced new translations of works by Plato's student ARISTOTLE, but these texts did not completely replace medieval Latin translations.

Several Renaissance scholars translated the writing of GALEN, a Greek physician from the A.D. 100s whose ideas formed the core of Renaissance medicine. A new, ten-volume Latin edition of Galen's works appeared in 1541. First published in Venice, it included several pieces that had never appeared in Latin before.

* **epic** long poem about the adventures of a hero

Various literary scholars produced Latin versions of the works of the ancient Greek poet Homer. In the 1430s Lorenzo VALLA translated part of Homer's epic* the *Iliad.* About 40 years later, Angelo POLIZIANO translated the entire poem, dedicating his edition to the Florentine statesman Lorenzo de' MEDICI. In Germany, the poet Helius Eobanus Hessus produced a verse translation of the *Iliad* in 1540.

From Latin and Greek to the Vernacular. Renaissance readers who did not know Latin or Greek also wanted information about ancient cultures. To meet this demand, vernacular translations of ancient works began to appear in the 1500s. Some writers made careers out of translating Latin and Greek classics into local languages. Ancient works on such topics as ethics* and rhetoric* often appeared in the vernacular, but professional works about science and law rarely did.

* **ethics** branch of philosophy concerned with questions of right and wrong

* **rhetoric** art of speaking or writing effectively

New Renaissance works in Latin might be translated into vernacular languages if they attracted enough attention. One example was *Utopia* (1516), a Latin work of social criticism by the English author Thomas MORE. Scholars also translated the Latin *Praise of Folly* (1511), by the Dutch humanist Desiderius ERASMUS. This work attacked human foolishness and corruption in the church and urged readers to live according to the example of Christ.

In Britain, learning to translate ancient works from Latin and Greek was an important part of a humanist education. Publishers issued English versions of many works of history, biography, and moral philosophy. William SHAKESPEARE used English editions of *Lives,* by the Greek biographer Plutarch, and *Metamorphoses,* by the Roman poet Ovid, as sources for his plays. In the early 1600s the scholar George Chapman translated both of Homer's epics, the *Iliad* and the *Odyssey,* into English.

Vernacular Works. Renaissance writers translated some popular works from one vernacular language to another. One example was *The Book of the Courtier* (1528), a book about courtly life by Baldassare CASTIGLIONE of Italy. Written in Italian, it later appeared in English,

French, Spanish, and Latin. At about the same time, the Spanish scholar Antonio de Guevara published *The Golden Book of Marcus Aurelius,* a partly fictional biography of an ancient Roman emperor. Translated into Dutch, English, French, German, Italian, and Latin, the book became a European best-seller.

Scholars translated some works because they viewed them as literary classics. In 1591 Sir John Harington published an English version of Ludovico ARIOSTO's epic *Orlando Furioso.* Nine years later Edward Fairfax produced an English edition of another Italian work, Torquato TASSO's epic *Jerusalem Delivered.* Fairfax gave his version a new title, *Godfrey of Bulloigne.* Changes of this sort were fairly common. In fact, many Renaissance translators freely added, removed, or rearranged material while preparing an edition in another language. (*See also* **Classical Scholarship; Greek Émigrés; Humanism; Ideas, Spread of; Latin Language and Literature; Literature; Poetry; Printing and Publishing.**)

Transportation and Communication

During the Renaissance, both merchants and governments depended on the regular flow of goods and information. In general, sea transportation was quicker and more efficient than land transportation. However, advances in both land and sea travel occurred over the course of the Renaissance. Communication also improved significantly during this period with the appearance of the first postal networks in Europe.

People traveled for a variety of reasons during the Renaissance. Explorers sailed far from Europe to discover new territories for their monarchs and to win glory and riches for themselves. Most voyages, however, were far more routine in nature. Business, politics, and diplomacy* accounted for much, if not most, travel at this time. Other reasons for trips included PILGRIMAGES (journeys to sacred places) and pleasure travel.

Land and Sea Transportation. The poor state of roads throughout Europe made overland travel slow and difficult, especially in winter, when many roads could not be navigated by wheeled vehicles. Most people traveling overland went on foot or rode mules or donkeys. Rich people tended to ride horses, although many of them preferred well-trained mules. Wealthy or sickly individuals might ride in litters or sedan chairs, carried either by animals or by several servants. People of all classes also accepted rides on carts carrying goods to market. Several models of wagons and carts existed for different road conditions. Pack animals, such as horses, mules, and oxen, were used to transport goods as well.

The first passenger coaches appeared in Hungary in the early 1400s. These were essentially heavy wagons pulled by two or more pairs of horses. More advanced coaches, which were easier to turn, came into use during the 1500s. These new models could carry up to eight people with luggage. Smaller and lighter coaches also became available at this time. They often had the passenger compartment suspended on straps to pro-

* **diplomacy** formal relations between nations or states

Wagons and carts were common modes of transportation for people of all social classes. In *Travelers in a Landscape* (1616) by Jan Brueghel the Elder, wagon drivers navigate the rough terrain of a country road.

vide a more comfortable ride. In the 1600s private carriages became fashionable among the upper classes. Despite their relative comfort, however, coaches often moved more slowly than foot traffic on Europe's poor roads. Overall, the speed of overland travel changed little until the late 1700s.

Sea travel increased during the Renaissance. Shipbuilders produced a variety of ships of different types and sizes for transportation, trade, fishing, exploration, or warfare. Ships ranged from single-person fishing vessels to large carracks that could hold 1,000 passengers and up to 2,000 tons of cargo. Travel time was difficult to estimate. The length of time it took to sail from one port to another varied according to the season, the weather, the tides, the cargo, the crew, and a host of other factors.

Communication. The merchants of the Middle Ages established the earliest communication networks in Europe. The Hanseatic League, an association of trading towns in northern Europe, set up regular courier services among its members in the 1200s. Venice also had a well-established trading network, and its couriers connected the Christian and Islamic worlds. By 1400 universities often ran their own messenger services to deliver letters for professors and students. Louis XI of France may have created the first national postal service in 1464. Spain founded its own national post not long afterward.

* **Holy Roman Empire** political body in central Europe composed of several states; existed until 1806

* **papacy** office and authority of the pope

During the reign of MAXIMILIAN I, the Holy Roman Empire* established an imperial postal service. This courier network, perhaps the most famous of its time, linked the far-flung territories of the HABSBURG family in Spain, the Netherlands, Germany, and Italy. The papacy* also ran its own postal service, which supplemented that of the Habsburgs. In the late 1550s Rome became the most important communications center in Europe.

Despite the existence of these established services, both governments and individuals often used private messengers. Independent couriers were more flexible than the official services and sometimes faster as well. Providing fresh horses at regular intervals helped speed couriers on their way. By changing to a new horse every 12 miles, the average courier could cover about 35 to 50 miles per day; a fast messenger might travel 75 miles or more per day under exceptional conditions. (*See also* **Economy and Trade; Exploration; Ships and Shipbuilding; Travel and Tourism.**)

Travel and Tourism

* **diplomacy** formal relations between nations or states

Renaissance Europeans had a passion for travel. They journeyed both within and beyond Europe for a variety of reasons, including religion, exploration, trade, and diplomacy*. Travel as a form of education also became popular at this time among the upper classes. Michel de MONTAIGNE, a French writer of the 1500s, declared that he had visited foreign countries "to notice unknown things."

Types of Travel. Many Renaissance travelers made their journeys as part of their jobs. Explorers and conquerors voyaged to the fringes of the known world seeking wealth, glory, and new territory for their countries. Merchants sailed in search of goods and markets, soldiers traveled to wars in other countries, and ambassadors represented their nations at foreign courts.

Some people traveled for religious reasons. Missionaries, for example, journeyed to Asia, Africa, and the Americas with the goal of spreading their Christian faith. Many of them wrote accounts of the distant lands they visited and the peoples they encountered on their journeys. Another form of religious travel was the PILGRIMAGE, a visit to a holy place. Many printers published guidebooks for pilgrims. Wynkyn de Worde's *Informacion for Pylgrymes unto the Holy Londe* (1498) was one of the first books published in England.

Pleasure travel was rare before the Renaissance. In 1336 the Italian poet PETRARCH wrote one of the first accounts of travel as a pleasurable experience, describing a trip he had made to the top of Mount Ventoux in France. Over the course of the Renaissance, the growing middle class began to view visits to foreign countries—especially Italy—as a desirable goal for learned people. Beginning in the mid-1550s, a growing number of young English noblemen rounded out their education with a "grand tour" of the European continent, lasting two or three years. While they often studied at European universities and met with local scholars during their travels, they also made time for sightseeing. Sir Philip SIDNEY's grand

Young men of the upper class often took a "grand tour" of Europe as part of their education. Such tours usually included a visit to the Italian city of Rome, where travelers could see ancient ruins such as the Colosseum, pictured here.

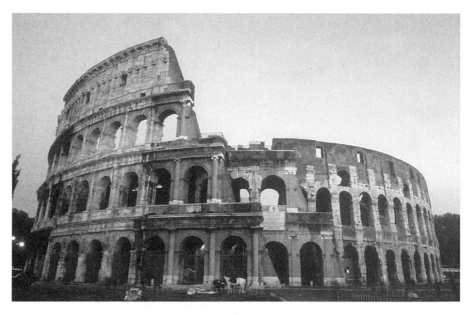

tour, which lasted from 1572 to 1575, included France, Germany, the Netherlands, and Italy. Over the course of his travels he learned languages, studied the ways of foreign courts, and admired scenery and architecture.

Parents, schools, and even the royal court might provide funds for the grand tour. ELIZABETH I sometimes paid the travel expenses of one of her subjects in the hope that the trip would make that person useful to her in the future as a diplomat or an expert in foreign trade. The grand tour almost always included the Italian cities of ROME and FLORENCE, and returning travelers brought back knowledge of ancient cultures and of the new styles of the Italian Renaissance. Architect Inigo JONES, who made the grand tour in 1613, introduced to England the pure classical style of Italian architect Andrea PALLADIO. Thomas Howard, the earl of Arundel, accompanied Jones on his tour and came home with a collection of ancient statues. Visits to Europe's chief cultural and artistic sites remained a vital part of the education of an English gentleman until the end of the 1700s.

Conditions of Travel. The journey from England to Italy was a difficult and uncomfortable one. Most people had to travel by land, as sea voyages between the two countries were rare due to the threat of piracy in the Mediterranean. Those who did venture out to sea ran the risk of encountering not just pirates but also storms, shipwreck, and disease.

The overland journey, however, had its share of hardships too. Travelers had to spend many days riding on horseback through unknown territories on barely marked roads, which could turn suddenly into rivers during the rainy season. They passed their nights in flea-laden inns, sleeping three or more to a bed, often in the company of bandits or rogues. Some English gentlemen disguised themselves as poor peasants in an effort to avoid being attacked or robbed on the roads.

Travelers bound for Italy could "post," renting horses from a series of stations along the road, or they could pay to join a convoy, a group traveling under the guidance of a director. Such groups sometimes included soldiers to protect the travelers in dangerous areas. At the end of the 1500s a new method of transportation appeared: coaches began to replace riding horses on the most level and well-used roads.

Money posed a practical problem for all travelers. Most countries had severe restrictions limiting the use of foreign currency. To get around these laws, travelers carried letters of credit from their own countries, which they could exchange for cash in the places they visited.

Travel was essentially a male activity during the Renaissance. Society looked on religious pilgrimages as the only respectable form of travel for a woman, and only a few women braved the dangers of such journeys. Lady Whetenall, one of the first Englishwomen to undertake the grand tour, died in childbirth in 1650 in the Italian city of Padua.

Travel Literature. Many Renaissance travelers wrote books about their journeys. Explorers returning from distant lands often shared their experiences in order to spread their own fame. Their accounts introduced knowledge of new regions, cultures, plants, and animals into Europe. Collections of these writings, such as Richard HAKLUYT's *Principal Navigations* (1589) and Pierre Bergeron's *Travel to the New World* (1629), enjoyed a great deal of success with the reading public.

Many forms of travel literature existed, ranging from guidebooks to personal narratives*, journals, and letters. Authors often combined descriptions of journeys with history, geography, or even fiction. Writers such as Miguel de CERVANTES SAAVEDRA of Spain and Luíz Vaz de CAMÕES of Portugal blended tales of their own travels into their fictional works. Spanish conquistador* Álvar Nuñez Cabeza de Vaca wrote a gripping account of his trip from Florida to Mexico in the mid-1500s. Dutch scholar Desiderius ERASMUS included lively descriptions of his wanderings through Europe in letters to his friends. After the grand tour became popular, many Englishmen published descriptions of their journeys to Italy.

By the end of the 1500s, writers and scholars had developed a travel journal method for formulating a precise picture of a foreign land. It told travel writers how to examine a new land, what order to follow in observing and reporting, and what questions to ask the local people. This method remained in use through the late 1700s and produced a large body of travel literature. (*See also* **Exploration; Missions, Christian; Transportation and Communication.**)

* **narrative**   story

* **conquistador**   military explorer and conqueror

Trent, Council of

* **theologian**   person who studies religion and the nature of God

In 1545 Pope Paul III called bishops and theologians* together in the northern Italian city of Trent to respond to the challenges raised by Protestants and by reformers within the Roman Catholic Church. This meeting, known as the Council of Trent, met over three distinct periods between 1545 and 1563. The decisions it reached had a major impact on the later history of the church.

Political, military, and religious conflicts threatened the council throughout its duration. When its first session opened in 1545, only 31

* **prelate**   high-ranking member of the clergy, such as a bishop

* **papal**   referring to the office and authority of the pope

* **sacrament**   religious ritual thought to have been established by Jesus as an aid to salvation

* **diocese**   geographical area under the authority of a bishop

* **humanist**   referring to a Renaissance cultural movement promoting the study of the humanities (the languages, literature, and history of ancient Greece and Rome) as a guide to living

* **medieval**   referring to the Middle Ages, a period that began around A.D. 400 and ended around 1400 in Italy and 1500 in the rest of Europe

prelates* attended, and the number present never exceeded 200. Although papal* delegates presided over the council, the popes were only partly successful in controlling its agenda. Moreover, the council was often torn by conflict and sharp debate. The council's first session broke up in 1547; the second session, which met in 1551, ended a year later, and the council took ten years to regroup. Many people believed it would never end successfully.

Reforms of the Council of Trent.   The council's two chief goals were to respond to questions of religious doctrine raised by Protestant reformers, especially Martin LUTHER, and to deal with demands from both Catholics and Protestants for church reform. By the time the council met, any real chance of healing religious divisions between Protestants and Catholics had faded. Instead, the council reaffirmed the Catholic position on disputed issues, making the break with Protestants final.

The Council of Trent did not try to issue a full statement of Catholic belief. Instead, it responded only to questions raised by the Protestant reformers. One of these concerned Martin Luther's view of the Scriptures as the only proper basis for religious teachings. The council's response to this issue was twofold. It established an official body of religious texts for Catholics, but it also affirmed the importance of church traditions in addition to Scripture. Next, the council dealt with Luther's idea that humans were saved solely through their faith in Christ and not through good works. The council declared that salvation involved both God's grace and human responsibility. Finally, the council discussed the sacraments*. Luther had reduced the number of sacraments from the traditional seven to two and had redefined the nature of those two. The Council of Trent reemphasized the traditional sacraments and declared that Christ had established all seven of them.

The council also had a clear goal of reforming the offices of popes, bishops, and priests. Attempts to reform the papacy met with little success, but the council set many new requirements for bishops. It issued a decree insisting that bishops live in their dioceses* and forbidding them to hold more than one office at a time. The council also tried to establish a closer relationship between bishops and the local clergy. It required bishops to hold regular meetings with their clergy, visit and oversee local parishes, be selective in choosing priests, and promote preaching on Sundays and feast days. The council emphasized the role of the parish as the proper site for tending to a congregation's spiritual needs and required every diocese to establish a seminary to train poor boys for the priesthood.

The Council of Trent and the Renaissance.   The Council of Trent gave the Catholic Church an opportunity to react to the new ideas of the Renaissance. Although the council issued no statement about the new humanist* learning, it focused on medieval* traditions in the language used in its own decrees. It also based its debates on the Latin Vulgate Bible, the version used throughout the Middle Ages. Many saw this decision as a warning against the new humanist emphasis on returning to original Greek and Hebrew texts of the Bible. The council

also failed to make any mention of new vernacular* Bibles, opening the door to later efforts to suppress such works. At the same time, its decision to keep Latin as the language of church ritual helped promote the study of classical* languages among Catholics.

At the same time, the Council of Trent reflected the influence of Renaissance ideas. The council said little about the humanist goal of applying principles of classical rhetoric* to the practice of preaching, but it did stress preaching as the chief duty of bishops and pastors. This emphasis contributed to a revival of preaching and to the writing of treatises* on how to preach that were based on humanist principles. The council also reaffirmed the value of "holy images," which many Protestants had criticized. This decision gave support to the outpouring of art, especially religious art, during the late Renaissance. At the same time, the council issued warnings about superstition and sexual elements in painting. These statements led to treatises on what was appropriate in "sacred art" and to attempts to censor it. (*See also* **Bible; Catholic Reformation and Counter-Reformation; Councils; Preaching and Sermons; Religious Thought.**)

Tudor Dynasty

See *Henry VII; Henry VIII; Edward VI; Grey, Jane; Mary I; Elizabeth I.*

Universities

Universities first appeared in Europe during the Middle Ages. By 1400, a total of 29 existed throughout the continent. Another 46 opened their doors over the next 200 years, mostly in Germany, Italy, France, and Spain. Like their modern counterparts, Renaissance universities offered advanced education and provided a setting for research. They made an immense contribution to scholarship and trained many of the leaders of society.

FUNCTIONS AND STRUCTURE

Cities and towns opened new universities for a variety of reasons. Some acted in response to the rising demand for trained professionals. Others gained political or economic benefits from having a school. Regardless of the reasons for their founding, all universities shared certain common features.

Functions. Renaissance universities trained many students for careers in government, law, medicine, and the clergy. The growing governments of the day required educated civil servants, lawyers, and judges. The demand for physicians to work in cities, towns, and royal households drew large numbers of students to study medicine. Other students earned degrees in theology* to prepare for careers in the church.

Some cities and towns founded universities for financial reasons. Attending a local school cost students far less than traveling to a distant town. Thus, building a university could help citizens save money. In addition, it might produce income for the town by attracting out-of-town students who would purchase food, lodging, and other necessities.

Universities in the Renaissance

- • Founded before 1301
- ○ Founded 1301–1400
- ○ Founded 1401–1500
- ● Founded 1501–1625
- * See notes

Universities in Spanish America

- ● Santo Domingo after 1538
- ● Mexico 1551
- ● Lima 1571
- ● Charcas 1622

Uppsala*

Baltic Sea

Aberdeen c. 1500
St. Andrews c. 1410
Glasgow 1451
Edinburgh 1582

Copenhagen 1475

Königsberg 1544

North Sea

Rostock 1419
Griefswald 1456

Groningen 1614

Frankfurt an der Oder 1506

Oxford 1190s
Cambridge 1233
Helmstedt 1575
Leiden 1575
Wittenberg 1502
Leipzig 1409
Erfurt 1379
Jena 1558
Cracow*

Cologne 1388
Louvain 1426
Marburg 1527

Trier 1473
Mainz 1476
Würzburg*
Prague 1348

Caen 1439
Heidelberg 1385
Ingolstadt 1472

Paris c. 1200
Strasbourg 1621
Tübingen 1472
Vienna 1365

Orleans c. 1235
Freiburg 1460

Nantes 1461
Angers 1229
Basel 1460

Bourges 1464
Dôle 1422

Poitiers 1431

ATLANTIC OCEAN

Padua 1222
Turin 1411
Pavia 1361

Bordeaux 1441
Grenoble 1339
Parma 1601
Ferrara*

Cahors 1332
Valence 1452
Bologna c. 1150–1200

Oviedo 1604
Toulouse 1229
Orange 1365
Avignon 1303
Florence*
Macerata 1540–1541

Montpellier 1220–1230
Pisa 1343
Siena c. 1240
Perugia 1308

Valladolid c. 1250
Huesca 1354
Perpignan 1379
Aix 1409

Salamanca*
Lérida 1300
Girona 1587
Rome 1240s

Sigüenza 1489
Saragossa 1583
Barcelona 1450
Naples 1224
Salerno c. 1592

Lisbon-Coimbra*
Acalá 1509

Valencia 1500
Palma 1483

Messina 1596
Catania 1445

Mediterranean Sea

N

| 0 | 100 | 200 mi. |
| 0 | 100 | 200 km |

Notes

Cracow: 1364, stopped 1370, renewed 1400
Ferrara: 1391, stopped 1402, renewed 1442
Florence: 1348, moved to Pisa 1473
Lisbon-Coimbra: 1290 at Lisbon; settled in Coimbra, 1537
Salamanca: 1400s
Uppsala: 1477, stopped 1515, renewed 1595
Würzburg: 1561–1583

UNIVERSITIES

The University of Paris was the largest European university of the Renaissance. This illustration from a French work of the early 1500s shows a gathering of Paris professors.

Universities also brought prestige to cities and their rulers by highlighting their commitment to learning. Many governments played an active role in higher education. They controlled the appointments and salaries of professors and the subjects taught. In many cases, they forbade citizens to study at foreign universities in order to increase enrollment at the local school. After the Protestant Reformation*, many towns set specific religious requirements for students and professors.

Structure. At all Renaissance universities, students attended lectures for several years and then took examinations to qualify for a degree. Receiving an advanced degree in a particular subject gave the student the right to teach it. A bachelor's degree in the arts required 1 to 3 years of study, a doctorate in law or medicine took 5 to 7 years, and a doctorate in theology required more than 12 years. In practice, some students graduated in less than the required time.

* **Protestant Reformation** religious movement that began in the 1500s as a protest against certain practices of the Roman Catholic Church and eventually led to the establishment of a variety of Protestant churches

All lectures, debates, and examinations were conducted in Latin. Professors focused on the great works in their field. For example, philosophy centered on the writings of ARISTOTLE and medicine on those of GALEN. Because of this uniformity in content, students could easily switch their studies from one university to another.

Some universities emphasized certain subjects and levels of training. Schools in Paris and Oxford focused on arts and theology. The Italian universities, by contrast, stressed law and medicine at the doctoral level. By the early 1400s they had completely ceased to offer bachelor's degrees. Universities also varied greatly in size. Paris, the largest, had 12,000 to 15,000 students and several hundred teachers. Large Italian universities boasted between 1,500 and 2,000 students and perhaps 100 professors. The typical university had 30 to 40 professors teaching 300 to 500 students.

Humanism. The influence of humanism* dramatically changed the course of studies at Renaissance universities. In the early 1400s professors began teaching ancient Latin and Greek texts and stressing the use of the original languages. For example, they read the works of Aristotle in Greek rather than relying on Latin translations from the Middle Ages. Some even produced new, more accurate Latin versions of these texts.

Humanist professors also considered texts in their historical context. Legal scholars, for instance, looked at Roman law against the background of ancient Roman society. French universities, in particular, favored this approach.

PROMINENT UNIVERSITIES

Three of the top universities of the Renaissance were Oxford University in England, the University of Paris, and the University of Padua in Italy. Founded in the Middle Ages, all three became major centers of scholarship and influenced intellectual activity across Europe.

Oxford. Formal lectures began at Oxford in the 1100s, and by 1310 the school had grown to some 2,000 students. During the Middle Ages, Oxford was largely free from government rule. The masters (teachers) elected their own head and voted on school regulations.

In the 1500s, however, the university lost most of its independence. At that time, the English king HENRY VIII became involved in a dispute with the Roman Catholic Church over his marriage to Catherine of Aragon. In 1530 the king asked Oxford for an opinion about the dispute, and the university hesitated to support him. When Henry broke with the church over the matter, Oxford found itself in an awkward position. As England became increasingly Protestant, Henry and his successors saw Oxford as a center of pro-Catholic feeling. They took measures to ensure that the university remained loyal to the English church. They also tried to control the curriculum. In 1570 Oxford lost the right to appoint its own leaders.

During the Renaissance Oxford's curriculum expanded, partly as a result of humanist influences. In the mid-1400s wealthy nobles introduced humanist ideas to Oxford by donating many books from their

* **humanism** Renaissance cultural movement promoting the study of the humanities (the languages, literature, and history of ancient Greece and Rome) as a guide to living

Student Nations

Beginning in the Middle Ages, university students formed themselves into groups called "nations" based on their homelands. Each nation elected a member to represent it to the host city. The University of Paris, for example, included four nations: France, Normandy, Picardy, and Germany. For a while, student nations exercised considerable power and were even able to help choose their own professors. However, during the Renaissance, the nations lost much of their influence. Civil governments took control of the appointment of professors and other aspects of universities.

* **ethics**   branch of philosophy concerned with questions of right and wrong

* **rhetoric**   art of speaking or writing effectively

libraries, especially Italian texts, to the school. Not long afterward, Oxford began hiring permanent lecturers to teach certain subjects, such as theology, in place of the recent graduates who had formerly served as teachers. During the 1600s the school added new professorships in several fields, including geometry, history, and Arabic.

Paris. The University of Paris included four faculties: arts, church law, medicine, and theology. Established around 1200, the school fell into a decline in the early 1400s. However, a series of reforms in the mid-1400s made it the best university in northern Europe.

Like Oxford, the University of Paris was caught up in the politics of the Protestant Reformation. Catholic clergy members controlled the course of study in Paris. They promoted a tradition known as Scholasticism, which stressed logic, natural philosophy, and ethics*. Humanist critics attacked this course of study. They called for the teaching of rhetoric* and ancient languages and literature. However, most members of the faculty opposed the humanists and warned against the dangers of allowing them to set the curriculum.

In 1521 the university condemned the teachings of the Protestant reformer Martin LUTHER. The king, FRANCIS I, who saw himself as a tolerant and cultured ruler, tried to protect humanists and religious reformers. He occasionally opposed the powerful Faculty of Theology, which had considerable influence over matters of faith. However, he also reacted against critics who went too far in attacking the Catholic Church. In 1543 Francis approved the Articles of Faith, a document that bound faculty members to uphold Catholicism. Despite reforms in the late 1500s that allowed new subjects in the curriculum, Scholastic thought dominated the University of Paris until the 1700s.

Padua. Founded in the 1200s, the University of Padua became the most famous university in Italy. Its importance grew after Venice conquered Padua in 1405. The leaders of Venice strongly supported the school in Padua. They decided that it would be the only university in the state and threatened to fine any Venetian who studied elsewhere.

After a drop in enrollment in the late 1400s, the state took measures to strengthen the school. They added professorships, raised salaries, recruited leading teachers from other universities, and restricted the number of local instructors on the faculty. These reforms helped keep key positions filled with distinguished scholars from around Europe.

The University of Padua suffered a severe setback in 1509, when the city's leaders briefly threw off Venetian rule. Professors and students fled the city, and the university closed down. It did not reopen until 1517, after Venice had recaptured Padua and all the other territory it had lost. The Venetians quickly rebuilt the school, and by the 1560s it boasted an enrollment of some 1,600 students.

Padua was particularly influential in the field of medicine. In 1537 the medical scholar Andreas VESALIUS came to the school to teach anatomy. Through techniques such as dissecting* human bodies, he revolutionized his field. Padua also established the first professorship in the study of "simples," or medicinal plants. In the 1540s it opened one of the first botanical gardens in Europe.

* **dissect**   to cut open a body to examine its inner parts

In addition to medicine, Padua had leading schools of natural philosophy (also known as natural science), law, and mathematics. Galileo GALILEI taught mathematics there from 1592 to 1610. Many famous thinkers studied at Padua, including Francesco GUICCIARDINI, Giovanni PICO DELLA MIRANDOLA, and Pier Paolo VERGERIO. The renowned German philosopher NICHOLAS OF CUSA obtained a doctorate from Padua in 1423. William HARVEY, the English scientist who discovered the circulation of blood, received his medical degree there in 1603. Other outstanding graduates hailed from Spain, Greece, Hungary, and even America. (*See also* **Academies; Classical Scholarship; Education; Humanism; Ideas, Spread of.**)

Urbanism

See *Cities and Urban Life.*

Urbino

See color plate 6, vol. 3

* **prince** Renaissance term for the ruler of an independent state

* **confraternity** religious and social organization of Roman Catholics who were not members of the clergy

The ancient Roman city of Urbino, located in central Italy, was an important administrative center in the Renaissance. In the 1400s the city enjoyed fame and great prosperity, due largely to the military reputation of the ruling princes* of the MONTEFELTRO FAMILY.

Urbino was a walled city that closed its gates at night. Officials divided the city into administrative quarters, each associated with particular crafts, religious orders, and confraternities*. The city's confined area and small population encouraged social unity.

When Count Antonio da Montefeltro became Urbino's ruler in 1375, he promised to uphold the city's laws. His pledge continued a tradition of self-rule with a council of elected citizens, subject to the prince. Citizenship was usually restricted to sons of citizens living in Urbino. The population also included a small community of Jews, who helped develop the city's commercial interests but had no citizenship rights.

For centuries the princes of Urbino came from the Montefeltro family. They commanded the military and supervised the city administration, holding public audiences to hear complaints and mediate disputes. The prince received a salary and dues of various kinds. He was expected to use some of his wealth for religious and civic buildings. Between 1465 and 1482, Duke Federico undertook extensive renovations in the city, and many of the city's leading families rebuilt their palaces in Renaissance style. After the death of the last Montefeltro prince in 1508, Urbino began a period of decline. (*See also* **Italy.**)

Utopias

In 1516 the English writer Thomas MORE published *Utopia,* his vision of an imaginary, ideal society. The book's title was a pun on Greek words meaning "no place" *(ou topia)* and "the good place" *(eu topia).* More's work became the first in a series of Renaissance texts that described various writers' ideas of the perfect society.

Utopias drew attention to the flaws of Renaissance states and offered visions of a better organized and more just society. Many Renaissance writers set their utopias in remote parts of the world, cut off from other societies. Their citizens tended to live highly ordered lives under the strict control of the government. Many utopias featured a communal lifestyle, with residents sharing all their property and raising their children as a group. Medieval* writers had also created portraits of ideal societies. These earlier visions depended either on a perfect world, in which nature provided everything humans could need, or on morally perfect human beings. More broke with these patterns and built his ideal state around institutions, such as law, government, and education, that would overcome the flaws of imperfect humans in an imperfect world. These institutions would control every aspect of life, keeping wealth, status, work, food, dress, leisure, marriage, and the household much the same for all citizens. The social structures of More's Utopia programmed its residents to be virtuous and dealt with those who strayed.

Two other major works about the idea of a utopia came in the 1600s. Italian writer Tommaso CAMPANELLA based his *The City of the Sun* (1623) on the idea that no one should own property. According to his views, private ownership damaged society by placing personal concerns above those of the group. Campanella's ideal city also rested on a perfect understanding of the natural world. All scientific knowledge was carved on the city's walls, eliminating the need for any further research. In Francis BACON's *The New Atlantis* (1627), by contrast, science was an ongoing and powerful activity. Scientific research had the power to reshape the relationship between society and the natural environment, thus changing the nature of the utopia itself. The power of science in society was a major theme in utopian writings of the late Renaissance.

Some utopias had strong religious elements. For instance, *Christianopolis* (1619), by Lutheran pastor Johann Valentin Andreae, addressed the problem of building a godly community in a sinful world. His answer centered on education as the force that held society together. Other utopias focused on designing the ideal constitution and government. In *Oceana* (1656), one of the last great utopian texts of the Renaissance, author John Harrington defined military service as the path to citizenship. In his utopia, all men between the ages of 18 and 30 followed a detailed course of military service. Harrington's state also featured elaborate structures at every level of government.

Valla, Lorenzo

1407–1457
Italian scholar and humanist

Lorenzo Valla, a central figure of the humanist* movement in Italy, focused his attention chiefly on the subjects of religion and language. Valla's writings greatly advanced the study of classical* Latin, the language of ancient Rome. They also encouraged the re-examination of many religious traditions dating from the late Middle Ages.

Born to a minor noble family in Rome, Valla studied under many of the Greek and Latin scholars who served at the court of Pope Martin V. At the age of 20 Valla produced his first scholarly work, a comparison of the ancient Roman writers Cicero and Quintilian. Valla favored Quintilian's detailed, grammar-based approach to rhetoric*. However, his support of Quintilian angered followers of Cicero, including the

* **classical**   in the tradition of ancient Greece and Rome

* **rhetoric**   art of speaking or writing effectively

* **philology**   scholarly study of language

* **papacy**   office and authority of the pope

* **heresy**   belief that is contrary to the doctrine of an established church

scholar Poggio Bracciolini. Poggio became a lifelong critic of Valla and influenced the pope not to employ him in his Curia (the body that aided the pope in governing the Roman Catholic Church).

Valla took up a career teaching rhetoric. He spent time in several Italian cities, including Naples, where he served at the court of Alfonso of Aragon, king of Naples and Sicily. There he completed one of his major works, *The Elegances of the Latin Language* (printed in 1471, after his death). This text analyzed the Latin tongue in detail and praised its immense variety. Valla stressed the importance of Latin as the basis for Europe's high level of civilization. He claimed that recovering the language in its ancient form would revive cultures that had fallen into decay during the Middle Ages. This emphasis on language has led some scholars to call Valla the founder of philology*.

In 1439 Valla completed the first version of another work on language that would come to be known as the *Dialectica*. This text challenged the views of the ancient Greek thinker ARISTOTLE, whose works had formed the basis of scholarship throughout the Middle Ages. Aristotle's philosophy had centered on abstract ideas such as "the good" and "the true." Valla, by contrast, focused on the concept of *verba et res,* or words and things. Thus, his work made grammar and rhetoric central to the study of philosophy. The *Dialectica* greatly influenced many later humanists, including Angelo POLIZIANO and Desiderius ERASMUS.

The following year Valla issued two works attacking powerful church institutions. The first revealed that the Donation of Constantine, an ancient document used by the papacy* to defend its political powers, was actually a FORGERY. The second criticized the idea that members of RELIGIOUS ORDERS had a better claim to salvation than ordinary Christians. Outrage over these works caused Pope Eugenius IV to ban Valla from Rome and investigate him for heresy*. Valla made a formal apology to the pope and earned the right to return to Rome in 1447. That same year, Eugenius died and the humanist NICHOLAS V became the new pope. Nicholas welcomed Valla back to his beloved Rome and showered him with honors and church offices. Valla remained in Rome until his death, writing texts on religion and translations of ancient Greek works. (*See also* **Classical Scholarship; Humanism; Latin Language and Literature; Logic.**)

Valois Dynasty

The ruling dynasty of France during much of the Renaissance, the Valois gained the throne in 1328 when the last king of the Capetian dynasty died without an heir. Philip of Valois, a cousin of the king, took the throne as Philip VI. Another cousin with a claim to the French throne, Edward III of England, challenged the legitimacy of the Valois. In 1337 he declared war, launching the Hundred Years' War between England and France.

After driving the English from most of France in 1453, the Valois king Louis XI focused attention on the dukes of BURGUNDY, his cousins and rivals. The rivalry lasted for decades. To protect themselves against France, the Burgundians made a number of marriage alliances with the

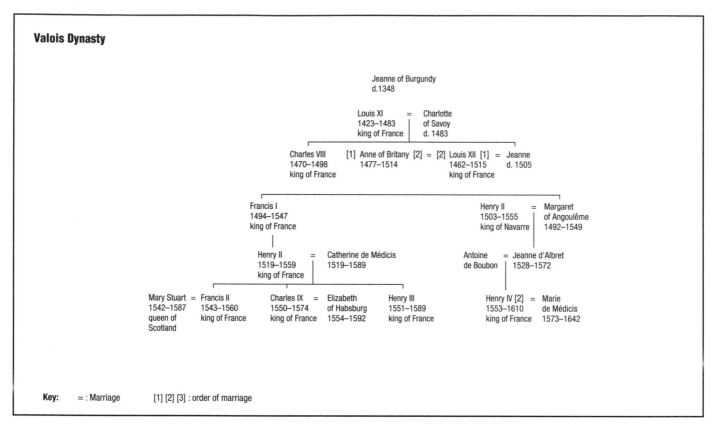

Valois Dynasty

Key: = : Marriage   [1] [2] [3] : order of marriage

* **duchy**   territory ruled by a duke or duchess

* **Holy Roman Emperor**   ruler of the Holy Roman Empire, a political body in central Europe composed of several states that existed until 1806

* **patron**   supporter or financial sponsor of an artist or writer

* **humanist**   Renaissance expert in the humanities (the languages, literature, history, and speech and writing techniques of ancient Greece and Rome)

HABSBURG DYNASTY. The family ties eventually led to hostility between the Valois and the Habsburgs. In the late 1400s and early 1500s, the Valois kings Charles VIII and Louis XII invaded Italy to assert French claims to the kingdom of NAPLES and the duchy* of MILAN. In response, Pope JULIUS II organized an alliance in 1509 known as the Holy League, which expelled the French from Italy by 1514.

Hostility between the Valois and Habsburg dynasties intensified during the reigns of FRANCIS I, successor to Louis XII, and the Holy Roman Emperor* CHARLES V. Francis I launched another invasion of Italy in 1515. His victory at Marignano restored Milan to French rule but provoked another round of fighting with Charles V. At the Battle of Pavia in 1525, Francis I was captured and held for ransom. He won his release the following year after promising to surrender Burgundy to Charles. Francis broke his word, however, and warfare resumed. It did not end until his death in 1547. Renaissance culture in France reached a peak under Francis I, who was a patron* of numerous artists, architects, and humanists*.

Henry II, Francis's son, had been married at age 14 to CATHERINE DE MÉDICIS in an effort to forge an alliance with the Medici pope. About a decade into his reign, Henry sent French forces back to Italy. King PHILIP II of Spain, son of Charles V, responded by invading northern France in 1557. However, concern over the spread of Protestantism led the two monarchs to make peace in 1559.

During the reign of Francis II, son of Henry II, control of the French monarchy fell into the hands of the Guise family, who were fervent Catholics. Many French nobles, including the BOURBON FAMILY, felt excluded from power and joined with French Protestants against the Guise. Four decades of civil war followed, and the worst mark against the Valois family occurred during this period. In 1572, during the rule of Charles IX, Catholic forces killed several thousand Huguenots* and others in the St. Bartholomew's Day massacre.

Henry III, the brother of Charles IX, took the throne in 1574. The best educated of the Valois kings, Henry sought a compromise between Catholics and Protestants. However, in 1584 Henry's brother and only heir died, leaving the Huguenot prince Henry of Bourbon next in line to the throne. Catholic forces took steps to prevent the Huguenot from becoming king. When Henry III tried to oppose them, he was forced out of Paris and later assassinated. His death in 1589 marked the end of the Valois dynasty, which had played such a significant role in shaping the French nation and monarchy. (*See also* **Dynastic Rivalry; France; Guise-Lorraine Family; Wars of Italy; Wars of Religion.**)

* **Huguenot** French Protestant of the 1500s and 1600s, follower of John Calvin

Vega Carpio, Lope Félix de

1562–1635
Spanish writer

The Spanish author Lope Félix de Vega Carpio was one of the most productive writers of the Renaissance. With hundreds of titles to his credit, he produced works in nearly every literary style of his time. Lope played a major role in transforming Spanish theater during the Renaissance, creating the popular "new theater" that drew large crowds to open-air performances in the city of Madrid.

A Dramatic Life. As a child, Lope composed poetry even before he could write. By age 5 he could read Latin as well as his native language, Castilian. He wrote his first play at the age of 12. At age 14 Lope attended the University of Alcalá, and at 21 he joined a military expedition to the Azores, a group of islands owned by Portugal in the north Atlantic Ocean. In 1588 Lope was banished from Madrid for eight years for libel* after circulating satiric* verses that attacked his former lover, the married daughter of a producer-director, and her family. He returned to Madrid illegally, however, and had his sentence lifted after serving seven years.

During his exile Lope became familiar with several dramatists from Valencia in eastern Spain. Their influence led Lope to introduce several innovations to theater in Madrid that challenged the classical* principles of the earlier Renaissance. Lope discussed these changes in his book *New Art of Playwriting in this Kingdom,* published in 1609. In one of the work's most important passages, Lope defended tragicomedy—the use of comic scenes, characters, and subplots in tragic plays.

Literary Achievements. At least 314 plays written by Lope have survived. Scholars have grouped these works into several broad, overlapping categories based on their themes and source material. One major grouping is Lope's honor plays, such as *The Sheep-Well.* This "peasant

* **libel** leveling false charges against someone, especially in writing

* **satiric** involving the use of satire, the ridicule of human wickedness and foolishness in a literary or artistic work

* **classical** in the tradition of ancient Greece and Rome

* **medieval** referring to the Middle Ages, a period that began around A.D. 400 and ended around 1400 in Italy and 1500 in the rest of Europe

* **adultery** sexual relationship outside of marriage

* **epic** long poem about the adventures of a hero

* **sonnet** poem of 14 lines with a fixed pattern of meter and rhyme

* **pastoral** relating to the countryside; often used to draw a contrast between the innocence and serenity of rural life and the corruption and extravagance of court life

honor play," based on an actual peasant uprising from the 1300s, celebrates revenge as an effective way to resolve questions of honor.

Historical dramas form another large group. Many of Lope's most powerful plays dramatized scenes from medieval* Castilian history, using such sources as legends and ballads. Examples include *The Knight from Olmedo,* based on a popular ballad about the murder of a young man by the servants of his rival, and *Punishment Without Vengeance,* a tragedy about the murder of a young wife who has committed adultery*. In a more comic vein, Lope wrote many cloak-and-sword plays, drawing on a long tradition of humorous dramas about secret schemes that dates back to the ancient Roman authors Plautus and Terence. Many of these, such as *The Prudent Woman in Love* and *Loving Without Knowing Whom,* ridicule the customs and prejudices of Spanish society in Lope's time.

Along with his plays, Lope wrote poetry in a variety of different forms. Unlike his fairly brief three-act plays, Lope's epics* gave him an opportunity to write in a grand, dramatic style. He based some of these long poems on earlier works by other poets. For instance, *Angelica's Beauty* continued the plot of Ludovico Ariosto's *Orlando Furioso* (Mad Roland), while *Jerusalem Regained* was a response to Torquato Tasso's *Jerusalem Delivered.* Lope also produced love sonnets*, popular ballads such as "Poor Little Boat of Mine," and extensive prose works, which often included large portions of verse. His *La Arcadia,* published in 1598, was the last major Spanish pastoral* novel. (*See also* **Drama, Spanish; Spanish Language and Literature.**)

Venice

* **republic** form of Renaissance government dominated by leading merchants with limited participation by others

See color plate 1, vol. 3

* **duchy** territory controlled by a duke or duchess

The republic* of Venice, one of the major powers of Renaissance Italy, built an extensive land and sea empire in the eastern Mediterranean. It became known for its distinctive form of government, stable society, and brilliant cultural achievements. When political turmoil and foreign invasions swept across the Italian peninsula during the 1400s and 1500s, Venice was the only state that remained independent.

The Venetian Empire. Venice was settled in the 500s and 600s by refugees from the Italian mainland. They built communities on mudflats and sandbanks in a lagoon off Italy's northeastern coast. By 1000 these communities had united to form a city ruled by an elected official (called a doge) and councils of merchants. Venetian traders sold fish and salt to towns along the coast and, later, to ports around the Mediterranean Sea.

As its commerce expanded, Venice became locked in rivalry with GENOA, another Italian trading city. The two went to war in 1379–1380. The Venetian admirals emerged victorious, and the city continued to dominate commerce in the Mediterranean.

After triumphing over Genoa, the Venetians expanded into northeastern Italy. The move brought Venice into conflict with the duchy* of MILAN.

In 1455 Pope NICHOLAS V attempted to avert war by forming the Italian League, an alliance that established a balance of power among Italy's five major states: Venice, Milan, Naples, Florence, and the Papal States.

Venice angered other members of the Italian League with its efforts to expand its territory and its trade routes. In 1508 the other Italian powers joined France, Spain, the Holy Roman Empire*, and the pope in a campaign to seize some of Venice's territories. Despite the forces joined against them, the Venetians resisted the takeover, and Venice emerged with its city and empire intact. By 1530 Venice was the only Italian city-state to remain a great and independent power.

Another challenge to Venice's rule came from the Ottoman Empire*, which had begun seizing Mediterranean lands in the mid-1400s. At first, Venice negotiated with the Ottomans to continue trading. Then, in 1571 the Venetians joined other European states to defeat the Ottoman navy in the Battle of Lepanto. In the late 1500s and early 1600s, Venice's maritime* empire declined in importance. European voyages to the Americas, along with growing demand for products such as sugar and tobacco, shifted the center of trade from the Mediterranean to the Atlantic.

Government. Venice was both a city and a nation. Its unique form of government combined features of monarchy, aristocracy*, and republic. The head of state, the doge, was elected through an elaborate series of committees designed to prevent any particular group from controlling the office. Every year the doge led official processions and performed ceremonies, such as casting a ring into the lagoon to symbolize Venice's marriage to the sea.

Venice's upper class kept a tight rein on the doge's powers through three councils—the Great Council, the Senate, and the Council of Ten—and many lesser councils. The Great Council consisted of the adult male members of the nobility. In 1297 membership on the Great Council was limited to the prosperous merchant families that made up the Venetian nobility. The Great Council elected most officials, including the doge, and made laws. The Senate, a smaller council, supervised ambassadors and city officials and managed the growth of the empire. The Council of Ten was responsible for state security. It became increasingly important in the late 1400s, and by the 1600s some considered its members the real rulers of Venice.

The Venetian government also included many lesser councils and committees. Only nobles could hold government office, but educated members of the middle class could serve as government secretaries. This group gained considerable status and was regarded as second only to the nobles.

Society. The nobility shaped civic life in Venice. Some nobles devoted themselves to political careers, leaving commerce to other family members. The wealthiest noble families built grand palaces and supported the arts.

* **Holy Roman Empire** political body in central Europe composed of several states; existed until 1806

* **Ottoman Empire** Islamic empire founded by Ottoman Turks in the 1300s that reached the height of its power in the 1500s; it eventually included large areas of eastern Europe, the Middle East, and northern Africa

* **maritime** relating to the sea or shipping

* **aristocracy** privileged upper classes of society; nobles or the nobility

The Myth of Venice

In civic ceremonies, letters, and art, Venetians promoted an image that historians call "the myth of Venice." The image portrayed Venice as ideally organized, well governed, peaceful, and productive. Citizens called Venice La Serenissima (the most serene—untroubled—republic). The myth was mostly true. Although Venice had crime, greed, and corruption, it did not have social conflicts, and its citizens did not try to overthrow the government.

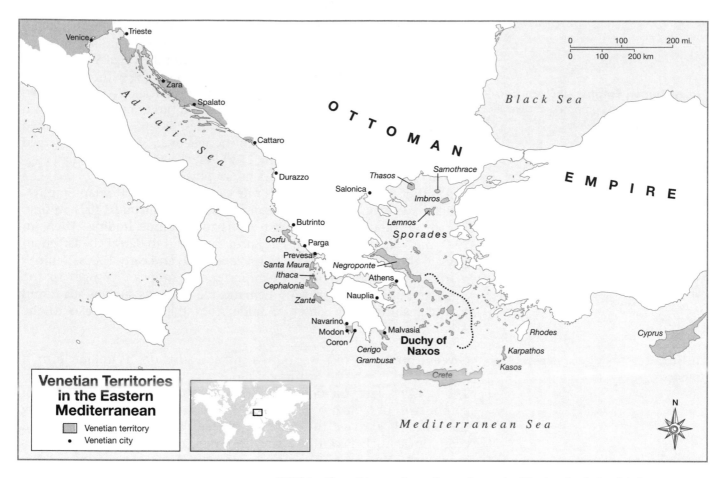

Venetian Territories in the Eastern Mediterranean

- Venetian territory
- Venetian city

Within the citizen class, those born in Venice had the highest status. Although citizens could not hold political office, they could freely pursue wealth. Many belonged to confraternities* called *scuole,* which provided fellowship as well as opportunities to display one's wealth and perform good deeds. The *scuole* commissioned artists to decorate their meeting halls and appeared in civic processions. They also took the lead in aiding the poor, providing money for orphans, widows, and others in need.

Venice had numerous professional and neighborhood organizations. Many artisans*, such as silkworkers and glassblowers, belonged to craft guilds*. The workers at Venice's immense shipbuilding center also joined guilds. Venice's neighborhood associations centered on the parish churches. Within each parish, special ceremonies strengthened neighborhood ties.

The Venetian government fought crime by closely supervising residents and promptly punishing wrongdoers. Criminals were fined, banished from the city, or executed. Justice was not uniform, however. Crimes against nobles were often punished with extra harshness, while crimes committed by nobles received light punishment.

Venice's many foreign residents formed organizations of their own. In the Greek and Slav communities, the churches served as both spiri-

Shipbuilding was a major industry in Venice. The Venetian Arsenal, shown here, was a complex of shipyards where several thousand builders assembled vessels with great speed and skill. It was the foremost technological center of its time, larger than any other industrial complex in the world.

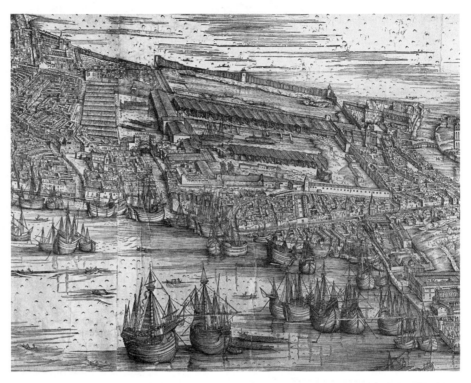

tual and social centers. German and Turkish merchants lived near the Rialto, the city's commercial center. After 1516 the Jews of Venice had to live within a closed, gated neighborhood called the ghetto, the first such confinement of Jews to a segregated neighborhood. Within the ghetto they followed their own laws and customs.

Religion and Culture. Religion played a major role in Venetian life. The primarily Roman Catholic city was filled with churches and had many priests, friars, and nuns. Venice took particular pride in its relics*, especially the body of St. Mark, the city's patron saint.

At the same time, however, Venice held itself apart from the papacy*. The Venetian Senate, not the pope, appointed the bishops and other major clergy of the city's mainland territories. Venice itself had no bishop. The city's highest-ranking religious officials were the clergy at the church of San Marco, which was attached to the doge's palace. Venice was also home to many heretics*. Individuals who wanted to obtain the writings of reformist thinkers such as Martin LUTHER and Desiderius ERASMUS could do so easily in Venice.

The nobles who governed Venice dominated its intellectual life. Most young nobles attended the nearby University of Padua. Venetian humanists* tended to be members of the upper class or to work for noble patrons. They discussed many popular subjects, but rarely addressed ideas such as political liberty, which might have threatened the ruling class.

* **relics**   pieces of bone, possessions, or other items belonging to a saint or sacred person

* **papacy**   office and authority of the pope

* **heretic**   person who rejects the doctrine of an established church

* **humanist**   Renaissance expert in the humanities (the languages, literature, history, and speech and writing techniques of ancient Greece and Rome)

* **classical** in the tradition of ancient Greece and Rome

Foreign humanists who came to Venice seeking employment could teach or could work in the city's printing industry. By 1500 the city had become Europe's major publishing center. Free-spirited and sophisticated, Venice was a magnet for writers of all sorts. Poetry, drama, and classical* studies flourished. In the 1500s many women writers lived and worked in Venice, including the humanist Cassandra Fedele and the poets Gaspara Stampa and Veronica Franco.

Venice produced many important artists during the Renaissance, including TITIAN, TINTORETTO, and the members of the BELLINI FAMILY. In addition, the city was itself widely regarded as a work of art, shimmering on the waters of the lagoon, adorned with hundreds of churches and palaces. Artists from all over Europe visited Venice to paint the magical cityscape. (*See also* **Art in Italy; Italy.**)

Vergerio, Pier Paolo

ca.1369–1444
Italian humanist

* **humanist** Renaissance expert in the humanities (the languages, literature, history, and speech and writing techniques of ancient Greece and Rome)

* **rhetoric** art of speaking or writing effectively

* **treatise** long, detailed essay

Pier Paolo Vergerio was one of the leading humanists* of his generation. His ideas on education influenced European thinkers for centuries. He placed a great deal of stress on skillful public speaking, an idea that became central to the humanist movement.

Vergerio was born in a small Italian town on the Gulf of Trieste. He received a degree in the arts from the University of Bologna and then spent seven years studying medicine and law at the University of Padua. In Bologna Vergerio developed an interest in the art of rhetoric* and in the best methods for educating young adults. In 1400 he laid out his ideas on the subject in a short treatise* on education. That work spelled out a new method of teaching adolescents that helped change the course of education in Europe.

Vergerio based his program on three core disciplines: history, moral philosophy, and rhetoric. He saw these subjects as the key to developing good moral character and sound political judgment. Moral philosophy, he claimed, taught students good values. History provided examples to illustrate these values. Finally, rhetoric offered the means to persuade others to make moral decisions in the political realm. Vergerio's program was widely copied by later educators. It formed the basis of European educational theory for many generations.

* **Holy Roman Emperor** ruler of the Holy Roman Empire, a political body in central Europe composed of several states that existed until 1806

Vergerio also influenced many people through his speeches and sermons. He defended the ideals of humanism and sought to heal divisions within the Roman Catholic Church. Vergerio spent the final years of his career in the service of the Holy Roman Emperor* Sigismund, retiring from public service after the emperor's death in 1437. He died in Hungary seven years later (*See also* **Education; Humanism.**)

Veronese, Paolo

1528–1588
Venetian painter

* **allegorical** referring to a literary or artistic device in which characters, events, and settings represent abstract qualities and in which the author intends a different meaning to be read beneath the surface

* **foreshortening** technique that involves changing the proportions of figures or objects to make them appear to be three-dimensional

Venetian painter Paolo Veronese, most renowned for his colorful, dramatic ceiling paintings, changed his artistic style towards the end of his career. His later works, such as this painting of a warrior from the 1570s, have darker, more expressive backgrounds than his earlier paintings.

Along with TITIAN and TINTORETTO, Paolo Veronese was one of the dominant Venetian painters in the late 1500s. Born Paolo Caliari in Verona, Italy, the painter became known as Veronese in honor of his native city. He gained a reputation as a master of ceiling painting, often of biblical or allegorical* subjects. These ceilings are notable for their dramatic treatment of space achieved through color and foreshortening*.

Veronese came from a family of stonecutters but turned to painting and studied with local masters. His family's craft may have influenced the artist, whose paintings reveal a strong sense of architectural form and space. His earliest works, dating from about 1546, are marked by sensitive brushwork and clarity of color. His figures, inspired partly by the Italian artist PARMIGIANINO, are elegant in style.

In 1551 Veronese ventured beyond Verona to paint fresco decorations for buildings in Venice. He moved to Venice permanently in 1553 to work on ceilings for rooms in the Ducal Palace. Veronese's skill as a designer of ceiling paintings flourished in Venice, with major projects for the church of San Sebastiano and the Library of St. Mark (Biblioteca Marciana). His allegorical painting of *Music* for the library earned Veronese the prize of a gold chain. For other churches and religious buildings in Venice, the artist created remarkable paintings that portray biblical feasts in monumental architectural settings. One of these works, a painting of the *Last Supper,* brought Veronese before the Venetian Inquisition to answer charges of including inappropriate subject matter—specifically dwarfs, drunkards, and other vulgar characters—in this sacred scene. The artist changed the title of the work to *Feast in the House of Levi.*

Veronese had a number of important patrons, including the prominent humanist writer Daniele Barbaro. From the beginning of his career in Venice, the artist also worked for the state in the continuing decoration of the Ducal Palace, most notably the Hall of the College (Sala del Collegio). The allegorical ceiling paintings for the room celebrate the power, prestige, and righteousness of the Venetian Republic.

Toward the end of Veronese's career, his painting became more Venetian in style. While still notable for clarity of color and fine brushwork, the artists later works have a darker, more expressive background. For many years Veronese ran a large family workshop. After the artist's death in 1588, his brother and sons continued the workshop, signing the works produced there *Haeredes Pauli* (heirs of Paolo). (*See also* **Art in Italy.**)

Verrocchio, Andrea del

ca. 1435–1488
Italian artist

See color
plate 4,
vol. 1

* **baptistery**   building where baptisms
are performed

* **mercenary**   hired soldier

* **altarpiece**   work of art that decorates
the altar of a church

Andrea di Michele di Francesco Cione, known as Andrea del Verrocchio, was a leading Florentine goldsmith, sculptor, and painter. Many younger artists, including LEONARDO DA VINCI, learned their craft in Verrocchio's workshop. As a sculptor, Verrocchio bridged the gap between DONATELLO and MICHELANGELO.

Verrocchio trained as a goldsmith before turning to sculpture. His first major sculptural work, the *Incredulity of St. Thomas* (ca. 1466–1483), was purchased by the merchants' court of Florence to replace a statue by Donatello. The large bronze piece shows the figures of Christ and the saint united in a dramatic way.

Verrocchio produced a number of important projects for the MEDICI family. In 1472 he completed a Medici tomb in the church of San Lorenzo in Florence. The sculptor's early training as a goldsmith can be seen in his treatment of the tomb's elegantly carved leaves. Verrocchio's work for the Medici includes two bronze statues: *David* and *Putto [infant boy] with a Dolphin.* The surfaces of both are finely carved with delicately worked details.

Verrocchio's concern with detail and surface texture appears in *Beheading of the Baptist,* a small silver sculpture for the Florentine baptistery*. The work reveals the artist's skill in depicting facial expressions. His busts (statues of head and shoulders) reflect the same skill. In *Lady Holding Flowers* (late 1470s), the beautifully carved features and graceful hands give the subject a noble air. Verrocchio's inclusion of the arms and hands was something new in Renaissance busts. About 1479 the artist received a commission from the city of Venice for a statue of the prominent mercenary* Bartolomeo Colleoni on horseback. The fierce expression on Colleoni's face and the horse's raised hoof give the imposing bronze monument a sense of menace. Verrocchio did not complete the work before his death.

In his own time Verrocchio was highly regarded as a painter as well as a sculptor. However, art historians have discovered that some pictures traditionally associated with Verrocchio were painted, entirely or in part, by others. Leonardo da Vinci touched up Verrocchio's *Baptism of Christ.* An altarpiece* in Pistoia Cathedral, long thought to have been painted by Verrocchio, is mostly the work of one of his pupils. Yet as both painter and teacher, Verrocchio influenced many central Italian artists, including Sandro BOTTICELLI, Pietro PERUGINO, and Domenico Ghirlandaio. (*See also* **Art; Art in Italy.**)

Vesalius, Andreas

1514–1564
Belgian anatomist

* **apothecary**   pharmacist

* **Holy Roman Emperor**   ruler of the
Holy Roman Empire, a political body in
central Europe composed of several
states that existed until 1806

Andreas Vesalius of Belgium made important contributions to MEDICINE, both as a physician-surgeon and as an anatomist (one who studies anatomy). His research on anatomy transformed the study of the human body. However, he made his greatest impact on science through his systematic method of collecting data, which he used to test the theories of earlier medical scholars.

Born in Brussels, Vesalius was the son of an apothecary* in the service of Holy Roman Emperor* CHARLES V. He attended school in Brussels and at the nearby University of Louvain, then went on to study medi-

* **dissect** to cut open a body to examine its inner parts

cine at the Universities of Paris and Padua. Vesalius became a professor of surgery at Padua, charged with performing human dissections*. The notes of a student who attended his first dissection are still preserved.

Before long, Vesalius gained a reputation as an excellent teacher and an expert anatomist. In 1538 he worked with an artist to produce a set of anatomical charts of the human body. These were based mainly on the ideas of GALEN, an ancient Greek physician whose writings had become the basis of medical theory in Europe. Galen, however, had dissected only animals, and many of his theories did not apply to human anatomy. A few years later, after gaining more experience in human dissection, Vesalius abandoned Galen's doctrines. He began preparing his own great work on anatomy, *On the Structure of the Human Body,* which he published in 1543.

Vesalius's text ran more than 650 pages and offered a complete study of the human body. Its most striking feature was its illustrations, created by draftsmen from the studio of the artist TITIAN in Venice. These included a series of 14 images showing the stages in the dissection of a muscle. Because the *Structure* was a vast technical work, Vesalius also issued a much shorter and simpler text on anatomy, the *Epitome.* Designed for medical students and readers with little or no knowledge of anatomy, the *Epitome* quickly became popular.

The *Structure* not only increased knowledge of the human body but also had a lasting influence on Renaissance science in general. Vesalius argued that the only reliable way to understand anatomy was to study the body directly. Because bodies tend to vary, the anatomist had to study many individuals before forming a theory or doctrine. Thus, Vesalius set out the basic scientific principle that an experiment must be repeated many times to confirm its results.

After publishing the *Structure,* Vesalius entered the service of Charles V. In addition to treating the emperor's many illnesses, he visited medical schools while traveling around the empire. He also continued to conduct dissections and developed several new surgical techniques. In 1555, Vesalius prepared a revised edition of the *Structure.* Soon after, he joined the court of Charles's son, PHILIP II, king of Spain and the Netherlands. In 1564 he made a long voyage, most likely a pilgrimage to the Holy Land. Shipwrecked during the return trip, Vesalius died from exhaustion on an island off the coast of Greece. (*See also* **Anatomy.**)

Vespucci, Amerigo

See *Exploration.*

Vienna

* **Holy Roman Empire** political body in central Europe composed of several states; existed until 1806

The Austrian city of Vienna was more influential during the Renaissance as a center of learning than as a showcase of the visual arts. Its artistic and architectural significance lagged behind its political importance as the chief city, and sometimes official residence, of the HABSBURGS who ruled the Holy Roman Empire*.

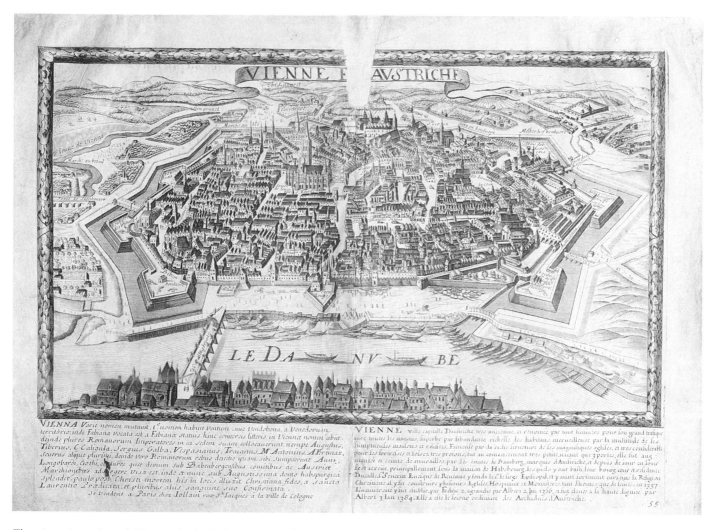

The Austrian city of Vienna lacked the resources to adopt new Renaissance styles of art and architecture. It remained a medieval walled city and expanded its defensive fortifications, as shown in this aerial view from the 1600s.

---

* **patron**   supporter or financial sponsor of an artist or writer

* **humanism**   Renaissance cultural movement promoting the study of the humanities (the languages, literature, and history of ancient Greece and Rome) as a guide to living

* **medieval**   referring to the Middle Ages, a period that began around A.D. 400 and ended around 1400 in Italy and 1500 in the rest of Europe

In the 1400s and early 1500s, Habsburg rulers undertook few major building projects in Vienna. Some had little interest in the city; others spent most of their time in other parts of the realm. Emperor RUDOLF II, an important patron* of Renaissance humanism* and painting, established his court in PRAGUE rather than Vienna.

Emperor FERDINAND I did some remodeling of the Hofburg palace in Vienna, and he built a graceful building on the palace grounds that was to be a residence for his oldest son, the future emperor MAXIMILIAN II. For his part, Maximilian II began several ambitious building projects, but completed little. Aside from some modest decorative features that reflected Renaissance style, Vienna remained a medieval* walled city.

Vienna also lacked wealthy citizens who could support Renaissance art and architecture. The city had been a trading center in the Middle Ages, but it no longer attracted much commerce. European trade patterns had shifted west, largely because of the threat of expansion by the Ottoman Turks* into southeastern Europe. As a result, instead of graceful Renaissance buildings, the city saw the expansion of defensive FORTIFICATIONS.

Although Vienna did not become a center of Renaissance art, it played a significant role in the new Renaissance learning. Its university, founded in 1365, was the second oldest in central Europe and attracted major scholars. Important work took place there in the natural sciences and in the development of instruments of measurement. Studies by university scholars on eclipses and calendars proved to be of great value to navigators of the time, such as Vasco da GAMA and Christopher COLUMBUS.

Vienna and its Habsburg rulers welcomed humanist writers and scholars. In 1497 Emperor MAXIMILIAN I established a special position at the university for Conrad CELTIS, the German poet. Celtis formed a literary society and brought various talented friends and students to Vienna. All of these individuals were greatly influenced by NICHOLAS OF CUSA, one of the leading philosophers and religious writers of the period.

Vienna became a major center of musical and theatrical life as well. Maximilian I hired some of the most prominent musicians and composers of the age for his court chapel, and his successors carried on this tradition. Maximilian was also an enthusiastic patron of the theater. Lavish productions of plays by ancient Greek and Roman writers were performed regularly, many with music, dance, and elaborate costumes. During the 1500s Catholic and Protestant groups used drama to bring the message of moral reform to Vienna's citizens, presenting biblical stories with local twists. (*See also* **Architecture; Austria; German Language and Literature.**)

Vignola, Giacomo Barozzi da

1507–1573
Italian architect and theorist

* **classical**   in the tradition of ancient Greece and Rome

* **perspective**   artistic technique for creating the illusion of three-dimensional space on a flat surface

* **papacy**   office and authority of the pope

* **villa**   luxurious country home and the land surrounding it

Giacomo Barozzi da Vignola was one of the most inventive and influential architects of the Renaissance. Vignola's lasting contribution, however, comes from his two famous texts on architecture. One of them, *The Five Orders of Architecture* (1562), is a practical manual on the decoration of classical* columns. The other, *Two Rules of Practical Perspective*, remains the most authoritative summary of perspective* theory of the 1500s.

Born to a family of artists in a small village in central Italy, Vignola was trained as a painter in Bologna. He excelled in drawing and perspective and began to study architecture, probably with Baldassare PERUZZI. By 1538 Vignola was working in Rome as an assistant on the redesign of St. Peter's church. He also produced drawings of ancient Roman ruins and made bronze replicas of ancient statues for King FRANCIS I of France, an activity that took him to France in 1541.

Returning to Bologna in 1543, Vignola was the architect of San Petronio church, and he redesigned the city's canal. In 1550 he went to Rome as architect to Pope JULIUS III, beginning two decades of almost continuous service to the papacy*. From 1565 until his death, Vignola directed work on St. Peter's. He also became architect for the House of FARNESE, for which he designed and decorated a magnificent villa*.

Vignola was the leading architect in Rome after MICHELANGELO. His buildings and writings exerted considerable influence on architects in Rome and throughout Europe. Vignola developed a forceful and original style based on the Renaissance principles, featuring restrained decoration and a clear, uncluttered design. Among his most famous works are the Villa Giulia, built for Julius III, the Palazzo Farnese, and the church of Il Gesù in Rome. (*See also* **Architecture.**)

Villon, François

1431–ca. 1463
French poet

* **stanza** section of a poem; specifically, a grouping of lines into a recurring pattern determined by meter or rhyme scheme

François Villon, the last major poet of the Middle Ages in France, attracted much admiration from French writers of the Renaissance. Clément Marot called him the greatest Parisian poet, and François RABELAIS quoted him in two of his own works. Villon wove elements from his own difficult life into his two major works, *Lais* and *Testament*.

Villon was born into a poor family and raised by a clergyman, whose name the poet adopted in 1456. This father figure helped Villon attend the University of Paris, where he received his bachelor's and master's degrees. In Paris Villon apparently fell in with some bad company and became involved in crime. He killed a man who had attacked him with a dagger, stole money from the College of Navarre, went to prison for another unidentified crime, and finally received a death sentence for his involvement in another fight. He escaped death in exchange for ten years of exile, and three days later he disappeared from Paris forever.

As a poet Villon was known for his biting humor, especially in his two major works: *Lais* (1456) and *Testament* (1462). In the 40 stanzas* of *Lais*, Villon painted himself as a wounded lover who, because his love is not returned, must leave town. The poet leaves his few belongings, such as his trousers and hair clippings, to his friends and fellow citizens. Villon's masterpiece, *Testament,* also deals with giving away possessions. In this lengthy work, which combines 158 stanzas of poetry with 16 ballads and three shorter poems, the poet looks back on his lost youth, poor background, and uncertain future as he makes his will. Villon's sarcastic wit appears in such details as the main character's decision to leave his glasses to the blind. In more thoughtful moments, the author reflects on himself and other victims of love, poverty, and time. *Testament* even has moments of tender sympathy, as when the poet leaves his most powerful gift, his poetic voice, to those who are not heard, such as his mother or an aging prostitute. (*See also* **French Language and Literature.**)

Violence

Violence against people and property was commonplace during the Renaissance. Society held conflicting attitudes about violent acts. It approved of some forms of violence, such as war and physical punishments for crimes, but punished other forms, including murder and rape. Still other types of violence, such as duels and feuds, were technically illegal but still widespread.

Violence could break out anywhere, but cities were generally safer than the countryside because they had walls, armed guards at gates, and police forces. When traveling in the country, merchants and other travelers often joined armed groups called convoys as a safeguard against

Violence was common at all levels of Renaissance society. In this copper engraving from the late 1500s, Spanish forces are killing rebels in the Dutch town of Harlem.

highwaymen. Unprotected peasants risked falling victim to bandits—or to violent nobles who preyed on the common people. Undisciplined soldiers posed another threat, often attacking and robbing helpless civilians. To protect themselves, most Renaissance men went about their daily business armed with some sort of weapon. Women without male protection faced the threat of rape.

Violent Crime. Renaissance society recognized several crimes of violence, and their punishments varied according to the nature of the crime. Authorities tended to view fighting as normal behavior. Those who engaged in brawls might receive a minor fine or escape punishment completely. If they had shed blood, however, the matter became much more serious. The punishment for violent crimes such as assault and murder depended upon the judge's interpretation of the attacker's motives and state of mind. "Crimes of passion," committed in the heat of the moment, generally received lighter sentences than cold-blooded crimes based on self-interest. Robbers and hired killers faced much more severe punishment than someone who committed a senseless murder during a drunken brawl.

Renaissance judges were especially concerned about speech as a form of violence. They believed that violent words gave rise to violent actions, such as feuds (ongoing battles between families) and attacks on public officials. Some communities outlawed specific insulting words and gestures. Punishments for verbal violence were very severe. In fact, in some cases, threatening someone could carry a more severe penalty than physically attacking the person.

The law treated sexual violence as a minor form of assault and punished it less severely than robbery or violent speech. Judges determined the seriousness of a rape by the age and social rank of the victim. The rape of a young girl or boy was a much more serious crime than an attack on a married woman or a widow. The rape of a single woman of marriageable age was generally viewed more as an outburst of uncontrollable male passion than a crime, and such rapists frequently escaped punishment altogether. Other rapists might have to pay a fine or marry their victims. Few were ever executed. By the late 1500s, however, women had begun to demand that officials take a sterner attitude toward sexual crimes.

Group Violence. Individual acts of violence often reflected the anger between larger groups. The family feud, for example, was a series of violent outbursts between individual members of warring families. This tradition had begun during the Middle Ages, when families, rather than governments, took the responsibility for punishing crimes committed against their members. The men of the family would hunt down men of their enemy's family, making no effort to conceal the attacks. Renaissance governments tried to stamp out feuds because these conflicts among leading families threatened the stability of the state. Feuds turned gentlemen into outlaws. Exiled for their crimes, these individuals often turned to theft or murder-for-hire to support themselves. Another danger came from the armed guards often employed by feuding families. These guards, called bravos, posed a threat not only to their employers' enemies but also to helpless peasants and citizens.

In the late 1500s the spread of the pistol and the rapier (a sharp, lightweight sword) made combat much more deadly. As a result, warring families gave up street brawls in favor of the DUEL, a ritual fight between two individuals. Dueling first became popular in Italy, and in the late 1500s it spread to the rest of Europe. The group violence of feuds gradually gave way to the individual violence of duels.

Political demonstrations could turn violent as well. Markets, public squares, and other urban gathering places often saw outbreaks of group violence, such as riots against public officials or brawls among the sup-

* **elite**   privileged group; upper class

porters of rival elite* families. Both men and women took part in these violent outbursts. Women with families to feed were especially likely to be involved in bread riots, which occurred when food was scarce or expensive.

Some acts of group violence occurred as part of social rituals. Gangs of young, single men, known as youth abbeys, sometimes terrorized the least powerful members of the community. For example, they engaged in noisy ceremonies called charivaris to mock people whose marriages or sexual relationships seemed to depart from community standards, such as old men who married young girls. Although the ritual mostly involved singing mocking songs and banging pots and pans, it could lead to arson*, assault, or even murder. The abbeys also subjected women to gang rapes. Women shamed in this way often had no choice but to turn to a life of prostitution.

* **arson**   deliberately setting fires that cause harm to people or property

Violence formed a part of certain SPORTS and public spectacles as well. In the Italian city of Venice, neighborhood gangs held "bridge battles" in which they fought to gain possession of a bridge. These fights with fists and heavy sticks could cause serious injuries and even deaths. The upper-class sport of jousting, in which mounted fighters tried to knock each other from their horses, also resulted in some accidental deaths. Many people enjoyed watching carnival sports that involved the torture of animals, such as bearbaiting, in which dogs attacked a chained bear. Crowds also gathered to witness the public torture or execution of criminals.

Lawful and Unlawful Violence. During the Renaissance the line between lawful and unlawful violence was often blurred. Many types of organized violence under state control could easily shift into unlawful forms. One gray area was PIRACY. The state authorized some sailors, called privateers, to attack and loot the vessels of enemy nations. However, many of those who referred to themselves by this name were really freelance pirates who preyed on both neutral and enemy ships.

* **picaresque**   refers to a type of fiction dealing with the adventures of a rogue or rascal

Soldiers could also cross the line into unlawful violence, turning into highway robbers. Because all governments faced critical shortages of manpower for their armies and police forces, they often recruited paupers, criminals, and outlaws. They also relied on mercenaries, professional fighters who offered their services for hire. The spread of professional soldiering in the 1400s and 1500s created a rootless class of people trained in violence. Many of them formed criminal bands. These shady figures—known as rogues in England, *pícaros* in Spain, and *ribaldi* or *vagabondi* in Italy—became the basis of the literary form called the picaresque* novel. (*See also* **Crime and Punishment; Sexuality and Gender; Warfare.**)

Virgil

70–19 B.C.
Roman poet

One of the greatest poets of ancient Rome, Virgil was also one of the most widely read classical* authors of the Renaissance. His best-known works were the *Eclogues,* a series of ten pastoral* poems; the *Georgics,* a set of four books on farming; and his famous *Aeneid,* an epic*

* **classical**   in the tradition of ancient Greece and Rome

* **pastoral**   relating to the countryside; often used to draw a contrast between the innocence and serenity of rural life and the corruption and extravagance of court life

* **epic**   long poem about the adventures of a hero

* **humanist**   Renaissance expert in the humanities (the languages, literature, history, and speech and writing techniques of ancient Greece and Rome)

* **fresco**   mural painted on a plaster wall

about the wanderings of the hero Aeneas, the legendary founder of Rome. Virgil's poetry became a key part of the school curriculum during the Renaissance and had a profound influence on the literature, art, and values of the period.

In the late 1300s, humanist* scholars began trying to recover the great works of ancient Greece and Rome. As humanism made its way into the schools, Virgil's works took a central place in education. By the end of the 1500s, almost everyone who received a humanist education was familiar with at least some of Virgil's poetry. Renaissance readers turned to Virgil's work for guidance in mastering Latin, the international language of the day. They drew on his poetry for well-turned phrases, figures of speech, and moral lessons, such as "fortune helps the bold and drives away the coward."

Virgil's works served as models for much of the literature written in Latin during the Renaissance. His poetry inspired generations of famous writers, including PETRARCH and Giovanni BOCCACCIO. The *Aeneid* was particularly influential. As a poem about exploration, it offered a literary model for Europeans coming to terms with the discovery and settlement of the New World. Renaissance artists and musicians also turned to Virgil's epic for ideas. The *Aeneid* inspired several sets of frescoes* (including one by the Italian painter RAPHAEL), as well as paintings, sculptures, and other artistic works. It also became the subject of musical works by such master composers as JOSQUIN DES PREZ and Orlando di LASSO. (*See also* **Classical Scholarship; Education; Latin Language and Literature.**)

Vittorino da Feltre

1378–1446
Italian humanist
and educator

* **humanist**   referring to a Renaissance cultural movement promoting the study of the humanities (the languages, literature, and history of ancient Greece and Rome) as a guide to living

* **rhetoric**   art of speaking or writing effectively

Vittorino da Feltre was a pioneer of humanist* education in Renaissance Italy. As a schoolmaster, he employed original teaching methods and showed concern for the welfare of his students. His school in the city of Mantua became an influential model for European boarding schools.

Vittorino studied at the University of Padua under the leading Latin scholar of his day, Gasparino Barzizza. In 1419 Vittorino settled in Padua and became a highly successful teacher. He taught students in his home, varying his fee based on the financial status of the pupil. Vittorino refused to accept more students than he believed he could responsibly teach. He also paid attention to his pupils' moral development.

In 1423 the ruler of Mantua invited Vittorino to the city to establish a school for the children of leading families in the region. This school, named "Pleasant House," accepted both children of nobles and promising children of lesser means. The curriculum included not only the standard humanist subjects, such as grammar and rhetoric*, but also mathematics, music, philosophy, and religion. Vittorino introduced several fresh approaches to learning at Pleasant House. He paid close attention to his students' personal needs and to the learning environment in general. He avoided crowded classrooms, presented material in stages so students did not get frustrated, and varied his courses to prevent boredom. He also made physical exercise a part of the daily routine. Unlike many other humanists, Vittorino left no treatises* describing his methods. What scholars know of them comes from the praise of his former students. (*See also* **Education; Humanism.**)

* **treatise**   long, detailed essay

Vives, Juan Luis

1492–1540
Spanish humanist

* **humanist**   Renaissance expert in the humanities (the languages, literature, history, and speech and writing techniques of ancient Greece and Rome)

* **Spanish Inquisition**   court established by the Spanish monarchs that investigated Christians accused of straying from the official doctrine of the Roman Catholic Church, particularly during the period 1480–1530

* **theological**   relating to theology, the study of the nature of God and of religion

The writings of Spanish humanist* Juan Luis Vives contributed to the study of language, education, and social reform. His works on education, in particular, had an influence on both Catholics and Protestants.

Vives grew up in a Jewish community in the Spanish city of Valencia. His parents and other relatives suffered under the Spanish Inquisition*, which executed his father by burning and removed his dead mother's body from its grave to burn it as well. Vives left Spain at the age of 17 and never returned. He eventually moved to Bruges in the Netherlands, where he met and worked with other humanists, such as Desiderius ERASMUS. In the 1520s Vives divided his time between the Netherlands and England, where he taught at Oxford University. He became friendly with many English humanists, including Thomas MORE.

In 1522 Vives published a lengthy commentary on *City of God,* a theological* work by the ancient religious scholar AUGUSTINE OF HIPPO. In this text, Vives criticized the sinful behavior of church officials. Four years later he addressed the topic of social responsibility in *On Aid to the Poor.* This work urged city governments to treat the war victims spread throughout Europe like native citizens.

Several of Vives's most important works deal with education. In *Education of the Christian Woman,* for instance, Vives argued that the education of women was consistent with female virtue. He pointed to More's daughters as examples. Schools throughout Europe used translations of many of Vives's other educational writings, including *Introduction to Knowledge* and *Latin Exercises.* Vives's most powerful works combined educational, social, political, and moral issues. His *Twenty Books on Education* not only set out a revolutionary educational program but also reflected on the corruption in human culture as a whole and on how to reform it. His *Three Books on the Soul and on Life* has been viewed as giving rise to the modern science of psychology. (*See also* **Education; Humanism; Inquisition.**)

Warfare

During the Renaissance, warfare became more frequent and much more destructive than in the Middle Ages. New technology, especially the introduction of gunpowder weapons and artillery, changed the nature of war. With the rise of more centralized states came the establishment of large standing armies. Some scholars have described the developments in the period between 1350 and 1600 as a military revolution.

New forms of technology changed warfare during the 1500s and 1600s. This 1526 painting of a battle in Siena shows the use of gunpowder cannons, one major advance of this period.

THE NATURE OF WAR

Medieval* warfare was limited in scope, often involving conflicts between individual nobles or between a noble and a prince*. However, during the Renaissance some princes, particularly in France and Spain, grew much more powerful than their neighbors. In addition, some European rulers pursued a policy of building their kingdoms by conquering independent territories. War ceased to be a local affair. It often involved troops from many different lands who fought on soil far from home.

Causes of Wars. In the Renaissance wars were generally fought to defend one's territory, to acquire more territory for the state, or to gain control of the monarchy. Many European wars of the period involved disputes over inherited titles and territories. For example, the WARS OF ITALY (1494–1559) began because King Charles VIII of France claimed to be the rightful heir to the kingdom of Naples. However, the English monarchy's campaigns of conquest against Ireland and Scotland did not rest on any claims of inheritance but were driven by the desire to

* **medieval** referring to the Middle Ages, a period that began around A.D. 400 and ended around 1400 in Italy and 1500 in the rest of Europe

* **prince** Renaissance term for the ruler of an independent state

* **annex**   to add a territory to an existing area

* **chivalric**   referring to the rules and customs of medieval knighthood

* **mercenary**   hired soldier

See color plate 13, vol. 2

* **Holy Roman Empire**   political body in central Europe composed of several states; existed until 1806

See color plate 11, vol. 4

enlarge the kingdom. The Spanish and French kingdoms also grew by annexing* territory, often by warfare.

Other factors had an impact on warfare. The chivalric* ideal, which flourished during the Renaissance, led many men to fight for honor or glory. This attitude was common among the nobility, and even some mercenary* captains, for whom war was a profession, would engage in combat for reasons of honor. Religious differences played a role in many Renaissance wars (most notably the THIRTY YEARS' WAR), but few conflicts were based solely on religion. Nevertheless, religious matters typically increased the bitterness of fighting and complicated the process of making peace.

While princes fought for power, glory, and honor, the common soldier often had different reasons for joining the military. Defending one's country was a powerful motive, but soldiers were often lured by the prospect of adventure and the opportunity to enrich themselves by looting towns or defeated enemies. Some men took up soldiering as a way to escape trouble, debts, or an unhappy family life. Many simply needed the employment and wages offered by military service.

Major Renaissance Wars.   Important wars occurred in almost every part of Europe during the Renaissance. The Hundred Years' War (1337–1453) between France and England was fought to determine how much control England would have over French territory. It ended with England holding only the port of Calais. Besides battling each other, both the French and English monarchies struggled to maintain control at home. English nobles fought one another for power in the civil wars known as the Wars of the Roses (1452–1487). France waged wars to add Brittany and Burgundy to the kingdom.

The Wars of Italy began as an attempt by France's King Charles VIII to claim Naples as his inheritance. His invasion in 1494 set off a series of wars for control over Italy that lasted for more than 60 years. The major combatants were France, Spain, and the Holy Roman Empire*. By 1525 Spain had emerged as the clear winner and the most powerful kingdom in Europe. At home, the Spanish monarchy waged war against the Muslim kingdoms that had existed in southern Spain for hundreds of years. Granada, the last Muslim stronghold, fell in 1492.

Religious violence in France led to a long civil war during the late 1500s. The WARS OF RELIGION (1562–1598), which went through various phases of fighting, were a particularly bitter chapter in French history. The conflicts resulted in the assassination of several noble figures and the killing of several thousand Protestants and others at the St. Bartholomew's Day Massacre in 1572. Religious differences also led to the Thirty Years' War (1618–1648). Although it began as a dispute between German princes and the Holy Roman Emperor, it grew into a war that involved almost every major power in Europe. Some scholars say that the Thirty Years' War marked the political end of the Renaissance.

CHANGING WARFARE

Historians generally agree that a military revolution occurred during the Renaissance, marking the start of the development of modern warfare. They have different views, however, on the timing of this revolution and

Heavy Metal

The design of Renaissance cannons differed significantly from those used in later eras. Early illustrations from around 1326 show cannons shaped like a vase or bottle that apparently fired projectiles resembling large arrows. Most cannons were cast in brass, bronze, or another alloy containing copper. This was because most early cannons were produced by bell makers, who used the techniques and materials with which they were familiar. Some cannons had barrels composed of flat bars of wrought iron arranged in a circle and held tightly together by iron hoops. The most famous large siege gun of the Renaissance, known as Mons Meg, was constructed by this method. It reportedly could fire a 330-pound stone ball a distance of up to two miles.

See color plate 12, vol. 2

propose dates ranging from the mid-1300s to the end of the 1600s. The first part of the military revolution was the growth in the size of armed forces. Armies expanded steadily from about 1350 to 1550. By 1500 all European states except England supported the idea of a standing army. Following the increase in military forces came the introduction of new, sturdier fortifications. Spain built a chain of fortifications to defend the state from internal and external attack. By 1600 the rest of Europe had begun developing costly defensive works along with larger armies.

Significant advances in military technology occurred during this period as well and profoundly changed the nature of warfare. Technology was applied to both offensive and defensive warfare, and the dominant military strategy shifted from defense to offense and then back again to defense during the Renaissance. In addition, the increasing use of mercenaries made war a more professional undertaking.

Soldiers. All adult male subjects of a kingdom were eligible for military service. However, armies consisted largely of people from two groups in society—the aristocrats who managed the war and the lower classes who fought it. In most states, captains recruited soldiers from certain areas, but there were never enough volunteers to fill out the ranks of the army. Many men were pressed into service, but others dodged the military or deserted as soon as they had the chance. As a result, states relied heavily on mercenaries to fight their wars. Many Italian states used hired soldiers in the 1300s and 1400s, and eventually the practice spread to northern Europe.

Mercenaries had many advantages over citizens as soldiers. They were better fighters and much better disciplined, which had benefits both on and off the battlefield. Soldiers dismissed at the end of a war were often penniless, and many of them formed outlaw bands to harass the peasants. Mercenaries, by contrast, could be trusted to return home with their pay and not cause problems. Many mercenary captains were nobles who had turned to military service because of the poverty of their lands.

Weapons and Tactics. Gunpowder and artillery dramatically changed the nature of warfare during the Renaissance. Defenders discovered that castles that withstood the attack of catapults (devices for hurling stones) and other forms of medieval artillery could be brought down by gunpowder artillery. During the Hundred Years' War, the French developed new artillery tactics. They used small, easy-to-move cannons to attack English castles and fortified towns, and the high, thin walls of medieval castles collapsed under the repeated battering of French cannons.

Because castles no longer provided a secure stronghold, armies were forced out into the open to fight. This led to offensive warfare involving battles fought by large armies that produced heavy casualties. The standard battlefield arrangement was a large square formation of soldiers with pikes (long poles topped by a blade). Cavalry stood alongside the pikemen, and a line of crossbowmen marched in front to provide covering fire for the infantry.

In the early 1500s the Italians developed a new type of fortress that could stand up to gunpowder artillery. Its walls were lower and thicker, making them harder to hit and to destroy. These fortresses were also designed to hold defensive guns. By the mid-1500s defensive tactics had the advantage again, and siege* warfare replaced open battlefield conflicts. A dense square made up of pikemen and soldiers carrying early firearms called harquebuses became the main military formation.

As firearms became more efficient, they began to take on an offensive role. Gunners arranged in lines rather than squares could concentrate their firepower and wreak havoc on tight formations of pikemen. As a result, new infantry formations emerged in which the men were deployed in shallower lines. By the late 1600s, thin lines of men with firearms had replaced the large bodies of pikemen in most armies. Heavy cavalry, which had dominated the medieval battlefield, never regained its importance. However, new formations of light cavalry emerged at this time. Finally, large standing armies were established in most countries.

Naval warfare also changed with the use of gunpowder. The main fighting vessel in the early Renaissance was the galley, a long, narrow ship driven by oars and sails. Naval battles involved trying to get close enough to put soldiers aboard an enemy's vessels and fight a sort of land battle at sea. By the 1400s, sailors were effectively adapting land cannons for use in naval warfare. However, galleys could carry very few cannons and little ammunition. Shipbuilders designed larger sailing ships such as caravels and galleons with separate decks to hold guns.

By the end of the 1500s, gunfire rather than close-range fighting was deciding most important sea battles. Cannon played a key role in the Battle of Lepanto, a famous conflict in 1571 between the Ottoman Turks* and Christian forces. More than 500 ships took part. The Christian ships, which had bigger guns, fired at point-blank range. The Turks lost about 200 ships and thousands of men in the ferocious one-day battle. (*See also* **Arms and Armor; Fortifications; Mercenaries; Ships and Shipbuilding.**)

Wars of Italy

The Wars of Italy—a series of conflicts between 1494 and 1559 for control of the Italian peninsula—involved much of Renaissance Europe. France, Spain and the Holy Roman Empire* took part, along with the papacy*, VENICE, FLORENCE, and NAPLES and mercenaries* from Switzerland and Germany. The wars ended with Spain in firm control over much of Italy.

The deaths of several Italian rulers in the early 1490s left Italy with little political leadership. In 1494 the duke of Milan invited King Charles VIII of France to come to Italy to establish order and support the duke's rule in Milan. Charles hoped to seize the kingdom of Naples, which he claimed as an heir of an earlier Neapolitan dynasty. Although the French army moved easily through Italy and took Naples, it was forced to withdraw in 1495.

In 1499 the French king Louis XII led another invasion. This time the French won both Naples and Milan, another city claimed by the French monarchy. Then Spain entered the contest for Italy. A series of battles between French and Spanish forces during the early 1500s brought Naples under Spanish control. In the following years the French lost Milan but regained it in 1515 with an important victory at Ravenna. But French control of Milan was short-lived.

In 1516 King Charles I became Spain's new king. He was also heir to the HABSBURG DYNASTY, which ruled Spain as well as the Holy Roman Empire. Using artillery and small arms effectively, Charles's army of Spanish and imperial troops triumphed over the French and their Swiss mercenaries in 1522. Three years later at the Battle of Pavia, imperial forces again defeated the French and took the French king FRANCIS I prisoner. Then in 1527, a combination of Spanish, Italian, and mercenary troops in the emperor's service sacked* Rome. Florence, too, had to submit to the emperor and accept the return of the MEDICI.

* sack to loot a captured city

In 1530 the pope crowned Charles I as Holy Roman Emperor CHARLES V in the city of Bologna. For all practical purposes this ended the wars and left much of Italy under the rule of Charles V and Spain. But more battles took place after 1530, including those at the Italian town of Ceresole in 1544 and at the French town of St. Quentin in 1557. Italians also made a few additional efforts to throw off Spanish rule. The city of SIENA expelled the Spanish troops stationed there in 1552 and asked the French for help. However, Spain reconquered the city and gave it to its ally, Cosimo I de' Medici, the ruler of Florence. Pope Paul IV began a war against Spain in 1556, but this too ended in failure.

The wars ended officially in 1559 with the Treaty of Cateau-Cambrésis. When the conflicts began, Italy had consisted of five major powers—Florence, Venice, Naples, Milan, and the papacy. By 1559 Milan and Naples had become part of the Spanish empire, Venice had been reduced to a minor power, and Florence was largely under Spanish influence. The years of fighting not only destroyed Italian independence, they also devastated the countryside.

* exploit to take advantage of; to make productive use of

Scholars have cited many reasons for the wars and for Italy's failure to maintain its independence. The Renaissance historian Francesco GUICCIARDINI argued that political intrigue by Italian rulers and the papacy led to Italy's fall. Others point out that many Italians were not loyal to their leaders, who often exploited* them or allowed the nobles to exploit them. Indeed, when Charles VIII of France left Milan in 1495, many Italians were genuinely sorry to see him go. In addition, political division weakened all the major Italian states except Venice. The desire for stability also led Italians to accept foreign military intervention if it promised to bring peace and quiet. (*See also* **Italy.**)

Wars of Religion

* patronage support or financial sponsorship

* heresy belief that is contrary to the doctrine of an established church

Between 1562 and 1598 France was torn apart by eight Wars of Religion. The conflicts began as a struggle between French Protestants who wanted freedom to practice their religion and Catholics who saw themselves as defenders of the true faith. The wars also had political roots in the rivalry among French nobles for royal patronage*.

The French monarchy was closely allied to the Roman Catholic Church, and kings of France took an oath to protect the faith and fight heresy*. When the church declared the teachings of Martin LUTHER to be heretical in 1521, the French monarch became the enemy of French Protestants. By the 1550s the more militant Protestantism of John Calvin had arrived in France, and King Henry II stepped up efforts to eliminate heresy. Henry's sudden death in 1559 put his son Francis II on the throne.

Francis was heavily influenced by his wife's uncles, the duke of Guise and cardinal of Lorraine, who were fervent defenders of the Catholic faith. Persecution of Protestants increased under Francis, particularly after the discovery of a plot by Calvinist nobles to kidnap the young king. When Francis died in 1560, the queen mother, CATHERINE DE MÉDICIS, declared herself regent* for the ten-year-old heir, Charles IX. Catherine's efforts to create a more tolerant atmosphere for religion led to even greater Catholic opposition. Violence against Huguenots* increased, and in 1562 Guise forces killed Protestants gathered for a service near the town of Wassy.

Catherine, torn between opposing factions, tried to maintain peace. The Peace of Amboise in 1563 allowed Protestants to worship openly in certain settings but imposed various restrictions. Many Catholics opposed the peace, and some of the king's advisers continued to call for persecution of Huguenots. This led to another plot to seize the king, which sparked a new war. Another unpopular and ineffective peace treaty followed in 1568.

New fighting erupted a few months later and lasted about a year. The treaty that followed expanded the religious rights of Protestants slightly and allowed them to hold certain fortified cities for their defense. Many Catholics reacted strongly against the terms of the treaty. In August 1572 they launched a wave of killings, called the St. Bartholomew's Day massacre, that left 2,000 people dead in Paris and an unknown number in a dozen other towns. In southern France, Protestants drew up a constitution that separated them from the monarchy. They formed an alliance with moderate Catholics who wanted to end the fighting and who supported the Huguenots' calls for freedom of worship.

Charles IX's death in 1574 put his brother, Henry III, on the throne and raised Catholic hopes for victory. However, the crown's poor finances limited Henry's ability to raise an effective army, and he was forced to sign another peace with the Huguenots. The terms of the peace angered Catholic nobles, who formed the radical Holy League to fight for defense of the faith. The fighting continued, debts mounted, and Henry became increasingly unpopular. In 1585 the Holy League pressured him into taking back the privileges granted to the Huguenots and starting a new war against Protestantism.

In renewed fighting, Protestant forces won the Battle of Coutras in 1587, but a Guise army unexpectedly defeated German mercenaries* arriving to help the Huguenots. Meanwhile, Henry came to fear his allies in the Holy League more than the Protestants. The king ordered them not to come to Paris, where the league was very popular, but they came anyway. When Henry tried to restrain the league's enthusiastic supporters, Parisians drove him from the city. The king then had Henri de Guise and his brother assassinated, causing the league members to revolt and take control of Paris. Henry planned a siege* of the city but was assassinated in August 1589 before he could begin the campaign.

Because Henry left no heirs, the throne passed to Henry de Bourbon, king of Navarre, who took the name HENRY IV. Henry IV started the siege

* **regent**   person who acts on behalf of a monarch who is too young or unable to rule

* **Huguenot**   French Protestant of the 1500 and 1600s, follower of John Calvin

* **mercenary**   hired soldier

* **siege**   prolonged effort to force a surrender by surrounding a fortress or town with armed troops, cutting the area off from aid

of Paris in 1590. Although a Protestant, he converted to Catholicism in 1593 in an effort to reduce Catholic opposition to his rule. Paris surrendered the following year, and over the next few years many towns surrendered voluntarily or fell to Henry's forces. By 1598 the last Catholic noble had lain down his arms. In April of that year, Henry signed the Edict of Nantes, which granted freedom of worship to Protestants. Despite Catholic resistance to the edict, a period of peace and relative stability returned to France after nearly 40 years of war. (*See also* **Catholic Reformation and Counter-Reformation; France; Guise-Lorraine Family; Protestant Reformation.**)

Weights and Measures

Europeans used a great variety of systems for weighing and measuring during the Renaissance. Even within the same kingdom or territory, standards could vary widely. The ancient Romans had imposed a single system of measurements throughout their empire, but when the empire collapsed, the Roman system fell by the wayside. Many localities developed their own systems, and by the Renaissance hundreds of thousands of different weights and measures were in use.

Most units of measurement were based on quantities people used in their daily life. For example, people might measure area according to how much land they needed to produce income for the year or on the amount of land they could rent for a certain fee. Other measurements depended on the physical qualities of humans and animals. Human body parts, such as the foot and palm, formed the basis for some units of length. Ale could be measured by the hogshead, which held about 63 gallons. Some units of volume depended on units of length, as in the case of units based on the length of string required to bind up a certain volume of a product. People also based units of capacity on the amount that a ship or pack train could carry.

Some units of measure had several applications. The French *aissin,* for instance, could measure areas of land or volumes of grain or wood. In other cases, a single unit had more than one name. The English measures *pint, jug,* and *stoup* were used interchangeably for the same volume of liquid. In Italy, the *grosso, dramma,* and *quarro* were equal units of weight.

Central governments laid out the standards for units of measurement, but they did not always define them in precise terms. In France, for instance, there were many different ways of calculating such measures as the *pied* for length and the *corde* for firewood. Also, local variations of measures sometimes became popular and replaced the national standard. The standards used inside a town might vary from those applied outside the town walls, and units of measurement often differed at land and at sea. The French *lieue* (league) ranged from 2,000 to 3,000 *toises* (3,900 to 5,850 meters), with the greater length being used at sea.

Governments also failed to produce enough physical prototypes (uniform models) to allow people to check the accuracy of their own measuring devices. Furthermore, these prototypes were not all made in the same place. Instead, individual manufacturers created models that often

varied from the original, or master, measure. Local craftsworkers further confused the issue by creating their own copies from the masters. In addition, measuring devices made of wood, lead, iron, and bronze could change with weather conditions and constant handling, further reducing their accuracy. Finally, standards of measurement changed over time. Europe did not develop a single unified system of measurement until the creation of the metric system in the late 1700s and early 1800s. (*See also* **Economy and Trade.**)

Weyden, Rogier van der

ca. 1399–1464
Flemish painter

* **Flemish** relating to Flanders, a region along the coasts of present-day Belgium, France, and the Netherlands

See color plate 10, vol. 2

A leading Flemish* painter of the early Renaissance, Rogier van der Weyden influenced artists in many areas of western Europe well into the 1500s. His expressive and finely detailed works were in great demand throughout much of Europe.

The son of a knife maker, van der Weyden was born in Tournai, a town in present-day Belgium. It is likely that he joined the workshop of the Flemish painter Robert Campin in 1427, probably as a partner rather than as a pupil. He may have trained earlier at the workshop of the Master of Flémalle and his works show the master's influence. However, many scholars believe that Campin and the Master of Flémalle were the same person.

Van der Weyden left Campin's workshop in 1432, and by 1435 he had moved to BRUSSELS. The following year he became the city's official painter, a position he kept for the remainder of his life. His notable works in Brussels include a series of four large paintings on the subject of justice painted for the courtroom of the town hall. In 1450 van der Weyden traveled to Italy, where he was already well known. Several of his works had reached collectors in Genoa, Ferrara, and Naples, and he won high praise at the court of Milan. However, Italian art had very little impact on the style and content of the artist's later works.

Van der Weyden's surviving works bear neither dates nor signatures, and few documents exist to identify certain paintings as his work. One exception is *Descent from the Cross*, which portrays the tragic figure of Christ surrounded by grief-stricken mourners after the Crucifixion. Various texts identify this piece as the work of "Rogier" and of "the great and famous Fleming Rogel." Probably painted in the Netherlands before 1443, the work eventually entered the collection of PHILIP II of Spain.

The *Descent from the Cross* and other religious paintings by van der Weyden present dramatic scenes in a vivid and emotional manner. Some of the artist's works reflect the influence of the great Flemish painter Jan van EYCK, and van der Weyden reinterpreted several van Eyck paintings. Van der Weyden was also an outstanding portrait painter. (*See also* **Art in the Netherlands.**)

Witchcraft

Renaissance Europeans defined witches as people who worshipped the devil and cast harmful spells. Both church and state authorities regarded witchcraft as a serious crime, punishable by death. Approximately

The word witchcraft applied to both "black magic," used to harm others, and "white magic," used to help and heal. In this illustration from a 1487 book, two white witches brew a potion to cure all diseases of the body and soul.

---

* **theologian**   person who studies religion and the nature of God

* **heresy**   belief that is contrary to the doctrine of an established church

* **treatise**   long, detailed essay

100,000 people stood trial for witchcraft between 1400 and 1700. As many as half of them were executed.

Ideas about Witchcraft. The most basic belief about witches was that they practiced harmful magic, also known as black magic or sorcery. According to this view, witches used mysterious powers to cause death, injury, illness, or some other misfortune. Sorcery could harm both individuals and entire communities, as in the case of a hailstorm that destroyed crops. The word "witchcraft" was also applied to practices regarded as "white" or helpful magic, such as healing. However, most authorities considered white magic a lesser crime than sorcery and punished it less severely.

The idea of witches as devil worshippers arose out of the early Christian belief that all magic drew its power from the devil. Theologians* of the 1200s and 1300s linked witchcraft to bargains with demons, making it a form of heresy*. Many people believed that witches not only made face-to-face bargains with the devil but also met in groups to worship him by night. According to legend, witches at these gatherings killed and ate children, danced naked, and had sex with demons. In some countries it was also a common belief that witches flew to and from their meetings.

By the early 1400s, church and legal authorities began to view witches as members of a new and dangerous religious group that defied the Christian church, rejected moral law, and destroyed life and property through magic. Religious scholars and church officials produced more than 30 texts on the subject of witchcraft during the 1400s. The most influential of these was *Malleus Maleficarum* (The Hammer of Witches), published in 1487 in Germany and widely read throughout Europe. The text brought together many scholarly ideas about witchcraft and argued for the vigorous prosecution of the crime. Several treatises* of the 1500s and early 1600s expanded on the ideas in this text.

Some learned Europeans of the 1500s rejected the standard view of witches. A number of authors argued that witches did not really make pacts with the devil but only imagined that they did so due to illusions cast by demons. Based on these views, the authors argued against the harsh treatment of witches. Such ideas did not become widespread until the late 1600s.

Witchcraft, Society, and the Law. About four out of five of the individuals accused of witchcraft were female. Women tended to engage in activities such as healing and assisting in childbirth, which often raised suspicions about the use of harmful magic. Many of their accusers described the women as loud, rude, or in some other way out of line with the accepted standards for female behavior. In the early 1400s, when witchcraft was commonly linked with other forms of heresy and ritual magic, many men also faced charges of witchcraft. Even later, after most people had come to view witchcraft as a female activity, men might fall under suspicion if they were related to female witches. Men were also accused of witchcraft in Russia, Finland, and parts of Spain and Italy, areas where magicians were generally thought of as male.

Most accused witches came from the lower levels of society. The poor, as the weakest and most vulnerable members of the community, made easy targets for those seeking someone to blame for their problems. Charges of witchcraft tended to be more common during periods of difficult social and economic conditions, when tensions and conflicts ran high. In such troubled times many people sought a supernatural explanation for the disruptions taking place around them. Rising prices, low wages, and widespread warfare led to a surge in witchcraft trials between 1560 and 1630.

Both church and civil authorities prosecuted those accused of being witches. Church law allowed officers of the court to bring a suspected witch to trial on the basis of rumor alone, without the need for a direct accusation. However, the law strictly required that all death sentences be based either on a confession or on the testimony of two witnesses to the crime. When no witnesses were available, the courts might resort to torture to force suspected witches to confess.

The earliest trials for witchcraft involving both sorcery and devil-worship occurred in the early 1400s in Switzerland and parts of what is now southeastern France. In the late 1400s witchcraft trials spread to other parts of western Europe. After a decline in the early 1500s, a second and more intense surge of trials began around 1560 and lasted until the 1630s. The most severe prosecutions took place in southern and western Germany, and large numbers of executions also occurred in eastern France, Switzerland, and Scotland. However, nearly every European country had at least one large-scale witch hunt. The judicial abuses common in witch trials eventually led to public calls for greater restraint in acting against witchcraft. Courts adopted stricter rules regarding the use of torture, as well as higher standards of proof. (*See also* **Magic and Astrology.**)

Wolsey, Thomas

ca. 1472–1530
English churchman and statesman

* **patron** supporter or financial sponsor of an artist or writer

* **humanist** Renaissance expert in the humanities (the languages, literature, history, and speech and writing techniques of ancient Greece and Rome)

* **theology** study of the nature of God and of religion

One of the most powerful figures in Renaissance ENGLAND, Thomas Wolsey played important roles in both the church and the government. As a chief adviser to HENRY VIII, he helped shape England's domestic and foreign policies. An active patron* of the arts, Wolsey supported many of the leading humanists* in England. He lived in splendid palaces filled with fine paintings and sculpture. However, he eventually fell out of favor with the king and died in disgrace.

The son of a butcher who also kept an inn, Wolsey was born in Ipswich, in eastern England. As a young man he studied arts and theology* at Magdalen College, Oxford. He served for a time as the financial officer of the college and as master of a school linked with it. In 1501 Wolsey left Oxford to serve as chaplain to a series of important individuals, including the king, HENRY VII. When Henry VIII took the throne in 1509, he appointed Wolsey royal almoner, the official in charge of distributing charity to the poor. A skilled administrator, Wolsey won the king's confidence. He also rose rapidly within the church, becoming bishop of Lincoln in 1514, archbishop of York six months later, and cardinal in 1515.

Shortly after Wolsey became cardinal, the king named him as chancellor, the highest official in the government. Wolsey remained King Henry's leading adviser for the next 14 years. In 1518 Wolsey negotiated a general European peace treaty and a settlement with France over territory captured by England. In 1521 he held peace conferences in an attempt to prevent war between France and the Holy Roman Empire*. From 1527 to 1529, Wolsey again tried to forge an agreement between France and the empire and also to end hostilities between England and France.

Wolsey also played major roles in England's judicial, social, and financial affairs. He presided over the king's council and the court of chancery, a division of England's High Court. Wolsey encouraged strict enforcement of the law and supported those who sought equal justice for all. He also established councils to oversee local governments in Wales and northern England. In terms of social policy, Wolsey took steps to control the spread of plague* through quarantine (the isolation of infected regions) and to prevent the hoarding of grain during times of famine. He also established commissions to investigate the conversion of fields to pastureland, which reduced the amount of land being farmed. As a financial advisor, Wolsey worked hard to increase the king's income. He imposed forced loans and high taxes on the people. However, he had to abandon some of his tax proposals when they provoked widespread anger and opposition.

Many of Wolsey's actions as a religious leader were unpopular. He held several church offices at once and kept a mistress, by whom he had two children. He also interfered in the affairs of other bishops and heavily taxed church officials. However, he also made some positive changes. He encouraged religious reform, sought to reduce tensions between the church and secular* courts, and worked to improve religious education for the clergy.

In general, other government officials cooperated with Wolsey. However, tensions developed over some of his policies and his treatment of nobles in the king's council. When Wolsey began to lose favor with the king in the late 1520s, many took the opportunity to criticize him. Wolsey's undoing came with his failure to obtain an annulment* of Henry's marriage to CATHERINE OF ARAGON. Despite Wolsey's skills as a diplomat, he was unable to persuade the pope to approve this action. As a result, Henry VIII removed Wolsey as chancellor in 1529. Wolsey retired to York and died the following year while on his way south to stand trial for treason.

* **Holy Roman Empire** political body in central Europe composed of several states; existed until 1806

* **plague** highly contagious and often fatal disease that wiped out much of Europe's population in the mid-1300s and reappeared periodically over the next three centuries; also know as the Black Death

* **secular** nonreligious; connected with everyday life

* **annulment** formal declaration that a marriage is legally invalid

Women

Women clearly played a secondary role in the political, social, and cultural life of the Renaissance. Since the Middle Ages, the major institutions of society—the family, the church, and the state—had placed restrictions on women's roles within them. However, these rigid limits began to relax in some ways during the Renaissance. Women found opportunities to take part in the widespread revival of art and scholarship. They also became more prominently involved in social

Single young women devoted much of their time to acquiring the skills they would one day need to manage a household. Among the skills they learned were spinning wool and weaving cloth, as shown in this painting by Francesco del Cossa from the late 1400s.

protest. As a result, women's views of themselves began to change during this period. A small but significant group of women drew attention to their unequal state and called for changes in the way society treated them.

WOMEN AND THE FAMILY

See color plate 2, vol. 2

In Renaissance society men were identified by their occupation or social status—as gentlemen, merchants, priests, peasants, and so forth. Women's identity, by contrast, depended on their relationships to men, as daughters, wives, mothers, or widows. The father served as the head of the Renaissance family, and property was passed down through the male line. Women played a supporting role within the family.

A daughter's most important duty was to preserve her virginity. Because identity and inheritance depended on fathers rather than mothers, a man had to know that his future wife had not conceived a child by another man before her marriage. Daughters also had to learn the skills they would one day need as wives and mothers. The older women of the household taught the girls to spin wool and weave cloth. They also showed them to manage the household economy, supervise servants, and nurse the sick.

Wives had many duties in the household, which varied according to their social status. Peasant women performed such tasks as tending to fowl and sheep, raising vegetables, brewing beer, and helping with the harvest. The wives of artisans* performed skilled craft work alongside their husbands. Occasionally they gained membership in guilds*, although this became less common over the course of the Renaissance.

* **artisan** skilled worker or craftsperson

* **guild** association of craft and trade owners and workers that set standards for and represented the interests of its members

Wives of merchants tended shops and helped keep accounts and other records. The chief job of upper-class wives was to run the household. They managed the purchasing of supplies, entertained their husbands' guests, and nursed sick family members and servants. They also did fine embroidery and other textile work for the home.

The chief responsibility of all wives, however, was bearing and raising children. Childbirth was risky for both infant and mother. Between 20 and 50 percent of infants died soon after birth. One in ten births resulted in the death of the mother, making childbirth a leading cause of death among women—especially those who had many children. Mothers were responsible for their children until they reached the age of six or seven, but society did not see children as belonging to their mothers. If a mother of young children died, the father and his family or servants raised the children. However, if a father of young children died, his male relatives became responsible for the children—although they might invite the mother to remain in the household to care for them.

Widowhood posed practical problems for a woman of any age. A woman whose husband died often found herself surrounded by competing interests. Her husband's family members might want her to stay in their household so that they would have the use of her dowry*. The members of her birth family, by contrast, might want her to return to her former home, along with her dowry. They might also urge her to remarry. The church and society in general worried that sexually experienced widows would behave immorally. In Catholic regions they would be urged to enter convents, in Protestant ones to remarry. Few believed that a widow could or should live alone, even if she could support herself. After 1600, however, it became more common for women to do so.

* **dowry** money or property that a woman brings to her marriage

WOMEN AND THE CHURCH

The role of women in religion differed significantly between the Roman Catholic Church and the various Protestant churches. Catholic women could pursue a career in the church by entering a convent, where they would live apart from the world. A Protestant woman, by contrast, had little choice but to spend her life within the family, under the control of male relatives. Catholic women might join a RELIGIOUS ORDER for many reasons. Some families placed their young daughters in convents on a permanent or temporary basis. Some grown women joined convents because they were drawn to the religious life, while others were widows or refugees seeking a haven.

Convents typically required an entrance fee, which they called a dowry, just as in a marriage. Those whose families could not afford this fee might join looser communities of religious women who did not live strictly apart from the world. A few women pursued holy careers as individuals, following a strict religious routine while remaining in the homes of male relatives. Others, usually wives and widows, devoted themselves to God through charity work. After the early 1500s, howev-

The Dowry

In many parts of Europe, a married woman could own no property except her dowry. Although technically her property for life, the dowry was managed by her husband during her lifetime and went to their children after his death. The dowry was a woman's inheritance. It served to cut her off from her birth family so that she would have no further claims on her father's estate. While families sought to limit the size of dowries to reduce their financial burden, they also tried to provide enough money to "purchase" desirable husbands for their daughters.

er, the Catholic Church severely limited these less structured forms of female religious life. The convent became the only approved religious path for a woman, and life within convents came under tighter control by male clergy.

Protestantism did away with the Catholic ideal of holy virginity and with religious communities for women. Protestant women had to live out their lives within the families of their fathers or husbands. Some modern historians see this as a change that placed women more firmly under male control, while others view it as a shift toward more equal marriages. In the earliest days of Protestantism, some women became religious leaders, publishing their views on reform. However, their voices had little lasting impact on the movement. Later, some women in minor Protestant groups such as the Anabaptists became famous as martyrs* for their faith.

WOMEN AND RENAISSANCE CULTURE

During the Renaissance, women began to play a larger role in the privileged world of power and ideas. Several women of this period governed their countries either as rulers or as regents*. Women also made inroads in other male domains, such as scholarship and the arts. Men often declared that women of notable learning or wisdom had "achieved the virtue of a man." Such remarks reveal that Renaissance society continued to view women as a group as inferior, even while acknowledging the accomplishments of a select few. Still, women's contributions to Renaissance culture helped lay the foundations for a new, more equal view of their abilities and rights.

Women of Power. Between 1400s and 1700 several bright and capable woman became rulers of their countries. ELIZABETH I of England, Christina of Sweden, and ISABELLA OF CASTILE all reigned as queens in their own right, while CATHERINE DE MÉDICIS and Anne of Austria acted as regents for their sons. These powerful women served as living proof that a woman could perform and even excel at male activities.

Female rulers often reinforced their power by surrounding themselves with images of armed women. The concept of the military maiden fascinated Renaissance artists and writers, appearing in the works of such authors as Edmund SPENSER and Ludovico ARIOSTO. Some Renaissance women actually served as soldiers by assuming male disguises. A few of them managed to keep their gender hidden for years.

Women as Scholars. Women had limited access to education during the Renaissance. Although no specific rule barred them from attending universities, the courses of study at these centers of learning were designed to prepare men for public and professional life. With the rise of humanist* education, however, other paths to knowledge became open to women. Some, for instance, gained access to learning through the culture of the Renaissance COURT. Female courtiers had the opportunity to talk with philosophers and scientists who came to the courts seeking patronage* for their projects.

* **martyr** someone who suffers or dies for the sake of a religion, cause, or principle

* **regent** person who acts on behalf of a monarch who is too young or unable to rule

* **humanist** referring to a Renaissance cultural movement promoting the study of the humanities (the languages, literature, and history of ancient Greece and Rome) as a guide to living

* **patronage** support or financial sponsorship

An Early Feminist

Laura Cereta (1469–1499) of Brescia, Italy, was one of the first female humanists. Widowed while still in her teens, Cereta devoted herself to writing essays in the form of letters to male scholars and leaders of the church and the state. Her works expressed ideas very unusual for the time. She rejected traditional views of men's and women's roles, argued that housework imposed limits on women's intellectual growth, and portrayed marriage as a kind of slavery. Cereta's bold writings had a strong influence on later feminists of the Renaissance and the centuries that followed.

* **vernacular** native language or dialect of a region or country

See color plate 14, vol. 2

Other women learned through private study. Some fathers, especially in northern Italy, educated their daughters in Latin and Greek, the foundations of humanist study. These vital language skills enabled a few Italian women of the 1400s to study philosophy. These early female humanists, such as Isotta Nogarola of Verona and Cassandra Fedele of Venice, produced letters, dialogues, poems, and other works. Many of their writings dealt with such issues as the mental abilities of women and their right to an education. Women also took part in learned debates through correspondence with male humanists.

Renaissance women were not very active in the sciences. A few, however, assisted their male relatives with scientific work. For example, Sophie Brahe, the sister of Danish astronomer Tycho BRAHE (1546–1601), helped him with his observations and took part in scientific discussions at the Danish court. Women did enjoy some independence in the field of medicine. Although without university degrees, they had little chance of practicing as physicians, many communities relied on female healers for their knowledge of herbs and other treatments. Some well-known healers, such as the French royal midwife Louise Bourgeois (1563–1636), published works that competed with those of male physicians. These women demonstrated that their hands-on experience could rival men's book learning about the human body.

Women in Art and Literature. The number of women writers grew enormously in the 1500s and 1600s. Italian humanism produced a dozen or so female writers, and by the end of the Renaissance there were hundreds and perhaps thousands of women writing in Italian, French, and English. Women penned religious poetry, love poetry, stories, novels, and plays. They also wrote diaries, family histories, and advice books for other women on topics such as cooking, fashion, child care, and herbal lore. A few women knew Latin and Greek and translated ancient works from these languages into the vernacular*.

Many female writers challenged the traditional view of women as physically and mentally inferior to men. For instance, in the early 1400s Christine de PIZAN of France proclaimed women's strength and envisioned a scholarly community for women. Two Venetian authors, Moderata Fonte and Lucrezia Marinella, published lengthy defenses of women in 1600. Their works attacked the idea of male superiority and laid the foundations for modern feminism. In the 1500s, female authors took part in the QUERELLE DES FEMMES, an ongoing debate about women's abilities and their proper place in society. This discussion, which continued beyond the end of the Renaissance, influenced later views on women's roles and rights.

A few women gained international fame as artists or musicians in the Renaissance. Two of the best known were Italian painters Artemisia GENTILESCHI and Sofonisba ANGUISSOLA. Wealthy women also contributed to the arts through patronage. Notable female patrons included CATHERINE OF ARAGON and MARGARET OF AUSTRIA. Some educated women became leaders of SALONS, circles of discussion among the learned and fashionable. Especially in France, but also in England, the Netherlands, and the Italian cities, salons helped spread new ideas and set standards of literary taste.

Images of Women. A few Renaissance artists portrayed women in ways that reflected the reality of the time. More often, however, women appeared in art as images of some abstract ideal—either good or bad. Some portraits flattered their subjects, such as the Italian artist TITIAN's painting of the 60-year-old noblewoman Isabella d'Este as a youthful beauty. Others placed women in mythical, historical, or religious settings. Whether the woman pictured was a saint or a temptress, a noble or a member of the working class, her image served as a model for female viewers, instructing them about morality and the right way to dress and behave.

Many works of art featured the Virgin Mary, who represented the ideal of Renaissance womanhood: chaste*, devout, humble, and motherly. Some pictures illustrated the events of Mary's life, while others presented her as an object of worship. Some artists glorified Mary, showing her surrounded by saints and angels. Others brought her down to earth, as in German artist Lucas CRANACH's 1519 woodcut* *The Holy Kinship,* which showed Mary in the company of her parents and extended family. These countless images of the Virgin Mary aimed to inspire Renaissance women and urge them to live up to her example.

Female saints also served as role models for women. Paintings that told the story of a saint's life often served an educational purpose, highlighting the themes of heroic virtue and self-sacrifice. Secular* paintings presented images of feminine perfection as well. Titian's *La Bella* (ca. 1536) reflected the concept of the ideal woman as described in works such as *The Book of the Courtier,* by Italian writer Baldassare CASTIGLIONE.

In other works, women appeared as temptresses. The chief such figure was the biblical Eve, often presented as the opposite of the Virgin Mary. In some pictures, Eve appeared with another troublesome female figure, such as Pandora, the character in Greek mythology who first brought human suffering into the world. *The Large Power of Women,* a series of woodcuts by Lucas van Leyden (ca. 1512) contained images of Eve and other women who brought trouble upon men. However, it is not always clear whether the artist meant these powerful women to be scorned as temptresses or admired as heroines.

* **chaste**   sexually pure

* **woodcut**   print made from a block of wood with an image carved into it

* **secular**   nonreligious; connected with everyday life

WOMEN AND SOCIAL PROTEST

Throughout history women have taken part in protests against injustice or other social problems. The political and economic conditions of the Renaissance brought many occasions for female protest. The most common form of protest for women of the lower classes was the bread riot, which erupted when shortages of food threatened women's ability to feed their families. Many such riots occurred in the 1500s and 1600s, when wars and instability led to severe grain shortages. In some areas, such as France, these shortages were worsened by new taxes on salt and other items. Famous riots led by women broke out in the French cities of Lyon in 1529 and Bordeaux in 1643.

Female artisans and workers also rose up in labor-related protests. In the 1300s, for example, low-paid wool spinners rebelled against the merchants who controlled trade in England. In addition, women played visible roles in religious riots, such as the peasant uprisings in Germany in the 1500s and the outbursts of violence that accompanied wars between Catholics and Protestants in France.

Women fought with whatever weapons came to hand. In 1695 French women in the town of Berry threw rocks to protest a new tax on tradespeople. Female violence often involved household items such as kitchen knives, dishes, and pots. One female baker in Lisbon, Portugal, led a group of armed female "soldiers" wielding a pan as a weapon. In addition, female protestors made violent verbal threats and sometimes publicly humiliated male officials by attacking them physically.

Some of these female-centered protests gave rise to a sense of unity among women and to early claims of equal rights with men. During the English civil war of the mid-1600s, for example, women protested martial law* by declaring their "equal interest with the men of this Nation" in protecting their rights and freedoms. In general, however, women's protests did not involve serious calls for a change in women's state. The protesters' views about gender took a back seat to other goals and concerns. Still, the Renaissance brought new visibility to outraged women, who—armed with household weapons and a strong moral sense—united against the forces that threatened them. (*See also* **Childhood; Family and Kinship; Feminism; Humanism; Love and Marriage; Patronage; Queens and Queenship; Sexuality and Gender; Violence.**)

* **martial law** situation in which the government places law enforcement in the hands of the military, often involving some restrictions on citizens' rights

Writing

* **humanist** Renaissance expert in the humanities (the languages, literature, history, and speech and writing techniques of ancient Greece and Rome)

* **medieval** referring to the Middle Ages, a period that began around A.D. 400 and ended around 1400 in Italy and 1500 in the rest of Europe

* **scribe** person who copies manuscripts

The art of calligraphy—elegant handwriting or lettering—evolved during the Renaissance. As humanists* stressed clarity and beauty in writing, they moved away from the cramped lettering of the Middle Ages. Instead, they looked toward ancient models of writing to create new styles of penmanship that were neater and clearer.

Many Renaissance scholars found medieval* calligraphy difficult to read. Two Italian humanists, Coluccio SALUTATI and PETRARCH, criticized the unclear handwriting of most medieval scribes*. Humanists wanted a new, clear form of writing that would express the ideals of their movement. Two followers of Salutati, Poggio Bracciolini and Niccolò Niccoli, helped create a well-defined humanist script.

Poggio developed a style of calligraphy known as humanist round hand or humanist book script. Compared to the script of the Middle Ages, the round hand employed more uniform spacing between words, used fewer abbreviations, and distinguished more clearly between different letters. Poggio's round hand had a strong influence on later styles of writing. After the invention of the printing press in the 1450s, his script became one of the most widely used types and the basis for typefaces used today.

Niccoli learned Poggio's writing and used it to create his own style, known as cursive. This form of writing, in which the letters connect and

have rounded angles, became the basis for modern italic script. Both styles of humanist calligraphy spread gradually throughout Italy and the rest of Europe. They had a major influence on the development of the writing style used in European manuscripts. (*See also* **Illumination.**)

Wycliffe, John

See *Bible; Christianity; Councils.*

Yiddish Language and Literature

See *Jewish Languages and Literature.*

Zwingli, Huldrych

See *Protestant Reformation.*

Suggested Resources

Asterisk denotes books recommended for young readers.

1. General Background

Breisach, Ernst. *Renaissance Europe 1300–1517.* New York: The Macmillan Company, 1973.

Burckhardt, Jakob. *The Civilization of the Renaissance in Italy.* Trans. by S. G. C. Middlemore. 2 vols. New York: Harper & Row, 1958.

Ferguson, Wallace K. *Europe in Transition 1300–1520.* Boston: Houghton Mifflin, 1962.

———. *The Renaissance in Historical Thought.* Boston: Houghton Mifflin, 1948.

Grendler, Paul F., ed. *Encyclopedia of the Renaissance.* 6 vols. New York: Scribners, 1999. Authoritative and thorough.

Hale, John, ed. *A Concise Encyclopedia of the Italian Renaissance.* London: Thames & Hudson, 1981. Short and useful.

Hay, Denys. *Europe in the Fourteenth and Fifteenth Centuries.* New York: Holt, Rinehart and Winston, Inc., 1966.

Rice, Eugene F., Jr. *The Foundations of Early Modern Europe 1460–1559.* New York: W. W. Norton and Co., 1970.

Ross, James Bruce and Mary Martin McLaughlin, eds. *The Portable Renaissance Reader.* New York: The Viking Press, 1953.

2. Humanism and Education

D'Amico, John F. *Renaissance Humanism in Papal Rome.* Baltimore: The John Hopkins Press, 1983.

Erasmus, Desiderius. *The Erasmus Reader.* Ed. by Erika Rummel. Toronto: University of Toronto Press, 1990.

Grendler, Paul F. *Schooling in Renaissance Italy. Literacy and Learning 1300–1600.* Baltimore: The Johns Hopkins University Press, 1989.

———. *The Universities of the Italian Renaissance.* Baltimore: The Johns Hopkins University Press, 2002.

Gundersheimer, Werner L., ed. *The Italian Renaissance.* Englewood Cliffs, N.J.: Prentice-Hall, Inc. 1965.

Houston, R.A. *Literacy in Early Modern Europe: Culture and Education, 1500–1800.* Rev. ed. New York: Longman, 2002.

Kristeller, Paul Oskar. *Renaissance Thought II. Papers on Humanism and the Arts.* New York: Harper & Row, 1965.

———. *Renaissance Thought: The Classic, Scholastic, and Humanist Strains.* New York: Harper & Row, 1961.

Nauert, Charles, Jr. *Humanism and the Culture of Renaissance Europe.* Cambridge: Cambridge University Press, 1995.

Woodward, William H. *Vittorino da Feltre and Other Humanist Educators.* New York: Columbia University Teachers College, 1963.

3. Nation, Politics, and War: General, Italy, Other Regions

General

Hall, Bert S. *Weapons and Warfare in Renaissance Europe: Gunpowder, Technology, and Tactics.* Baltimore: The Johns Hopkins University Press, 1997.

Mattingly, Garrett. *Renaissance Diplomacy.* Boston: Houghton Mifflin, 1955.

Skinner, Quentin. *The Foundations of Modern Political Thought.* Vol. 1: *The Renaissance.* Cambridge: Cambridge University Press, 1978.

Italy

Brucker, Gene A. *Renaissance Florence.* Rev. ed. Berkeley: University of California Press, 1983.

*Chambers, D.S. *The Imperial Age of Venice 1380–1580.* London: Thames & Hudson, 1970. Illustrated popular account.

Hale, John R. *Florence and the Medici: The Pattern of Control.* London: Thames & Hudson, 1977.

Lane, Frederic C. *Venice: A Maritime Republic.* Baltimore: The Johns Hopkins University Press, 1973.

Laven, Peter. *Renaissance Italy 1464–1534.* London: Methuen & Co. Ltd., 1971.

Machiavelli, Niccolò. *The Letters of Machiavelli.* Trans. and ed. by Allan Gilbert. New York: Capricorn Books, 1961.

———. *The Prince and selected Discourses.* Trans. by Daniel Donno. New York: Bantam Books, 1966. There are many other translations of this important work.

Mallett, Michael. *Mercenaries and their Masters: Warfare in Renaissance Italy.* Totowa, N.J.: Rowman and Littlefield, 1974.

Other Regions

Baumgartner, Frederic J. *France in the Sixteenth Century.* New York: St. Martin's Press, 1995.

Elliott, John H. *Imperial Spain 1469–1716.* New York: New American Library, 1963.

Elton, G. R. *England Under the Tudors.* 3rd. ed. New York: Routledge, 1991.

Evans, R. J. W. *The Making of the Habsburg Monarchy, 1550–1700: An Interpretation.* New York: Oxford University Press, 1985.

Guy, John. *Tudor England.* New York: Oxford University Press, 1988.

Holt, Mack P. *The French Wars of Religion, 1562–1629.* Cambridge: Cambridge University Press, 1995.

Israel, Jonathan. *The Dutch Republic: Its Rise, Greatness, and Fall, 1477–1806.* Oxford: Oxford University Press, 1995.

Mattingly, Garrett. *The Armada.* Boston: Houghton Mifflin, 1959.

Youings, Joyce. *Sixteenth-Century England.* Harmondsworth, England: Penguin Books, 1984.

Zophy, Jonathan W. *The Holy Roman Empire: A Dictionary Handbook.* Westport, Conn: Greenwood Press, 1980.

4. Society and Economy [includes Women and Jewish Life]

Bell, Rudolph. M. *How To Do It. Guides to Good Living for Renaissance Italians.* Chicago: University of Chicago Press, 1999.

Bonfil, Roberto. *Jewish Life in Renaissance Italy.* Trans. by Anthony Oldcorn. Berkeley: California University Press, 1994.

Brown, Judith C., and Robert C. Davis, eds. *Gender and Society in Renaissance Italy.* London: Longman, 1998.

*Brucker, Gene. *Giovanni and Lusanna: Love and Marriage in Renaissance Florence.* Berkeley: University of California Press, 1986.

Burke, Peter. *Popular Culture in Early Modern Europe.* Rev. ed. Brookfield, Vermont: Scolar Press, 1994.

Cipolla, Carlo M. *Before the Industrial Revolution. European Society and Economy, 1000–1700.* New York: Norton & Co., 1976.

———, ed. *The Fontana Economic History of Europe: The Sixteenth and Seventeenth Centuries.* Glasgow: Collins/Fontana Books, 1974.

Davis, Natalie Zemon. *Society and Culture in Early Modern France.* Stanford, Calif.: Stanford University Press, 1975.

Huppert, George. *After the Black Death. A Social History of Early Modern Europe.* Bloomington: Indiana University Press, 1986.

Israel, Jonathan I. *European Jewry in the Age of Mercantilism.* 3rd ed. Portland, Or: Valentine Mitchell, 1998.

King, Margaret L. *Women of the Renaissance.* Chicago: University of Chicago Press, 1991.

Origo, Iris. *The Merchant of Prato, Franceso di Marco Datini, 1335–1410.* New York: Knopf, 1957,

with many reprints. Excellent account of the family life and business of a merchant.

Roth, Cecil. *The Jews in the Renaissance.* New York: Harper & Row, 1959.

Swetz, Frank J. *Capitalism and Arithmetic. The New Math of the 15th Century.* La Salle, Ill.: Open Court, 1987.

Warnicke, Retha M. *Women of the English Renaissance and Reformation.* Westport, Conn: Greenwood Press, 1983.

5. Art and Architecture: General, Italy, Other

General

Aston, Margaret. *The Panorama of the Renaissance.* New York: Abrams, 2000.

Holmes, George. *Renaissance.* New York: St. Martin's Press, 1996.

*Janson, H.W., and Anthony F. Janson. *History of Art for Young People.* 5th ed. N.Y.: Abrams, 1997.

Levey, Michael. *Early Renaissance.* Harmondsworth, England: Penguin, 1967.

McCorquodale, Charles. *The Renaissance: European painting, 1400–1600.* London: Studio Editions, 1994.

Murray, Linda. *The High Renaissance and Mannerism: Italy, the North and Spain, 1500–1600.* New York: Thames & Hudson, 1985.

Murray, Peter, and Linda Murray. *The Art of the Renaissance.* London: Thames & Hudson, 1985.

Shearman, John. *Mannerism.* Baltimore: Penguin, 1967.

Italy

Avery, Charles. *Florentine Renaissance Sculpture.* London: J. Murray, 1970.

Baxandall, Michael. *Painting and Experience in Fifteenth Century Italy. A Primer in the Social History of Pictorial Style.* 2nd ed. New York: Oxford University Press, 1988.

Hartt, Frederick. *History of Italian Renaissance Art.* 4th ed. Rev. by David G. Wilkins. New York: Abrams, 1994.

Hopkins, Andrew. *Italian Architecture: from Michelangelo to Borromini.* New York: Thames & Hudson, 2002.

Pope-Hennessy, J. *Italian Renaissance Sculpture,* 3rd ed. Oxford: Phaidon, 1986.

Rosand, David. *Painting in Sixteenth-Century Venice: Titian, Veronese, Tintoretto.* Rev. ed. Cambridge: Cambridge University Press, 1997.

Rowe, Colin. *Italian Architecture of the 16th Century.* Princeton: Princeton Architectural Press, 2002.

Seymour, Charles. *Sculpture in Italy, 1400–1500.* Harmondsworth, England: Penguin, 1966.

Taylor, Pamela, ed. *The Notebooks of Leonardo da Vinci.* New York: New American Library, 1960.

Vasari, Giorgio. *Lives of the Artists.* Trans. by George Bull. Baltimore: Penguin, 1965.

Other Regions

Białostocki, Jan. *The Art of the Renaissance in Eastern Europe: Hungary, Bohemia, Poland.* Ithaca: Cornell University Press, 1976.

Blunt, Anthony. *Art and Architecture in France 1500–1700.* 4th ed. New Haven: Yale University Press, 1982.

Brown, Jonathan. *The Golden Age of Painting in Spain.* New Haven: Yale University Press, 1991.

Chastel, André. *French Art: The Renaissance, 1430–1620.* Paris: Abbeville Press, 1995.

Cuttler, Charles D. *Northern Painting: From Pucelle to Bruegel.* Fort Worth, Tex.: Holt, Rinehart and Winston, Inc., 1991.

Gent, Lucy, ed. *Albion's Classicism: The Visual Arts in Britain, 1550–1660.* New Haven: Yale University Press, 1995.

Moffitt, John F. *The Arts in Spain.* New York: Thames & Hudson, 1999.

Snyder, James. *Northern Renaissance Art.* New York: Abrams, 1985.

6. Music and Theater

Atlas, Allan W., ed. *Renaissance Music: Music in Western Europe, 1400–1600.* New York: W. W. Norton, 1998.

Brown, Howard Mayer, and Louis K. Stein. *Music in the Renaissance.* 2nd ed. Upper Saddle River, N.J.: Prentice Hall, 1999.

*Charney, Maurice. *All of Shakespeare.* New York: Columbia University Press, 1993.

Doughtie, Edward. *English Renaissance Song.* Boston: Twayne Publishers, 1986.

Fenlon, Iain. *Music and Culture in Late Renaissance Italy.* New York: Oxford University Press, 2002.

———, ed. *The Renaissance from the 1470s to the End of the 16th Century.* Englewood Cliffs, N.J.: Prentice-Hall, 1989.

Hunter, George K. *English Drama, 1586–1642.* New York: Oxford University Press, 1997.

McKendrick, Melveena. *Theater in Spain 1490–1700.* Cambridge: Cambridge University Press, 1989.

Palisca, Claude V. *Baroque Music.* Reprint, Englewood Cliffs, N.J.: Prentice Hall, 1991.

*Yancey, Diane. *Life in the Elizabethan Theater.* The Way People Live Series. San Diego: Lucent Books, 1997.

7. Literature: General, English

General

Ariosto, Ludovico. *Orlando Furioso (The Frenzy of Orlando).* Trans. by Barbara Reynolds. 2 vols. Harmondsworth, England: Penguin Books, 1975.

Bentley, Eric, ed. *The Genius of the Italian Theater.* New York: The New American Library, 1964. Seven Italian plays, four from the Renaissance.

Bishop, Morris. *Petrarch and His World.* Bloomington: Indiana University Press, 1963.

Boccaccio, Giovanni. *The Decameron.* Trans. by G.H. McWilliam. Harmondsworth, England: Penguin Books, 1972.

Cervantes Saavedra, Miguel de. *The Portable Cervantes.* Trans. by Samuel Putnam. New York: The Viking Press, 1951.

Hardin, James, and Max Reinhart, eds. *German Writers of the Renaissance and Reformation, 1280–1580. Dictionary of Literary Biography,* vol. 179. Detroit: Gale Research, 1997. Has biographies of 40 writers.

McFarlane, I.D. *Renaissance France, 1470–1589.* New York: Barnes and Noble, 1974.

Montaigne, Michel de. *Montaigne's Essays and Selected Writings. A Bilingual Edition.* Trans. and ed. by Donald M. Frame. New York: St. Martin's Press, 1963.

More, Thomas. *Utopia.* Trans. by Paul Turner. Harmondsworth, England: Penguin Books, 1965. Many reprints and other translations.

Pascal, Roy. *German Literature in the Sixteenth and Seventeenth Centuries: Renaissance, Reformation, Baroque.* New York: Barnes and Noble, 1968.

Rabelais, François. *The Histories of Gargantua and Pantagruel.* Trans. by J. M. Cohen. Harmondsworth, England: Penguin Books, 1955.

English

*Andrews, John F., ed. *Shakespeare's World and Work.* New York: Charles Scribner's Sons, 2001.

Bacon, Francis. *The Advancement of Learning and New Atlantis.* Ed. by Arthur Johnston. Oxford: Clarendon Press, 1974. Many other editions of these works.

Boyce, Charles. *Shakespeare A to Z. The Essential Reference to His Plays, His Poems, His Life and Times, and More.* New York: Dell Publishing, 1990.

Donne, John. *John Donne: A Selection of His Poetry.* Ed. by John Hayward. Baltimore: Penguin Books, 1950.

Haydn, Hiram, ed. *The Portable Elizabethan Reader.* New York: Viking Press, 1955.

Lewis, C.S. *Preface to Paradise Lost.* N.Y.: Oxford University Press, 1961.

Marlowe, Christopher. *The Complete Plays.* New York: Viking Press, 1969.

Milton, John. *Paradise Lost.* Ed. by John Leonard. New York: Penguin Books, 2003.

Shakespeare, William. *The Complete Works of Shakespeare.* Ed. by David Bevington. 4th ed. New York: Scott, Foresman, 1997.

Schoenbaum, Sidney. *Shakespeare: The Globe and the World.* New York: Oxford University Press, 1979.

Sidney, Philip. *Selected Prose and Poetry.* Ed. by Robert Kimbrough. 2nd edition. Madison: University of Wisconsin Press, 1983.

Spenser, Edmund. *The Faerie Queene.* Ed. by A.C. Hamilton. New York: Longman, 1977.

8. Religion

Bireley, Robert. *The Refashioning of Catholicism, 1450–1700.* Washington, D.C: The Catholic University of America Press, 1999.

Chadwick, Owen. *The Reformation.* Baltimore: Penguin Books, 1964.

O'Connell, Marvin. *The Counter Reformation 1560–1610.* New York: Harper & Row, 1974.

O'Malley, John W. *The First Jesuits.* Cambridge, Mass.: Harvard University Press, 1993.

Spitz, Lewis W. *The Protestant Reformation 1517–1559.* New York: Harper & Row, 1985.

9. Philosophy, Science, and Technology [includes printing]

*Baigrie, Brian S., ed. *The Renaissance and the Scientific Revolution.* New York: Charles Scribner's Sons, 2001.

Copenhaver, Brian P., and Charles B. Schmitt. *Renaissance Philosophy.* New York: Oxford University Press, 1992.

Febvre, Lucien, and Henri-Jean Martin. *The Coming of the Book: The Impact of Printing 1450–1800.* Trans. by David Gerard. London: N.L.B., 1976.

Hall, Maria Boas. *The Scientific Renaissance, 1450–1630.* New York: Dover Publications, 1994.

Kapr, Albert. *Johann Gutenberg. The Man and his Invention.* Trans. by Douglas Martin. Brookfield, Vt: Scholar Press, 1996.

Koyre, A. *The Astronomical Revolution.* Trans by R.E.W. Maddison. Reprint, New York: Dover Publications, 1992.

Kristeller, Paul Oskar. *Eight Philosophers of the Renaissance.* Stanford, Calif.: Stanford University Press, 1964.

*Spangenburg, Ray. *The History of Science from the Ancient Greeks to the Scientific Revolution.* New York: Facts on File, 1993.

*Stefoff, Rebecca. *The Young Oxford Companion to Maps and Mapmaking.* New York: Oxford University Press, 1995.

10. Exploration

*Allen, John Logan, E. Julius Dasch, and Barry M. Gough. *Explorers: From Ancient Times to the Space Age.* 3 vols. New York: Simon & Schuster Macmillan, 1999.

Boxer, C.R. *Portuguese Seaborne Empire.* London: Hutchinson, 1969.

*Gough, Barry M., ed. *Geography and Exploration.* New York: Charles Scribner's Sons, 2002.

Hale, J.R. *Renaissance Exploration.* London: British Broadcasting Corporation, 1968.

Parry, J. H. *The Age of Reconnaissance.* New York: New American Library, 1963.

Penrose, Boies. *Travel and Discovery in the Renaissance 1420–1620.* New York: Atheneum, 1962.

Subrahmanyam, Sanjay. *The Portuguese Empire in Asia, 1500–1700: A Political and Economic History.* New York: Longman, 1993.

11. Biographies

Alberti, Leon Battista. Gadol, Joan. *Leon Battista Alberti: Universal Man of the Renaissance.* Chicago: University of Chicago Press, 1969.

Borgias. Mallett, Michael. *The Borgias: The Rise and Fall of a Renaissance Dynasty.* Chicago: Academy Chicago Publisher, 1987.

Catherine of Aragon. Mattingly, Garrett. *Catherine of Aragon.* New York: AMS Press, 2003.

Charles V. Brandi, Karl. *The Emperor Charles V: The Growth and Destiny of a Man and a World-Emperor.* Trans. by C.V. Wedgewood. London: J. Cape, 1980.

———. Maltby, William S. *The Reign of Charles V* New York: Palgrave, 2002.

Columbus, Christopher. Phillips, William D., Jr., and Carla Rahn Phillips. *The World of Christopher Columbus.* Cambridge: Cambridge University Press, 1992.

Donne, John. Bald, R.C. *John Donne: A Life.* New York: Oxford University Press, 1970. Reprint, with corrections, 1986.

Dürer, Albrecht. Panofsky, Erwin. *The Life and Art of Albrecht Dürer.* 4th ed. Princeton: Princeton University Press, 1971.

Elizabeth I. MacCaffrey, Wallace. *Elizabeth I.* New York: E. Arnold, 1993.

———. Weir, Alison. *The Life of Elizabeth I.* New York: Ballantine Books, 1999.

———. *Williams, Neville. *The Life and Times of Elizabeth I.* Garden City, N.Y.: Doubleday & Company, 1972. Well-illustrated popular biography.

Erasmus. Bainton, Roland H. *Erasmus of Christendom.* New York: Charles Scribner's Sons, 1969.

———. Sowards, J. Kelley. *Desiderius Erasmus.* Boston: Twayne Publishers, 1975.

Francis I. Knecht, R.J. *Renaissance Warrior and Patron: The Reign of Francis I.* New York: Cambridge University Press, 1994.

Galileo. Drake, Stillman. *Galileo at Work: His Scientific Biography.* Chicago: University of Chicago Press, 1978.

———. Reston, James, Jr. *Galileo: A Life.* New York: HarperCollins Publishers, 1994.

Guicciardini, Francesco. Ridolfi, Roberto. *The Life of Francesco Guicciardini.* Trans. by Cecil Grayson. London: Routledge & Kegan Paul, 1967.

Habsburg. Wandruszka, Adam. *The House of Habsburg: Six Hundred Years of a European Dynasty.* Trans. by Cathleen Epstein and Hans Epstein. Garden City, N.Y.: Doubleday, 1964.

Henry VIII. *Dwyer, Frank. *Henry VIII.* World Leaders Past and Present Series. New York: Chelsea House, 1988.

———. Scarisbrick, J. J. *Henry VIII.* Berkeley: University of California Press, 1968.

Isabella of Castile. Liss, Peggy K. *Isabel the Queen.* New York: Oxford University Press, 1992.

James I. Carrier, Irene. *James VI and I: King of Great Britain.* Cambridge: Cambridge University Press, 1998.

Jonson, Ben. Kay, W. David. *Ben Jonson: A Literary Life.* New York: St. Martin's Press, 1995.

Leonardo da Vinci. Clark, Kenneth. *Leonardo da Vinci.* Rev. by M. Kemp. New York: Penguin, 1993.

Luther, Martin. Bainton, Roland H. *Here I Stand: A Life of Martin Luther.* New York: Abingdon-Cokesbury Press, 1950.

Machiavelli, Niccolò. Ridolfi, Roberto. *The Life of Niccolo Machiavelli.* Trans. by Cecil Grayson. Chicago: University of Chicago Press, 1963.

———. Viroli, Maurizio. *Niccolò's Smile: A Biography of Machiavelli.* Trans. by Antony Shugaar. New York: Farrar, Straus, and Giroux, 2000.

Maximilian II. Fichtner, Paula Sutter. *Emperor Maximilian II.* New Haven: Yale University Press, 2001.

Michelangelo. Hibbard, Howard. *Michelangelo.* New York: Harper & Row, 1985.

Milton, John. Brown, Cedric C. *John Milton: A Literary Life.* New York: St. Martin's Press, 1995.

More, Thomas. Ackroyd, Peter. *The Life of Thomas More.* London: Chatto & Windus, 1998.

———. Marius, Richard. *Thomas More: A Biography.* New York: Knopf, 1984.

Philip II. Kamen, Henry. *Philip of Spain.* New Haven: Yale University Press, 1997.

Rubens, Peter Paul. *McLanathan, Richard. *Peter Paul Rubens.* New York: Abrams, 1995.

Shakespeare, William. *Stanley, Diane, and Peter Vennema. *Bard of Avon: The Story of William Shakespeare.* New York: Morrow Junior Books, 1992.

———. Holden, Anthony. *William Shakespeare: The Man Behind the Genius.* Boston: Little Brown, 2000.

———. Shoenbaum, Sidney. *William Shakespeare: A Compact Documentary Life.* New York: Oxford University Press, 1977.

Titian. Hope, Charles. *Titian.* New York: Harper & Row, 1980.

Vesalius, Andreas. O'Malley, Charles D. *Andreas Vesalius of Brussels 1514–1564.* Berkeley: University of California Press, 1965.

12. Novels and Films

Shellabarger, Samuel. *Captain from Castile.* Boston: Little, Brown, 1945. Novel about Cortes's invasion of Mexico, 1519–1521. Made into a film starring Tyrone Power in 1947.

Stone, Irving. *The Agony and the Ecstasy: A Biographical Novel of Michelangelo.* Garden City, N.Y.: Doubleday & Co., 1961.

Hamlet. 1948. Shakespeare's play. Directed by and starring Laurence Olivier.

Henry V. 1989. Shakespeare's play. Directed and starring Kenneth Branagh.

Henry V. 1944. Shakespeare's play. Directed by and starring Laurence Olivier.

Macbeth. 1948. Shakespeare's play. Directed by and starring Orson Welles.

A Man for All Seasons. 1966. Directed by Fred Zinnemann. Starring Paul Scofield. Life of Thomas More.

Mary Queen of Scots. 1971. Directed by Charles Jarrott. Starring Vanessa Redgrave and Glenda Jackson.

Prince of Foxes. 1949. Directed by Henry King. Starring Tyrone Power and Orson Welles.

Cesare Borgia is the villain in a swashbuckling story set in Italy ca. 1500.

Return of Martin Guerre. 1982. Directed by Daniel Vigne. Starring Gerard Dépardieu and Nathalie Baye. Case of assumed identity in a village in France of the 1500s.

Richard III. 1956. Shakespeare's play. Directed by and starring Laurence Olivier.

Romeo and Juliet. 1968. Shakespeare's play. Directed by Franco Zeffirelli. Starring Leonard Whiting and Olivia Hussey.

Shakespeare in Love. 1998. Directed by John Madden. Starring Joseph Fiennes and Gwyneth Paltrow. Shakespeare has writer's block until he meets Paltrow and writes *Romeo and Juliet.*

The Taming of the Shrew. 1966. Shakespeare's comedy. Directed by Franco Zeffirelli. Starring Richard Burton and Elizabeth Taylor.

West Side Story. 1961. Directed by Robert Wise and Jerome Robbins. Music by Leonard Bernstein. Starring Natalie Wood and Richard Beyman. Musical loosely based on Shakespeare's play *Romeo and Juliet.*

13. On-Line Resources

16th Century English Renaissance Literature (1485–1603). *Information on the leading English writers of the era, including biographies, essays, and works.* http://www.luminarium.org/renlit/

Art History Resources on the Web. *An informative and in-depth look at art, architecture, and sculpture from throughout Renaissance Europe.* http://witcombe.sbc.edu/ARTHLinks2.html

Encyclopaedia Britannica's Shakespeare and the Globe: Then and Now. *Explores the history and*

legacy of Shakespeare, his plays, and other important Elizabethans. http://Shakespeare.eb.com

The Internet Encyclopedia of Philosophy. *A searchable database of the philosophers and ideas of the Renaissance.* http://www.utm.edu/research/iep/r/renaiss.htm

Web Gallery of Art. *A searchable guide to European art from 1150–1800.* http://gallery.euroweb.hu/

Acknowledgments

Volume 1

Color Plates for Art and Architecture

1: Detail from *Legend of the True Cross,* fresco painting by Piero della Francesca, © David Lees/Corbis; **2**: *Portrait of Agnolo Doni,* painting by Raphael, © Arte & Immagini srl/Corbis; **3**: *The Story of Joseph,* individual panel from the *Gates of Paradise* gilded bronze doors made by Lorenzo Ghiberti for the Baptistery in Florence, © Ted Spiegel/Corbis; **4**: *David,* by Verrochio, © Michael Nicholson/Corbis; **5**: Santa Maria Novella, facade designed by Leon Battista Alberti, © Archivo Iconografico, S.A./Corbis; **6**: *Sacred Allegory,* painting by Vincenzo Bellini, © Archivo Iconografico, S.A./Corbis; **7**: *The Penitent Magdalen,* painting by Titian, photograph, © Archivo Iconografico, S.A./Corbis; **8**: *Last Judgment,* by Michelangelo, 1508—1512, The Art Archive; **9**: *Etienne Chevalier and St. Stephen,* painting by Jean Fouquet, 1450, Staatliche Museen Gemdldegalerie at Berlin, photograph, © Francis G. Mayer/Corbis; **10**: Château Chambord, palace built by King Henry II, painting, © Adam Woolfitt/Corbis; **11**: *God the Father,* detail (center panel) from *The Ghent Altarpiece,* painting on wood panel by Hubert van Eyck and Jan van Eyck, © Archivo Iconografico, S.A./Corbis; **12**: *The Deer Hunt of Friedrich III, the Wise, Elector of Saxony,* painting by Lucas Cranach the Elder, © Ali Meyer/Corbis; **13**: *Return of the Hunters,* painting by Pieter Brueghel the Elder, The Art Archive/Kunsthistorisches Museum Vienna/The Art Archive; **14**: *View of Toledo,* oil painting by El Greco, © Francis G. Meyer/Corbis.

Black-and-White Photographs

7: *The Labours of the 12 Months,* manuscript painting by Pietro de Crescenzi, Le Rustican, © Giraudon/Art Resource, New York; **10**: *Malatesta Temple,* Rimini, with facade by Leon Battista Alberti, photograph, Alinari-Art Reference/Art Resource, New York; **15** From *The Herbal,* by J. Gerarde, © Corbis; **21**: *The Anatomy Lesson,* by John Banister, photograph, © Bettmann/Corbis; **27**: St. Peter's Basilica, aerial view, Vatican City, Rome, Italy, photograph, © Alinari/Art Resource, New York; **28**: *Vitruvian Man,* drawing by Leonardo da Vinci, photograph, Corbis Corporation; **31**: *Beatrice d'Este,* panel painting by Giovanni Ambrogio Predis, © Scala/Art Resource, New York; **37**: German armor for man and horse, 16th century, horse armor attributed to Kunz Lochner, painting, The Metropolitan Museum of Art, Bashford Dean Memorial Collection, Gift of Mrs. Bashford Dean, 1929, (29.15/.29), Rogers Fund, 1932, (32.69), photograph, all rights reserved, The Metropolitan Museum of Art, New York; **39**: *The Annunciation,* painting attributed to Antoniazzo Romano, ca. 1475–1485, © Burstein Collection/Corbis; **48**: Sigismund Chapel in Cracow, Poland, illustration, Rysinski Studio Inc. Edward Rysinski, New York; **50**: Exterior View of Château de Fontainebleau, designed by Gilles Le Breton, painting, © Archivo Iconografico, S.A./Corbis; **54**: *Self-Portrait,* painting by Albrecht Dürer, 1500, photograph, Giraudon/Art Resource, New York; **57**: *David,* sculpture by Michelangelo, photograph, Scala/Art Resource, New York; **59**: *The Tribute Money,* detail of fresco painting by Masaccio, © Sandro Vannini/Corbis; **64**: *Saint Eligius as a Goldsmith,* painting by Petrus Christus, © Francis G. Mayer/Corbis; **68**: Palace and monastery of El Escorial, built ca. 1562–1584, Madrid, Spain, photograph by Ruggero Vanni, © Vanni Archives/Corbis; **76**: Rudolf I (center) with two sons Albert and Rudolf, photograph, Osterreichische Nationalbibliothek, Vienna; **79**: *Francis Bacon,* engraving, © Leonard de Selva/Corbis; **86**: *The Madonna of the Meadow,* painting by Giovanni Bellini, © National Gallery, London/Corbis; **89**: Gutenberg printed bible on display, photograph, © Bettmann/Corbis; **93**: *Boccaccio,* painting by Andrea del Castagno, 1449–1451, © Arte & Immagini, SRL/Corbis; **103**: *Allegory of Spring,* painting by Sandro Botticelli, Uffizi Gallery, Florence, photograph, Corbis-Bettmann; **109**: View of the Tempietto di San Pietro in Montorio, Rome, Italy, designed by Donato Bramante, painting, © Archivo Iconografico, S.A./Corbis, Corbis, New York; **113**: *The Peasant Wedding,* painting by Pieter Breughel the Elder, photograph, Art Resource, New York; **115**: The octagonal dome of the Duomo, church designed by Filippo Brunelleschi, photograph, © Scala/Art Resource, New York; **121**: Philip III, Duke of Burgundy, print, Archive Photos, Inc.; **128**: *The Cardsharps,* oil painting by Caravaggio, © Kimbell Art Museum/Corbis; **132**: *Baldassare Castiglione,* oil painting on canvas by Raphael, in the collection of the Musée du Louvre, Paris, France, © Scala/Art Resource, New York; **136**: *Fishing for Souls,* oil painting by Adriaen van de Venne, © Rijksmuseum Amsterdam; **139**: Saltcellar of Francis I, 1539–1543, artwork by Benvenuto Cellini, Kunsthistorisches Museum, Vienna, Austria, © Francis G. Mayer/Corbis; **149**: The Emperor Charles V at the Battle of Muhlberg, painting by Titian, © Gianni Dagli

ACKNOWLEDGMENTS

Orti/Corbis; **152:** *Children's Games,* oil painting by Pieter Breughel the Elder, © Francis G. Mayer/Corbis; **157:** Engraving of St. Peter's Square and Basilica, by Giacomo della Porta, © Corbis; **163:** Detail from *The Allegory of Good Government: The Effects of Good Government in the City,* fresco cycle by Ambrogio Lorenzetti, © David Lees/Corbis; **169:** *The School of Athens,* mural by Santi Raphael, photograph by Erich Lessing, Erich Lessing/Art Resource, New York; **178:** *The Princesses Sibylla, Emilia*

and Sidonia of Saxony, painting by Lucas Cranach the Elder, © Ali Meyer/Corbis; **182:** Etching of *Christopher Columbus on Hispanola,* © Corbis; **190:** Painting of Nicolaus Copernicus, © photograph by Erich Lessing/Museum of Torun, Torun, Poland/Art Resource, New York; **195:** Painting of Ludovico Gonzaga, his family and court, © Arte & Immagini srl/Corbis; **199:** *Comfort the Prisoner,* altar panel from Altmunster in Upper Austria, ca. 1490, © Brandstatter, Dr. Christian/Corbis.

Volume 2

Color Plates for Daily Life

1: *Precious Metal Workshop,* painting by School of Agnolo Bronzino, © Archivo Iconografico, S.A./Corbis; **2:** From German manuscript *Splendor Solis,* illustration, The Art Archive/British Library/British Library; **3:** *Portrait of a Merchant,* by Jan Gossaert, National Gallery of Art; **4:** *Manufacturing Wool,* painting by Mirabello Cavalori, 1570–1572, illustration, © Archivo Iconografico, S.A./Corbis; **5:** *Summer,* painting by Francesco Bassano, 1570–1580, © Alexander Burkatowski/Corbis; **6:** *Fruit Vendor,* oil painting by Bernardo Strozzi, © Arte & Immagini srl/Corbis; **7:** *The Egg Dance,* painting by Jan Mostaert, The Art Archive/Museo Civico Cremona/Dagli Orti; **8:** *The Fortuneteller,* oil painting attributed to Caravaggio, © Archivo Iconografico, S.A./Corbis; **9:** *The Conjuror,* painting on panel by Hieronymus Bosch, © Scala/Art Resource, New York; **10:** Single panel from a triptych of the *Seven Sacraments,* by Rogier Van de Weyden, illustration, © Scala/Art Resource, New York; **11:** *Temple de Lyon, Nomme Paradis,* painting, The Art Archive/University Library Geneva/Dagli Orti; **12:** *The Joust in the Piazza Santa Croce, Florence, 1555,* fresco painting by Jan van der Straet, The Bridgeman Art Library; **13:** *Battle of San Romano,* tempera and silver foil on wood, by Paolo Uccello, ca. 1455, National Gallery, London, England, The Art Archive/Eileen Tweedy; **14:** *Game of Chess,* oil painting on canvas by Sofonisba Anguisciola, The Bridgeman Art Library; **15:** *An Old Man and His Grandson,* painting on panel by Domenico Ghirlandaio, The Art Archive/Musée du Louvre Paris/The Art Archive.

Black-and-White Photographs

2: The *Labours of the 12 Months: October,* fresco, © Alinari/Art Resource, New York; **4:** *The Indoor Wedding Dance,* oil painting by Pieter Brueghel the Younger, © Christie's Images/Corbis; **7** *Mercury,* bronze sculpture by Giambologna, © Alinari/Art Resource, New York; **13:** Vittore Carpaccio's *Return of the Ambassadors to England,* ©Archivo Iconografico, S.A./Corbis; **14:** John Donne, photograph of painting, courtesy of the National Portrait

Gallery, London; **17:** *Cityscape,* by Adriaen Collaert, British Museum, London, ©Snark/Art Resource, New York; **20:** Illustration from *Chronicle of Scotland,* The Folger Shakespeare Library; **26:** Engraving of Robert Garnier, The Bridgeman Art Library; **31:** Study of *Praying Hands,* drawing by Albrecht Dürer, © Classic Illustrations/Corbis; **34:** *De Sphaera,* 15th century illuminated Lombard manuscript, © Gianni Dagli Orti/Corbis; **38:** Woodcut of classroom from a 1573 Latin grammar text, The Folger Shakespeare Library; **45:** The Armada portrait of Elizabeth I, painting by Marc Gheeraedts, The Granger Collection, New York; **48:** *The Allegory of the Tudor Succession: The Family of Henry VIII,* oil on panel, ©Yale Center for British Art, Paul Mellon Collection USA/Photo: Bridgeman Art Library; **55:** Woodcut from *Shepheardes Calendar,* by Edmund Spenser, The Granger Collection, New York; **59:** *Desiderius Erasmus,* oil on panel, by Hans Holbein the Younger, ca. 1523, Louvre, Paris, France, The Art Archive/Dagli Orti; **66:** Map of the Indian Ocean dedicated to King Manuel I of Portugal, 1519, illustration, Bibliothèque Nationale de France, Paris; **70:** *The Madonna of Chancellor Rolin,* panel painting by Jan Van Eyck, photograph, © Francis G. Mayer/Corbis; **73:** Dutch marketplace in Anvers, Netherlands, oil painting, Musées royaux des Beaux-arts de Belgique, Bruxelles; **86:** *Cosimo de Medici,* painting by Pontormo, © Archivo Iconografico, S.A./Corbis; **90:** Early Renaissance fresco painting with figures displaying fruit, © Archivo Iconografico, S.A./Corbis; **94:** Map of Nancy, France, in 1617, engraving after Claude La Ruelle, The Art Archive/Musee Historique Lorrain Nancy/Dagli Orti; **99:** Antoine Macault, painting, © Giraudon/Art Resource, New York; **108:** Engraving of Michel de Montaigne, The Library of Congress; **112:** Oil painting of Galileo Galilei by Justus Sustermans, © Bettmann/Corbis; **115:** *Villa Este and gardens, Tivoli, Italy,* color engraving, The Art Archive/Biblioteca Nazionale Marciana Venice/Dagli Orti; **119:** Map of America, from the 1633 copy of *Atlas of the World,* by Gerardus Mercator, The Art Archive/Biblioteca Nacional Madrid/Dagli Orti; **128:** *Triumphal Entry into Jerusalem,* fresco by Giotto, 1305–1306, Arena Chapel

(Cappella Scrovegni), Padua, Italy, The Art Archive/Dagli Orti; **133:** Engraving of Henry IV, King Of France, by Delannoy Staal, © Bettmann/Corbis; **141:** Johannes Gutenberg and his printing press, photograph of an A. Menzel painting, Corbis-Bettmann; **150:** *Henry VIII,* portrait painting on panel by Hans Holbein the Younger, © Gianni Dagli Orti/Corbis; **160:** *Homage to Emperors Albrecht II, Friedrich III, Maximilian I, and Karl V,* © photograph by Erich Lessing, Art Resource; **166:** Detail from *Angel Appearing to Zacharias,* fresco cycle by Domenico Ghirlandaio, © Sandro Vannini/Corbis; **169:** *Sir Thomas More,* painting by Hans Holbein the Younger, © Francis G. Mayer/Corbis; **174:** Bas relief sculpture of Matthias Corvinus, © Archivo Iconografico, S.A./Corbis; **178:** Frontispiece with commentary by Averroes, to *Opera (Works),* Volume I, by Aristotle, © The Pierpont Morgan Library/Art Resource, New York; **185:** Burning of Jewish men accused of heresy and witchcraft by the Spanish Inquisition, a contemporary illustration, Granada, Spain, © Bettmann/Corbis; **188:** Portrait of Hugh O'Neill, photograph, The New York Public Library; **194:** *The Triumph of Death,* Florentine manuscript illumination, 15th century, from *Rime i Trionfi,* by Petrarch, photograph, © Archivo Iconografico, S.A./Corbis; **197:** *View of Rome,* painting by anonymous artist, © Scala/Art Resource, New York; **199:** *James I, King of England,* oil painting by Paul Van Somer, © Bettmann/Corbis; **202:** Page from the Hebrew Book of Abraham, printed by Elieser Toledano, © Christel Gerstenberg/Corbis; **206:** From *Haggadah for Passover; Collection of Texts on the Script and Prayer,* German manuscript painting, © Giraudon/Art Resource, New York; **210:** Bridal casket, illustration, © The Israel Museum, Jerusalem; **217:** *Ben Jonson,* painting by Isaac Oliver, © Bettmann/Corbis, New York.

Volume 3

Color Plates for the Renaissance City

1: Venice canal, painting by Carpaccio, ca. 1486, David Lees/Corbis; **2:** *Pope Urban VIII in Il Ges&graveu;,* painting by Andrea Sacchi, © Scala/Art Resource, New York; **3:** *View of an Ideal City,* designed by Luciano Laurana, © Arte & Immagini srl/Corbis; **4:** *Portrait of Cosimo I in Armor,* tempera painting by Agnolo Bronzino, © Arte & Immagini srl/Corbis; **5:** *Ferdinand of Aragon's Fleet in Naples Harbor,* painting by Francesco Pagano, © Archivo Iconografico, S.A./Corbis; **6:** *Portrait of Federigo da Montefeltro,* tempera painting by Piero della Francesca, © Archivo Iconografico, S.A./Corbis; **7:** *View of Perugia, Italy,* painting, © Archivo Iconografico, S.A./Corbis; **8:** Clock Pavilion wing of the Palais du Louvre, designed by Pierre Lescot, The Art Archive/Dagli Orti; **9:** *Civitates Orbis Terrarum: View of London,* hand-colored prints, part of book by Francis Hogenberg, © Archivo Iconografico, S.A./Corbis; **10:** *Seven Acts of Mercy,* Master Alkmaar feeding the hungry, painting, © Rijksmuseum, Amsterdam; **11:** *General View of the Port and Town of Amsterdam,* engraving by D.G. Hucquier, The Bridgeman Art Library; **12:** *Pierre Gilles,* portrait by Quentin Massys, Konkinklijk Museum Voor Schone Kunsten, Antwerp, Belgie; **13:** Exterior of the Plaza Mayor, Madrid, © Jim McDonald/Corbis; **14:** Cathedral of St. Michael the Archangel, the Kremlin, photograph, © Neil Beer/Corbis; **15:** The Vitava River flowing past Prague Castle and the Hradcany (castle district), Prague, Czech Republic, illustration, © Chris Bland, Eye Ubiquitous/Corbis.

Black-and-White Photographs

2: Johannes Kepler with globe, photograph, © Bettmann/Corbis; **10:** From *Consilia,* Part 4, illustration by Bartolomeo Sozzini, courtesy of Special Collections, Biddle Law Library, University of Pennsylvania Law School; **14** *Lady with an Ermine,* oil painting by Leonardo da Vinci, © Edimedia/Corbis; **17:** Pope Sixtus IV and Platina in the Vatican Library, painting by Melozzo da Forli, © Scala/Art Resource, New York; **22:** Painting by Botticelli from *The Decameron,* by Giovanni Boccaccio, © Archivo Iconografica, S.A./Corbis; **30:** *Wedding of Ottavio Farnese and Margaret of Austria,* fresco by Taddeo Zuccaro, © Scala/Art Resource, New York; **35:** *Art and the Curio Cabinet,* oil painting, © photograph by Eric Lessing, Art Resource, New York; **39:** Niccolo Macchiavelli, painting by Santi di Tito, © Archivo Iconografico, S.A./Corbis; **43:** Celestial map with signs of zodiac and mythological characters, illustration, The Art Archive/Bodleian Library Oxford/The Bodleian Library; **50:** Portrait of Christopher Marlowe, The Granger Collection, New York; **56:** Fra Luca Pacioli with mathematical instruments, photograph, Achivo Iconografico, S.A./Corbis; **64:** *Portrait of Lorenzo the Magnificent,* painting by Giorgio Vasari, © Archivo Iconografico, S.A./Corbis; **66:** Doctor giving treatment to sick man with cut on leg, fresco by Domenico di Bartolo, The Art Archive/Santa Maria della Scala Hospital Siena/Dagli Orti (A); **74:** *Pieta,* sculpture by Michelangelo Buonarroti, © Araldo de Luca/Corbis; **80:** Woodcut depicting copper smelting process, © Bettmann/Corbis; **82:** Portuguese Jesuit missionaries in Japan, screen painting, The Art Archive/Museo de Arte Antiga Lisbon/Dagli Orti; **87:** *The Banker and His Wife,* oil painting by Quentin Massys, © Bettmann/Corbis; **94:** Woodcut by Ambrosius Holbein from *Utopia* by Thomas More, from the March 1518 edition printed in Basel by John Froben, W.W. Norton & Company, Inc; **100:** *Four Musicians Playing in a Meadow,* by Erich Lessing, Art Resource, New York; **104:** *The Concert,* oil painting by

Master of the Female Half-Lengths, © Francis G. Mayer/Corbis; **109:** Choir Panel from *Cantoria,* by Luca Della Robbia, illustration, © Ted Spiegel/Corbis; **115:** *Birth of Venus,* tempera on canvas by Sandro Botticelli, ca. 1482, Galleria degli Uffizi, Florence, Italy, The Art Archive/Dagli Orti; **123:** Pieter Corneliszoon Hooft, photograph, The New York Public Library; **131:** *History of the Spedale: The Hospital and the Social Practices of Marriage and Adoption,* fresco painting by Domenico di Bartolo © Archivo Iconografico, S.A./Corbis; **136:** Palazzo Piccolomini, constructed by Bernardo Rossellino, painting, The Art Archive/Dagli Orti; **139:** Villa Rotonda (formerly the Villa Capra), designed by Andrea Palladio, ca. 1566–1570, near Vicenza, Italy, © Sandro Vannini/Corbis; **141:** Procession of knights passing before King Henry II of France, The Art Archive/Bibliotheque Municipale Rouen/Dagli Orti; **144:** Hotel Nevers, Nesle Tower, and Grand Gallery of the Louvre seen from Pont Neuf bridge, painting, The Art Archive/Musée Carnavalet Paris/Dagli Orti; **148:** Henry Wriothesley, Earl of Southhampton, illustration, Henry E. Huntington Library and Art Gallery; **155:** *Portrait of Francesco Petrarch,* © Archivo Iconografico, S.A./Corbis; **156:** *Philip II of Spain,* painting by Titian, © Arte &

Immagini srl/Corbis; **159:** Detail from *Miracle of the Sacrament,* fresco by Cosimo Rosselli, Scala/Art Resource, New York; **165:** Bas relief sculpture of 15th century religious pilgrims, painting, © David Lees/Corbis; **173:** *The Plague,* painting by Marcantonio Raimondi, © Historical Picture Archive/Corbis; **177:** Pope Pius II (as Eneas Silvio Piccolomini), being crowned, painting, The Art Archive/Piccolomini Library Siena/Dagli Orti; **183:** Portrait of Edmund Spenser, Library of Congress; **187:** *Stephen Bathory and Sigismund III,* engraving, © Historical Picture Archive/Corbis; **189:** *Jean Bodin,* engraving, Art Resource; **189:** *Pope Julius II,* oil painting on wood by Raphael, © National Gallery Collection, by kind permission of the Trustees of the National Gallery, London/Corbis; **200:** *Peasant Dance,* painting by Pieter Bruegel the Elder, © Francis G. Mayer/Corbis; **205:** Detail of a view of Lisbon from *Civitates Orbis Terrarum,* painting by Georg Braun, © Archivo Iconografico, S.A./Corbis; **209:** *History of the Spedale: Distribution of Alms,* fresco painting by Domenico de Bartolo. © Archivo Iconografico, S.A./Corbis; **213:** *Dr. King Preaching at Old St. Paul's before James I,* painting by J. Stow, The Bridgeman Art Library.

Volume 4

Color Plates for New Frontiers

1: Colorplate from *Harmonia Macrocosmica,* an atlas of the heavens written by Andreae Cellarius, © Archivo Inconografico, S.A./Corbis; **2:** Vasco de Gama, 16th century Portuguese print, © Stapleton Collection/Corbis; **3:** Illustration from *Brevis Narratio Eorum Quae in Florida Americae,* written and illustrated by Theodor de Bry, © Archivo Iconografico, S.A./Corbis; **4:** Decorated world map by Jan Blaeu, 16th century, illustration, © Archivo Iconografico, S.A./Corbis; **5:** Detail from *The Port of Seville,* showing Magellan's fleet, painting by Alonso Sanchez Coello, © Giraudon/Art Resource, New York; **6:** *Colchium and Ephemerum,* botanical prints and text by Girolamo Mattioli, © Araldo de Luca/Corbis; **7:** Portuguese carracks off a rocky coast by Joachim Patinir, The National Maritime Museum; **8:** Model of aerial screw, built after a sketch, invention by Leonardo da Vinci, © Scala/Art Resource, New York; **9:** Manuscript illumination of the dissection of a cadaver by Bartholome l'Anglais, translated by Jehan Corbichon, photograph, © Archivo Iconografico, S.A./Corbis; **10:** Jakob II Fugger, portrait by Dosso Dossi, The Art Archive; **11:** Metal foundry for the production of cannons, fresco, 16th century, The Art Archive/Galleria degli Uffizi Florence/Dagli Orti (A); **12:** *Martin Luther and the Wittenberg Reformers,* oil painting by Lucas Cranach the Elder, Toledo Museum of Art; **13:** *Philip II on Horseback,* oil painting on canvas by Peter Paul Rubens, © Archivo

Iconografico, S.A./Corbis; **14:** *Betrothal of the Virgin,* oil painting by Raphael, © Archivo Iconografico, S.A./Corbis; **15:** *The Sense of Hearing,* oil painting on panel by Jan Brueghel, The Art Archive/Museu del Prado Madrid/Dagli Orti.

Black-and-White Photographs

2: Engraving of a printing press in 1520, © Bettmann/Corbis; **8:** *Martin Luther,* painting on wood panel, © Bettmann/Corbis; **12:** Isabella Queen of Spain, detail of *Virgin of the Fly,* painting attributed to Gerard David, © Archivo Iconografico, S.A./Corbis; **18:** Detail from *Madonna of the Fish,* oil painting on canvas by Raphael, © Francis G. Mayer/Corbis; **22:** Ignatius de Loyola, engraving ca. 1550, photograph, Hulton/Archive; **27:** Thomas à Kempis, woodcut, Corbis-Bettmann; **32:** *Self Portrait,* painting by Giorgio Vasari, Arte Video Immagine Italia srl/Corbis-Bettmann; **38:** Elizabeth I before Parliament, hand-colored engraving, © The Folger Shakespeare Library; **42:** Peasants taking up arms, engraving, © Bettmann/Corbis; **63:** Title page of *Dialogus Systemate Mundi,* written by Galileo Galilei, © Bettmann/Corbis; **65:** Illustration of engraving of rhinoceros by Albrecht Dürer, Library of Congress; **73:** Painting of Santorio Santoro's weighing chair, painting by Christel Gerstenberg, Corbis; **78:** *Mary Magdalene,* by Donatello, ca. 1454–1455, Museo dell Opera del Duomo,

Florence, Italy, The Art Archive/Dagli Orti; **82:** *The Prodigal Son with Courtesans,* painting, © Gianni Dagli Orti/Corbis; **84:** William Shakespeare, engraving by Martin Droeshout, AP/Wide World Photos; **89:** Elizabethan galleons at sea, engraving, Corbis; **92:** Illustration from Toggenberg Bible of people suffering with bubonic plague, 15th century painting, © Bettmann/Corbis; **95:** Galley slave, engraving by Vecellio, 16th century, © Christel Gerstenberg/Corbis; **102:** *Civitates Orbis Terrarum: Sevilla,* painting by Georg Braun, © Archivo Iconografico, S.A./Corbis; **105:** Lithograph of Garcilaso de la Vega, photograph, The Library of Congress; **110:** *A Game of Football in the Piazza Santa Maria Novella,* fresco by Giovani Stradano, William L. Clements Library, University of Michigan; **112:** James I of England, painting by Paul van Somer, © Gianni Dagli Orti/Corbis; **118:** *Le Diverse et Artifiose Machine,* illustration/figure LXXV, by Agostino Ramelli, © Corbis; **121:** Teatro Olimpico, view of stage and amphitheater, designed by Andrea Palladio, painting, © Scala/Art Resource, New York; **130:** *Tournament,* manuscript illustration by Ogier le Danois, © Archivo Iconografico, S.A./Corbis; **133:** *Travellers in a Landscape,* painting by Jan Brueghel the Elder, © Victoria & Albert Museum, London/Art Resource, New York; **135:** The ruins of the Colosseum, built by the Emperor Vespasian, 72–80 b.c., Roman Imperial Period, Rome, Italy, painting, © Timothy McCarthy/Art Resource, New York; **140:** Meeting of Doctors of the University of Paris, engraving, The Art Archive/Bibliotheque des Arts Decoratifs Paris/Dagli Orti; **151:** *The Arsenal,* detail from *Map of Venice,* drawing by Jacopo de Barbari, © Erich Lessing/Art Resource, New York; **153:** *Warrior Handing a Letter to a Page,* painting by Veronese, © Christie's Images/Corbis; **156:** *View of Vienna, Austria,* painting by Jollain, © Archivo Iconografico, S.A./Corbis; **159:** Tortures and executions of Dutch freedom fighters and protestants, copper engraving, © Christel Gerstenberg/Corbis; **164:** *The Victory of Camollio,* painting by Giovanni di Lorenzo Cini, © Alinari/Art Resource, New York; **172:** Medieval woodcut of two witches standing at a cauldron, taken from a 15th century book on alchemy, photograph, © Bettmann/Corbis; **175:** Details from *Allegory of March: Triumph of Minerva,* fresco by Francesco del Cossa, © Archivo Iconografico, S.A./Corbis.

Index

Note: Volume numbers precede each page number, separated by a colon. Page numbers in boldface type refer to main discussions of a topic.